Transylvania

History and Reality

Milton G. Lehrer
edited and with a foreword by
David Martin

Bartleby Press

Silver Spring, Maryland

Printed in the United States of America

Published and distributed by:
Bartleby Press

Library of Congress Cataloging-in-Publication Data

Lehrer, Milton G., 1906–
   Transylvania, history and reality.

   Translation of: Adealul, pămînt românesc.
   Bibliography: p.
   1. Transylvania (Romania)—History. 2. Transylvania (Romania)—Ethnic relations. I. Title.
DR280.L4513   1986   949.8′4   86-25861
ISBN 0-910155-04-6

CONTENTS

"The Hungarians have been carrying on a violent, blind policy toward the nationalities which are subject to the Hungarian Crown, especially toward the Romanians."

Lord Edmond Fitzmaurice
British cabinet minister and
representative of the Foreign Office
to the House of Lords, 1905-1909

"Un état de choses, soit-il millenaire, ne mérite pas de durer s'il est contraire à la justice." [A state of affairs, even if it has lasted for a thousand years, does not deserve to be perpetuated if it is contrary to justice.]

Alexandre Millerand
Premier and
President of
France, 1920-1924

FOREWORD

Some time ago a Romanian friend asked me whether I would be interested in polishing the English and editing a book about Transylvania which had originally been printed in Romanian and had been translated from the Romanian into English by a translator with a less than perfect knowledge of English vocabulary and syntax. The book, "The Transylvanian Problem as Seen by an American," bore the subtitle, "Transylvania: Romanian Land." It was written the year before the end of World War II by Milton G. Lehrer, whose biography is given elsewhere.

Apart from the challenge of putting rough English into reasonably readable English prose, I also felt challenged by the subject matter. It was clear from the title that Lehrer was a partisan of a Romanian Transylvania. Although I had majored in foreign policy during the twenty-odd years I had worked for the U.S. Senate, and although I was vaguely aware of the arguments on both sides—the Romanian side and the Hungarian side—in the case of the Transylvanian dispute, I had been prone to regard it as a minor and remote European problem which, in a world beset by so many crises, hardly warranted the time and effort required for careful study.

My initial impression from the English text that was given to me was a questioning one. Lehrer, like most Europeanized Americans who become caught up in European politics, was not merely a partisan, but a highly passionate partisan. On the other hand, having been born in New York, he could obviously lay legal claim to the title, "The Transylvanian Problem as Seen by an American". But the fact that he was a Jew, if anything, strengthened his claim to objectivity on the Transylvanian issue, because traditionally the Jews have not tended to side either with the Romanians or the Hungarians in their disputes.

In the post-World War II period, especially during the 1956 events in Hungary and for several years thereafter, I worked closely with a number of Hungarians whom I still count as close personal friends. Some of them, I know, would differ violently with Lehrer's thesis that Transylvania was basically a Romanian land, and that the Hungarian claim to it was based on its subjugation by the armies of the Hungarian tribes which invaded the area from the steppes of the Caucasus in the 9th century A.D. Others of my Hungarian friends, more tolerant of national rights that were not strictly Hungarian, would be disposed to agree that Hungarian treatment of the Romanians over the centuries left much of which to be ashamed.

As I read further into the Lehrer manuscript, I sometimes found myself irked by the lack of footnotes—a product no doubt of the fact that as a practicing journalist Lehrer had been unaccustomed to annotating his prose. But, simultaneously, I became convinced that the book contained much vital historical information; that the issue of Transylvania rated a much higher political importance than I had previously been prepared to accord it; that, historically, there was much more to be said for the Romanian side of this controversy than most informed Americans or western Europeans are aware; and that, as passionately anti-Hungarian as Lehrer's text might appear to be, his strongly partisan attitude was one of the modern realities born of centuries-old conflict and oppression.

When a text is translated from Romanian into imperfect English prose, and when this English prose is then rewritten with a view to making it more readable, even the most painstaking editor is bound to miss out on a word or two. This problem was in part solved by having a knowledgeable Romanian, Petru Buzescu, Senior Legal Specialist, European Law Division, Library of Congress, check my edited text against the original Romanian text of the Lehrer book. Whatever minor imperfections there may be, I feel they in no way detract from the basic merit of Lehrer's historical and polemical presentation. In addition, I have conscientiously endeavored to adhere to the intended substance of the various quotes from languages other than Romanian—Hungarian, German, French, Russian—although I must freely concede that they are not literal translations.

Despite the mental reservations to which I have referred, I undertook the task of editing Lehrer's manuscript because I felt that its availability in an English language edition would put the western world, especially the English-speaking world, in a better position to pass informed judgment on the issues of the Transylvanian conflict. Indeed, fairness demands that it be read and the arguments made by this study be weighed. The fact that this account was not written by a native Romanian but by a native of America reinforces its claim on our attention.

The first part of Lehrer's book has to do with the very early history of the Romanian people. According to Lehrer and other historians, the Romanians are descended from the inhabitants of the ancient Roman province of Dacia and from the legionaries of the Roman Emperor Trajan, who conquered the land and then settled on it. Toward the end of the ninth century, A.D., the greater part of Dacia was overrun by the Hungarian tribes who, under the leadership of King Arpad, migrated to the area from the Caucasus. In the centuries after the Hungarian conquest, there were repeated revolts of the Transylvanian peasants directed primarily against the Hungarian nobility, who constituted the bulk of the privileged land-owning class. The better part of Lehrer's history, however, has to do with the increasing embitterment of Hungarian-Romanian relations over the past several centuries.

The lot of the Romanian peasant was indeed an onerous one.

Lehrer quotes a 1773 letter from Empress Maria Theresa, consort of the Holy Roman emperor, Francis I. Anticipating the visit to Transylvania of the future emperor, Joseph II, Maria Theresa demanded of Transylvania's governor that he "clear the road of the corpses of those killed by hanging, impaling, or quartering, which the Hungarians, to the travelers' horror, have purposely let rot alongside these roads." Lehrer's book contains a dramatic account of the great Romanian peasant revolt of 1784, led by Nicolae Horia and Ion Closca, which demanded the abolition of serfdom, redistribution of the land, and taxation of the nobles. One of the numerous Romanian petitions which preceded the 1784 revolt said:

> We cannot help wondering why it is that you, the Hungarians, in addition to forcing us to bear the yoke of serfdom, place so many pressures on us Romanians. We have been and we still are more numerous than you are.

What is even more important, we have existed for a much longer time in this country, since we are the descendants of the ancient Dacians.

Although initially successful, the revolt of Horia and Closca was brutally suppressed in December of 1784. Horia and Closca were among the many who were ordered executed by quartering.

The next high point in Lehrer's history has to do with the great Hungarian revolution of 1848 under the leadership of Lajos Kossuth. Kossuth favored a whole array of reforms for the Hungarian people—but on the issue of self-determination for the Romanians and the other minorities in Hungary, his stand was indistinguishable from that of the Hungarian conservatives. Later, when his own revolution had failed, he came to see that one could not ask for the right of self-determination for the Hungarians and, at the same time, deny this right to the Romanians. This moral inconsistency, he realized, may well have cost him the success of his revolution.

Still another landmark in Lehrer's history is the Apponyi law of 1907 which basically called for the Magyarization of the Romanian majority in Transylvania. This was to be accomplished primarily through the Magyarization of the schools. But the process also involved the elimination of Romanian credit institutions, the Magyarization of geographic and village names, and powerful pressures to compel individuals to change their names to Hungarian equivalents.

Lehrer quotes a December 1907 statement by Ludovic de Mocsany, whom he describes as "one of the most enlightened Hungarian politicians of the beginning of the 20th century":

> Excessive fear makes us commit actions which are really imprudent. I refer to the general tendency to support Magyarization. I know very well that here and there, in the four corners of our country, there is frenzied applause whenever that great chauvinist, Desider Banffy, repeats unremittingly that our motherland will never be happy until the last person belonging to the Romanian or Slovak races is turned into a genuine Magyar. And why is it that in our Parliament one could declaim, without fear of punishment, that the Magyar language has to be made the exclusive instrument of public education?

What is the rationale of the law which stipulates that half of the classes in all of the elementary schools which belong to the other nationalities should be dedicated to the study of the Magyar language?

Mocsany was one of the many prominent Hungarians who felt guilty or uneasy about the continued repression of the Romanian people and the repeated attempts at Magyarization. Lehrer also quotes this telling statement from "The Downfall of the Danubian Monarchy" by the Hungarian diplomat Baron Szilassy:

Under the protection of a common army, Hungary—that is, its masters, the Hungarian magnates—put into practice the policy of the Magyarization of the non-Hungarian nationalities, believing that a policy that had proved impossible elsewhere in the world could be applied successfully in Budapest. We, the Hungarians, refused to learn anything. We did not wish to take into account that eastern Hungary was inhabited by the Romanians, who represented the majority of the people there. In 1864, Austria granted the Romanians their national independence. Three years later, Hungary violated this independence. To torture a people like this was, in the 20th century, simply intolerable. The federal system was the only system which could have avoided disaster. But still we rejected it.

The conclusion of World War I represented a watershed. Despite powerful pressures to enter the war on the side of the Central Powers, Romania originally remained neutral. Transylvanian-Romanians, however, were impressed into service with the Austro-Hungarian forces by the tens of thousands. This recruitment was accompanied by increasingly harsh measures directed against the Romanians in Transylvania. According to Decree no. 4,000, for example, which was put out in 1917 in the name of the presidency of the Hungarian council of ministers, Romanians could no longer buy a plot of land anywhere in the country without the prior permission of the ministry of agriculture in Budapest. Since such permission was rarely, if ever, granted, the decree had the effect of prohibiting Romanians from buying land in a country where they had resided for more than a thousand years.

The Allies entered into negotiations with a Romanian state that was increasingly driven by overwhelming popular sympathy for the Romanian cause in Transylvania. On August 17, 1916, Romania signed a treaty of alliance with the Allies. In return for an Allied guarantee that the end of the war would result in a definitive solution to the Transylvanian problem, Romania agreed to enter the war against the Central Powers by August 28. The meeting of the Austro-Hungarian Crown Council which took place in Vienna on October 15, 1918, made a serious effort to prevent the downfall of the monarchy by attempting to turn Austria-Hungary into a federal state where all nationalities would be independent and equal. But it was too late. On December 1, 1918, a vast Romanian assembly convened in the town of Alba-Julia, and proclaimed the unification of Transylvania with Romania.

When World War I was over, Transylvania was annexed to Romania by treaty. The dividing line remained a bone of contention for the simple reason that there were many basically Hungarian areas that had a sizeable quota of Romanian residents—and vice versa. But Lehrer makes the point that the Hungarian delegation brought with it to the peace conference a map supposedly suggesting frontier concessions significantly to the west of the border finally agreed to under the Trianon treaty. He denies the charge that Hungary was "mutilated" by the peace treaty. He says that "what was taken away from the Hungarians was only equal to what they had conquered over the centuries by arbitrary methods and by violence." He also flatly contradicts the Hungarian charges that the Romanian government persecuted its new Hungarian subjects, pointing out that, under Romanian rule, the number of Hungarian publications and schools and cultural organizations in Transylvania increased dramatically and that the Hungarian peasants were the beneficiaries, at least to the same degree as the Romanians, of the land reform measures that were enacted.

In August 1940, history reversed itself. Hungary demanded that the Axis governments act as arbitrators of its historic differences with Romania over the question of Transylvania. Acting on this demand, Count Galeazzo Ciano, Mussolini's foreign minister, and Hitler's foreign minister, Count Joachim von Ribbentrop, summoned the representatives of Romania and Hungary to a meeting in Vienna at the end of August 1940. They informed the Romanians that "they had

only forty-eight hours at their disposal to settle the Transylvanian problem, and that no delay could be tolerated for a
debate of the issue." The outcome of the conference was fore-
ordained. The "arbitration" awarded the northern part of Transylvania to Hungary. Commenting on the decision, Count
Ciano said: "We have settled a very difficult problem, not only
with scrupulous impartiality but with the certitude that our
decision will result in complete trust for the future between
the two countries which have addressed us."

Nothing, of course, could have been further from the truth.

In the wake of World War II, both Hungary and Romania
were victims of Soviet expansionism. The Soviet Union annexed Bessarabia and most of Bukovina from Romania and
"compensated" Romania by permitting it to reannex Transylvania on its west.

For the time being, the prime issue in all of central Europe
has to do with the imposition of totalitarian communist regimes
which violate all the rules of human rights and which have led
to economic disaster. But one day the countries of central Europe will be free. When that day arrives, it would be distinctly
advantageous if the West were armed with well-informed and
carefully considered opinions on issues such as the Transylvanian problem.

I have to the best of my ability adhered faithfully to the
thrust of Lehrer's text. It is my feeling that Lehrer's frequently
excessive criticism of the Hungarians has a strange ring at this
juncture in history. But then one must remember that this
book was written before the end of World War II, when all the
pent-up hatred resulting from hundreds of years of Hungarian
oppression had been reactivated by Hungary's incorporation
of northern Transylvania under the auspices of Hitler and
Mussolini. The change that can be wrought in a relatively short
period of time is evident from the contrast between the attitude
of the French people toward the Germans in 1944, at the time
Lehrer wrote his book, and their attitude toward the Germans
today.

It is also to be pointed out that Lehrer distinguishes repeatedly between the Hungarian nobility and the Hungarian
peasant masses. Indeed, the nobility, as owners of vast estates,
imposed a regime that was almost as repressive for the Hungarian peasant masses as it was for the Romanians. Lehrer
also gives full credit to the many more generous Hungarian

spirits who shared the international indignation over Hungary's treatment of its Romanian citizens.

In a more moderate vein, Lehrer said in his concluding remarks: "On the day when the despotic regime in Budapest is replaced by a sincere and democratic regime, nothing will stand in the way of cooperation between the two neighboring European peoples, the Hungarians and the Romanians. But the condition sine qua non for such cooperation is the unity of Transylvania within the natural frontiers of Romanianism."

With the reservations outlined above, I believe that Lehrer's book makes an important contribution to the understanding of a fascinating and complex historical situation and should be read by all to whom Transylvania is somewhat more than the fabled home of Dracula.

David Martin

INTRODUCTION

On the occasion of his campaign in Egypt, Napoleon brought with him a score of famous scholars, including scientists and philosophers, in order to conduct an on-the-spot investigation of the relics of an ancient past—the proofs of a civilization which had flourished on the banks of the Nile a long time ago. On the deck of the ship which was taking them to Egypt, the French scholars were talking—with the vivaciousness which is characteristic of all peoples of Latin origin—about the most controversial scientific and philosophical problems. In these discussions, the future emperor of France quite often took an active part, with that common sense which represented the fundamental trait of his genius.

One starry night, while the ship was gliding smoothly over the waters of the Mediterranean Sea, the philosophers were arguing animatedly about problems which had always tormented the human mind: spiritualism, materialism, and the existence of God. Napoleon came up in the thick of the battle. An atheist was pompously expounding his theory concerning the nonexistence of divinity, defending the concept of an absolute materialism. Another atheist followed him, adding even more subtle and complicated arguments to those of the men who had spoken before him.

Napoleon listened attentively to the presentations by these two very learned men, and then, pointing to the starry sky, addressed the representatives of science and philosophy with the following words, superb in their simplicity: "Gentlemen, you can go on as long as you wish—but answer this question: Who has made all these?"

I recalled this incident in Napoleon's life—which was mentioned by Emerson—after returning from a research trip in Transylvania during the summer of 1940, a short while before

1

the Vienna agreement. I had read the various writings which the opponents of Romanian continuity in Transylvania had sponsored after the appearance in 1871 of Robert Rossler's famous work *Rumänische Studien* ("Romanian Studies"). This was the first attack on the principle of Romanian continuity in Transylvania and the other territories which had once constituted the ancient Roman province of Dacia.

Historians, pseudo-historians, philologists, publicists, and newspaper writers—some of them honest-minded people, others of more questionable motivation, some seeking to be objective, others not troubling to conceal a quite passionate partisanship—all wanted to have a word to say on this delicate problem. More often than not their writings transgressed the framework of scientific argument to reach into the more flexible area of political ideas.

I have investigated all of the theories on this subject, from the most learned ones to the most childish. I have studied all the arguments invoked. I have listened to ardent pleadings. At a certain moment, after listening to countless sophisms and dialectical subtleties and after witnessing numerous exhibitions of tightrope walking and chauvinistic *tours de force*, I had the impression that every new book I read carried me deeper and deeper into the thick of a tropical forest.

So different were the arguments invoked by the supporters of the anti-Romanian thesis, so contradictory were the conclusions reached by these supporters, that I must confess I set foot on Transylvania's soil with a lot of trepidation in my heart.

But the deeper I went into Transylvania, the stronger became my belief that the detractors of the Romanian continuity in this province beyond the Carpathians had created a false Baedeker for the confusion of those who had no way of knowing the real facts of the situation.

Imagine a guide for the blind, starting from the presence of Algerian and Moroccan mosques on the banks of the Seine, populating the 20 *arondissements* of Paris with a few thousand fez-wearing Moslems, especially on the Boulevard de la Gare. What an image of Paris would form in the mind of the blind traveler who is offered such a description of the city, which ignores all of its eternal cathedrals and its ancient Latinity!

Traveling in Transylvania, one can't help recalling, sometimes with sad amusement, all the phantasmagorias and aberrations and all the chauvinist lies which characterize the arguments of those who deny the Romanian continuity in the area. Indeed, one cannot restrain oneself from saying to those who slander what should be an indisputable reality: "Go on talking as long as you wish, gentlemen, but who else created the eminently Romanian aspect of this land? Who else but the Romanian people?" What a different appearance this battle of the Transylvanian thesis and antithesis acquires when one takes a good on-the-spot look at things. Think of a tropical plant, which is withering because of the artificial light in the hothouse, coming back to life in the light and warmth of a natural climate.

I have sought to be as objective as possible in writing this book. My goal is the establishment of the truth. In striving toward this goal, I shall be content if I have contributed to clarifying this ostensibly intricate, but in fact very simple central European problem. And if I succeed in convincing the reader of the objectivity of my research and my reasoning, I shall have the satisfaction of not feeling lonely at the end of my trip.

I would like to stress the fact that the book was finished before August 23, 1944. But the political atmosphere at the time it was written did not prevent me from revealing to public opinion in the West the true face of the so-called Vienna arbitration—an arbitrary, unjust, and politically inane act, sponsored and forcibly imposed by the two partners, Il Duce and the Führer, who believed that the thousand-year-old culture of Europe had fallen into such decay that Europe's destiny could be written by them—by two adventurers, posing as leaders.

Diktats imposed by dictators have always shared the fate of their creators. Indeed, nothing can be achieved by violence—nor by dictatorships, nor *Diktats*—it is like trying to erect a building on sand.

1. THE HUNGARIAN SUBJUGATION OF TRANSYLVANIA

The Alfold

Toward the end of the ninth century, the early Hungarians, following the valleys and rivers of the region and crossing the pathways in the forest-covered northern Carpathians, got as far as Pannonia. The seven Magyar tribes set up their final settlements on the plains, avoiding the mountain regions which were not in harmony with their way of life.

On the ample plains of Pannonia—the Alfold, as the Hungarians call it—dominated to the east and north by the Bihor and Maramures mountains, the forefathers of today's Hungarians found the most favorable conditions for harmonious historical development and ethnic unity. This much goes unchallenged by all Hungarian writers.

"On this plain, which looks like a sea to me," says the great Hungarian national poet, Petofi, "I feel at home." The Frenchman Sayons paints this picture of the indestructible connection existing between the Hungarian people and the open plains they live on: "The true motherland of the Hungarians is the Alfold, a low plain. It is there that the conquerors settled their people under Arpad. It is especially there that their history should have come to fruition through the centuries. It is there that this history exists in all its fullness."

. . . and Transylvania

Thus, Transylvania, with its plateau and mountain depressions and mountain ranges which surrounded it on all sides, was neither a geographic nor historic fulfillment for the Hungarian people, who were preeminently a people of the plains—of the Hungarian steppes. In the life of the Hungarian people, Transylvania was an accident. Originally the mountains separated the Hungarians from this land. For them, Transylvania was a land "over the mountains"—*Ultrasilvaniae.* The Hungarian is *Erdely*—("ero," silva; and "elu," ultra).

If the Hungarians had been luckier in their expeditions to the West, Transylvania would never have come under Hungarian rule.

This is what Transylvania means to the Hungarians.

On the other hand, for the Romanians Transylvania was the heart of ancient Dacia itself, pulsating with the same blood for thousands of years.

What the Alfold meant to the forefathers of today's Hungarians, the land of Transylvania meant to the ancestors of today's Romanians. In the forest-covered mountains and their fortresses on the hills, the peaceful people of Trajan Dacia were able to hold out for centuries against the invasions which succeeded each other with relentless regularity. This impenetrable fortress is the place where the very existence of the Romanian nation was conceived.

The Conquest of Transylvania

The whole history of this land, from the moment when the Hungarian conquerors extended their rule over it to the contemporary epoch, gives living proof of its regional will to preserve its Romanian spirit unaltered. The conquest of Transylvania took place long after the conquest of Pannonia by the Magyar tribes. It was carried out in stages, and many fierce battles were fought by the Romanian populace against the new invaders.

These battles, which ended in the submission of the Romanian populace in the three principalities of Transylvania (which corresponded to the three Dacias—*Porolissensis, Apulensis,* and *Malvensis*) are related at length in the ancient Hungarian folksongs and ballads and constitute the source of inspiration of the famous *Gesta Hungarorum*, which was written by an anonymous chronicler.

It was not until the time of Ladislau the Holy, who ruled from 1077 to 1095, that Transylvania was brought under the suzerainty of Hungary (Robert Rossler).

The Extensively researched memoranda that the

Hungarian delegation brought to the peace conference in 1920 contained this statement: "The history of Transylvania from St. Stephen's death up to the epoch of St. Ladislau is shrouded in deep darkness."

The old Hungarian chronicles have largely removed the veil which shrouded those days in mystery. But it is a curious fact that the Hungarians themselves have shown little interest in these old chronicles, which constitute the principal Hungarian source regarding the conquest of Pannonia and the submission of the eastern territories.

The Battles with the Romanians

The much-quoted anonymous chronicler of King Bela offers a detailed description of the battles which the three Hungarian tribes of Tuhutum, Tosu, and Elend fought with the dukes of the Romanian provinces which they subjugated: Menumorut (in *Dacia Porolissensis*), Gelu (in *Dacia Apulensis*), and Glad (in *Dacia Malvensis*).

Hungarian views differ with respect to the historical value of the anonymous chronicler of King Bela, especially with regard to the extensive description of the native Romanian populations which the Hungarians found in Transylvania.

The Hungarians were never able to forgive the anonymous chronicler of King Bela for the passages he wrote concerning the indigenous Romanian population of Transylvania. There was no shortage of epithets. The chronicler has been referred to as a "narrator of fables," as an "inventor of etymologies," as a "poet and writer of legends," as a "flatterer." He encountered different treatment, however, when it came to other aspects of his history. Then he became a "matchless geographer" and a "keen scholar of history." For instance, Janos Melich states that the anonymous chronicler was "one of the most outstanding Hungarian historians," while E. Jakobowich writes that "the data presented by the despised anonymous chronicler contains very important information about the history of Hungary."

But, no matter what opinion the Hungarians of today may hold concerning the work of the anonymous chronicler, what is certain is that in the 13th century a Hungarian writer flatly asserted that the Romanians were present in Transylvanian territory when the Hungarians invaded the province.

A professor at the University of Budapest, Eugen Horvath,

attempted to argue the matter with Professor Arthur Seton-Watson (Scotus Viator), one of the most profound scholars of the history of the Hapsburg monarchy. In a paper published in Budapest in 1936, he completely misrepresented what the anonymous chronicler had written concerning the Romanians. In this way he perhaps thought he could settle for all time the troublesome reference to the Romanian precedence in Transylvania. Thus, he declared that the anonymous chronicler had said that the Hungarians found "a certain number of Romanians, isolated on the snow-capped mountains of Transylvania." In fact, the anonymous chronicler spoke about the Wallachians* who lived in all regions which the Hungarians had conquered by the sword.

There is one other matter. If the Romanians were only poor miserable shepherds who lived in gorges between those mountains that were always covered by snow, what shall be said about the illustrious Hungarian leader, Arpad, described by modern historians as a political personality of first importance, who consented to the marriage of his son, Zulta, to the daughter of Menumorut, the duke of these shepherds?

Hungarian historians overlook the fact that *Gesta Hungarorum* is not the only chronicle that contains references to the indigenous Romanian population of Transylvania prior to the Hungarian conquest. Similar references are to be found in the chronicle of Simonis de Geza (*Chronicon Hungaricum*), in the illustrated chronicle published in Vienna (*Chronicon pictum Vindobonensis*), and in the Hildeschein chronicle published in Germany. Similar references are also to be found in all the documents of the Hungarian monarchs which deal with Transylvania.

The Romanians whom the Hungarians found in Transylvania had their own political organizations. According to certain Hungarian documents, such as those dealing with the military expeditions of the Transylvanian Saxon leader Ioachim, in the county of Sibiu, the Transylvanian Wallachians had their own military organization.

The Political Organizations of the Romanians in Transylvania

The essence of the Romanian political organization was represented by the *knezats*—small administrative units within

---

Strictly speaking the Wallachians, a Romanian people, were the residents of the southern principality of Wallachia. The term was commonly used in Hungary to mean Transylvanian Romanians or Romanians in general.

which the Romanian peasants and shepherds lived a life which was perhaps not marked by outstanding historical events, but was not without drama and unrest.

The *knezats* had judicial and administrative duties. They administered justice according to the Romanian law, *jus valachicum*, in so-called "seats," and they also recruited "braves"—brave young men who were always ready to defend their inheritance against invaders of all kinds.

The *knezats* were not limited to Transylvania. They were in fact spread all over those regions, on either side of the Carpathians, where the Romanians had lived. But the *knezats* were specific to the Romanians; they were social organizations which were not to be found either among the Hungarians or among the Slavs.

Above the *knezats*, as a sort of central organization of the political life, were the principalities, whose main duty was the organization of territorial defense but which also had other administrative duties.

Today, when history possesses irrefutable evidence about the Romanian presence in Trajan Dacia, it is clear that the Romanians could not have held out against so many barbarian invasions if the defense of their territory had not been assured by the leaders of their political organizations, the *voivodes*.

Although they bore Slavic names, these political organizations were, in their essence, purely Romanian. The Romanians adapted these names, borrowed from the Slavs, to ancient institutions which some investigators trace back to a Latin origin. The *kneazs*, who administered justice, bore for a long time the title of *judicius* (*knezii vel judices*). There is reason for believing that this was equivalent to *duumvirii iuredicundo* (two-man judicial board) of ancient Dacia.

The works of some researchers, such as N. Iorga, Lupas, and Nistor demonstrate that the title *kneaz* had a completely different meaning with the Slavs than it did with the Romanians. Similarly, the term *voivode* was more all-inclusive with the Wallachians than with the Slavs.

Thus, the Slav *kneaz* was a sort of king, while with the Romanians he was a *primus inter pares*, elected from among the well-to-do peasantry. A *kneaz* could often rise to the highest political rank and become a *voivode*. According to Hurmuzaki, this was the case of the well-known *voivode*, Litovoi.

At the time the Hungarians invaded Transylvania, these

political organizations had deep roots among the Wallachian populace of Transylvania. Under Arpad, the Hungarians endeavored to replace the indigenous political institutions with administrative divisions, as they had done in Pannonia. These administrative divisions were known as *comitats*, and they were led by *comits*. The Hungarian efforts were in vain with the Romanians. The only *comits* the Hungarians managed to appoint in Transylvania were those of the Transylvanian Saxons and the Transylvanian Szecklers* (*comes Saxorum, Sachsengraf*, and *comes sicularum*). The *comitat* at Solnoc existed for so short a time that it hardly constitutes an exception to the rule.

The Transylvanian Saxons' and Szecklers' political organization, although it was modeled on the administrative division characteristic of the *comitats*, was very much inspired by the Transylvanian political organization; their seats, which were called *szek* and *Stuhl*, were a real counterpart of the seats (*sedes*) in the Romanian *knezats*.

Taking these facts into consideration, it becomes questionable to assert, as Professor Horvath of the University of Budapest did, that it was Hungarians who taught the Romanians the art of political organization.

The Latin-Hungarian documents speak about Romanian districts (*districtus valachales*) at Deva, Hateg, and Fagaras as well as about the Romanian law (*jus valachicum*).

If the Hungarians had introduced their own political organizations in Transylvania, then, of course, instead of the *knezats*—whose detailed description is to be found in *Carmen miserabile* of the Italian monk, Rogerius—*comitats* on the Hungarian style would have existed.

Horvath tries to find support for his assertions in philological data. The Romanians, he said, borrowed from the Hungarians the words which express concepts of political organization. Consequently, he added, they must have adopted the organizations themselves. In order to illustrate his theory, the Budapest professor listed words which have nothing to do with the political organization of the country, such as *mester*

The Szecklers, who speak a Hungarian dialect, are today generally considered part of the Hungarian people. But it was not always so. As this book makes clear, the Szecklers for many centuries regarded themselves as a national entity distinct from the Hungarians and on occasion even made common cause with the Romanians against them.

("master") or *gazda* ("host"), or words which had been borrowed by both the Romanians and the Hungarians from the Slavs. Examples of this latter category are *hat* ("frontier path") of north Slavic origin, *pecete* ("seal") of old Slavic origin, and *ban* ("money") which is of southern Slavic origin. But Horvath forgot that the Romanian language is the only Romance language which has preserved the word *dominus* with its original meaning of *Domn*, that is, a king, and that the Latin *imperator* is still in usage today, after 2,000 years, in the slightly revised form of *imparat* ("emperor"). He also forgot that in Byzantine documents the Hungarian leaders were mentioned using the Slav word *voevod*, and that the lofty *kiraly*, which expresses the notion of royalty, comes in fact from the Slav word *kral*.

As Sayons remarked, the Finno-Ugrian vocabulary of the Hungarian tribes which settled in Europe was extremely limited, an indication of a backward civilization. This is another reason why it is questionable to speak of a Hungarian influence on early Romanian political organizations.

The historian, Iorga, says that "the assimilation of the Slavs, and the extended German influence, and the strong efforts of the Catholic church were necessary to raise this people, so much like the Huns and the Avars, to a level corresponding to that of the barbarians, who became more civilized only as a result of their exposure to western civilization."

Far from exercising an influence over the political organizations of the nations that shared Transylvania with them, most of the Hungarian cultural notions, according to the Romanian historian, were borrowed from the Slavs.

The Principalities (Voivodates)

The first *voivodes* of Transylvania are mentioned in documents that go as far back as the 12th century. The list of the *voivodes* who ruled beyond the mountains is comprehensive. It misses virtually no names, beginning with the year 1103, when *voivode* Mercurius of Ultrasylvania is mentioned for the first time, until 1555, when two *voivodes* are mentioned by Ferdinand of Hapsburg.

Beyond this there is no doubt that there were *voivodes* even before the year 1103—a fact that was accepted by Paular in the year 1888—but their names have not come down to us. Some *voivodes* such as Leuca-Voda (1219) and Posa (*Pousa Woyvoda Ultrasilvano*) in 1227 had genuine Romanian names.

The Permanence of Autochthonous Ways of Life

The Hungarians were obliged to accept the quasi-independent situation of the Romanian *voivodates* and to content themselves with their rule over Transylvania, which was more Romanian than Hungarian. Hungary proper and the *voivodate* of Transylvania were two distinct entities, the only link between them being represented by the *voivodes'* oath of obedience. Two facts confirm the nominal relationship which characterized Hungarian rule over the Romanian people of Transylvania. Giula *cel Mic* ("Giula the Small"), the *voivode* of Transylvania, who was the fourth in chronological order (his three predecessors were Tuhutum, Horca, and Giula), adopted the Christian Orthodox rite against the will of the Catholic king, Stefan *cel Sfint* ("Stephen the Holy") and, because his attitude was hostile to Hungary, he was attacked by the army of the Hungarian king, and his country was "joined to the kingdom" (*Adiuncto Panoniae*). It is clear, therefore, that for a century after the conquest of Pannonia, Transylvania was not under Hungarian rule.

In the Banat region, in the former *Dacia Malvensis*, the situation was virtually the same. After Glad, the duke of the Wallachians, swore his oath of obedience, the Romanians continued to have ties with the eastern Roman Empire. *Voivode* Ahtum, one of Glad's successors, was accused for this reason of dishonesty toward the Hungarian crown, and the Banat *voivodate* was also joined to Hungary after the battles led by Sunad, King Stephen the Holy's nephew.

A Hungarian writer, Ion Nistor, said of this period in history that "Even after the territories of the two Dacias (*Porolissensis* and *Apulensis*) had been annexed by Hungary, the Hungarian kings respected the Dacian political and military organizations, maintaining the ancient *voivodal* institutions in these regions."

The relations between Hungary and Transylvania varied with the difference in power between the *voivode* and the king. If the *voivode* was weak, then the king of Hungary exercised his rule more forcibly. And, similarly, if the *voivode* was strong, Hungary's attitude was a more moderate one.

Hungarian historians themselves admit that such a state of affairs existed. In *The History of the Magyar Nation under the Arpad Kings*, Gyula Pauler asserts that Transylvania had always been ruled by *voivodes*. Alexandru Szilagy in *The His-*

tory of Transylvania, published in 1866, firmly declared that Transylvania was never completely joined to Hungary, Hungary and Transylvania being "two completely different countries."

This fact is completely understandable, from the geographical point of view and from the viewpoint of Hungarian foreign policy, both during and after the monarchy.

Before the various invaders reached the territory of Pannonia, they invariably had to cross Transylvania. Since the Hungarian element was not able to provide Transylvania with a secure defense—in fact, the Hungarians were very poorly represented in the defending forces—Transylvania had to defend itself with the men and means at hand. This fact naturally contributed to the strengthening of the province's autonomy.

On the other hand, because of Hungarian involvement in western expansion, the eastern part of Transylvania was neglected. The problems of this region, indeed, were among the last to command the attention of the Arpad kings, because, as the Hungarian writer Ladislau Kovary, suggestively remarked, "Transylvania has always been looking to the East," that is, to the Eastern Roman Empire.

Even before the conquest of Transylvania, says Balint Homan, the Hungarians had to answer the central question whether they wished to expand toward the east or toward the west. The Magyars chose the west (*Das Ungartum wahlte den Westen*). Janossy Denes affirms that the Hungarian leaders were preoccupied with the same choice even after the conquest of the land. "Hungary," he says, "chose the west, which brought about its independence and a life of its own." (*Alleinherrschaft und Selbstandigkeit.*)

Another factor which contributed dramatically to the continuity of the old Romanian ways in Transylvania and to the continuity of the autochthonous ethnic element over the years was the remarkably meager number—even for those days—of the Hungarian invaders.

According to the old Hungarian chronicles, when the Hungarians conquered the area between the Carpathians and the Danube, they numbered all told some 200,000. Of this number, 25,000 were warriors. The plundering war expeditions with which the Hungarians commenced their history resulted in the decrease of these numbers. After the battles with the Moravians and the Bulgarian troops of Tzar Simion, after Bulgaria was devastated and Byzantium was invaded, after northern Italy was plundered and Croatia and Corinth were conquered, after the victories of Brenta (899) and Ennsburg (907) and the retreats from Mersburg (933), from the Leech plain (955), and from Adrianopolis (970)—after all these costly experiences, it is inconceivable that the initial number of Hungarians did not decrease quite substantially.

"Only extremely fortunate circumstances," said C. Sassu in his work *The Romanians and the Hungarians,* "due to the fact that Otto I was quite taken up with other problems—such as the subjection and Germanizing of the Slavs on the eastern banks of the Elbe and his campaigns in Italy for the purpose of assuring his future imperial dignity—protected the Hungarians from complete ruin, which was the fate their relatives, the Huns and the Avars, had met before."

So the Hungarians did not manage to populate all of Pannonia, nor did they manage to expand to the east.

Tibor Eckhardt admitted this fact, stating that at the beginning the Magyars could not adequately populate even the territory which became Hungarian after the Trianon Treaty. "Their number," said Eckhardt, "was too small to achieve that."

In fact, this is the natural explanation of the numerous colonists whom the Hungarians brought to Transylvania, and whom the ancient chroniclers called "guests." According to a later Magyar viewpoint, the mission of these "guests" was to drive out the centuries-old owners of the newly colonized land.

It would be an error, however, when referring to those days, to give the word "colonists" the meaning that it has today.

The places where these "guests" settled were not uninhabited. They were, in fact, inhabited by ancient autochthonous populations who were capable of defending their small pieces of land, but who were not ready to serve as a sort of protective shield for the Alfold settlements of the Hungarians.

Military reasons, in the first place, and economic and political ones, in the second place, were the factors responsible for the existence of these foreign settlements amid the native Romanian populations of Dacian-Roman origin.

2. COLONIZATION AND DENATIONALIZATION

The Szecklers

The first colonists the Hungarians settled in the eastern and south-eastern regions of Transylvania were the Szecklers. Their settlement had a well-defined goal: to defend the eastern borders of the territory ruled by the Hungarians against the Petchenegs and the Cumans, peoples who were masters of the land on the eastern side of the Carpathians and who, on occasion, extended their rule over the Transylvanian regions beyond the Carpathians.

We do not have the precise data concerning the colonization of the Szecklers. What is known for certain, however, is that they came before the German colonists. It is most likely that they came to the regions populated by the Szecklers today, either at the end of the 11th century or at the beginning of the 12th century. The first German colonists are mentioned approximately 1140 A.D.

According to an early opinion, which is also supported by old Hungarian chroniclers and which was brought to light in recent years by the historian Balint Homan, the Szecklers were the descendants of the Huns—that is, of the 3,000 Huns who did not follow Attila's son Chaba, into Scythia. This body of Huns must have been waiting somewhere in the Carpathians for almost six centuries for their blood relatives, the Hungarians, even helping them to conquer Pannonia.

"After conquering Pannonia together [with the Hungarians], the Szecklers received a part of the land—but not in the Pannonian plain. In this respect they shared the fate with their mountain neighbors, the Wallachians, with whom they mingled and from whom, it is said, the Szecklers borrowed the alphabet."

The above quotation is from *Gesta Hungarorum* by Simonis de Geza, a priest at the court of Ladislau IV (1278-1290). This quotation, according to the modern Hungarian historians, had to do with the epoch of Ladislau the Holy, who was king of the Hungarians at the beginning of the 11th century A.D.

It is a curious fact that it is from these chroniclers that the Hungarians borrow the traditional Hun belief concerning the Szecklers' origin, in order to prove the autochthonous character of the enclave in eastern Transylvania. The same Hungarians reject the statements of the chroniclers regarding the priority of the Romanians, both with regard to the Hungarians and the Szecklers. The assertion of this priority, indeed, is expressed firmly and repeatedly in the old Hungarian documents. I have mentioned this matter in order to emphasize once more the passion displayed by Hungarian historians when they wrote or commented on the history of Transylvania.

The Hungarian historian Hunfalvy rebelled against this assertion of the Szecklers' origin, saying that they were no less Hungarian than the Hungarians themselves and that "they were transplanted from their mother country as defenders of the eastern boundary." The theory that the Szecklers colonized the eastern part of Transylvania is supported by many historians who do not accept the Hunnish theory of their origin. But not all the Hungarian historians agree on the Magyar origin of the Szecklers. Dozens of theories were designed to solve the mystery which surrounded the Szecklers' origin, but none of them could withstand serious historical analysis.

An English monk of the 17th century ventured the hypothesis that the Szecklers were a branch of the Scythians, brought to Transylvania by the Huns.

The historian Gyula Pauler, maintains, however, that the Szecklers were of Magyar origin. Carol Szabo expresses the opinion that they are the descendants of the Cabars and belong to the nomadic Chazars. Ladislau Rethy asserts that the Szecklers could be a branch of the Petchenegs, and Iosif Thury considers them of Hunnish-Avaric origin, while I. Karacsonyi, after first theorizing that the Szecklers were descendants of the Bulgarians, then rejects this first theory and speculates that the Szecklers could be direct descendants of the Gepidae, a people of Germanic origin.

D. G. Popa-Lisseanu, one of the outstanding Romanian scholars of the problem, to whom we are indebted for much information regarding the Szecklers, sees in Karacsonyi's change of attitude after World War I a deliberate attempt to create a connecting bridge between the German and Magyar peoples, thus introducing a political substratum into a problem which should be governed by scientific considerations only.

But no matter what their origin might be, we know as a fact that, before settling in the regions adjacent to Transylvania, the Szecklers could be found in other regions of Hungary. Indeed, there are documents which speak of their presence in the northern region and in other parts of Hungary. In every case they are referred to as defenders of the camps and burghs.

"The Szecklers," said the Romanian writer Popa-Lisseanu, "are not so much a tribe as a profession. In those days they were *servientes regis*—that is, the king's servants."

Szecklers were thus mercenaries who defended the established order, in return for which they were granted the right to establish their own settlements. They represented a social class, not a people. If matters had developed normally, the Szecklers—colonizing elements within the Romanian populace (from whom they borrowed the alphabet)—should have become part of the indigenous populace by assimilation. But a contrary phenomenon took place. The indigenous people disappeared almost completely, while the colonizers became the dominant people of the area. This happened throughout the so-called Szeckler region consisting of the three border counties of Ciuc, Odorhei and Trei-Scaune, to which a part of the neighboring county of Mures should be added.

In 1930, the census registered almost 1,500,000 Hungarians in the entire territory of Romania. One-third of them (496,184) were Szecklers. Living in a restricted area, they managed to give this ancient Dacian land the appearance of an eminently Hungarian territory, in the first place because they were densely concentrated in a limited territory, and, in the second place, because they had adopted the Hungarian language as their own a long time previously. In fact, this region has a more genuinely Hungarian appearance than Hungary proper, where there still exist old Slavic and Germanic elements.

That there were Romanians in the regions today populated by the Szecklers is recognized by Simonis de Keza, by the old Hungarian documents which speak of the Romanian *knezats* set up in the midst of the Szecklers, and by all statistics that are historically available. Today, of the 496,184 inhabitants who are of Szeckler origin, only 68,423 declare themselves to be Romanian, and of this number, 11,042 cannot speak the Romanian language.

The Denationalization of the Romanians in the Szeckler Region

We shall review the means used by the Hungarians to denationalize the Romanians in the Szeckler region. This will help us to understand how, characterized by much violence, a deceptive state of affairs was created—which was enough to offer justification for the fragile edifice erected in Vienna in 1940.

Anyone tracing the boundary between the two countries will easily note that the concentration of the Szeckler population should have been regarded as the fundamental element for marking the boundary between Romania and Hungary. "One of the greatest gains of the new settlement," said Vilmos Siegler in his book *The Return to the Mother Country in the East*, "is without any doubt the return of the Szecklers to their mother country, since these people represent one of the most valuable branches of the Hungarian race." Siegler was one of the officials of the ministry of external affairs of Hungary.

Among those Romanians who were "denationalized" as a result of pressures and temptations of all kinds, the upper class occupied first place. It was from their ranks that the *voivoides* (some of whom had under their rule only a very limited territory), the *kneazs*, and the gentry were chosen. Their elevations to the nobility and their endowments from the king's domains (according to the medieval concept, all land was the king's property) were conditioned by their Magyarization and their conversion to the Catholic church. The only Transylvanian *boyards* who preserved their ancient faith unaltered were those in Fagaras County, and that was only thanks to their close contacts with the Romanians on the other side of the Carpathians, as well as to a special political situation that existed in the area. The large number of special rites and privileges which the Szecklers enjoyed, according to Popa-Lisseanu, resembled more than anything else the temptation of the apple. This was a trap into which the native Romanian inhabitants fell.

Religion as an Instrument of Denationalization

The lower class, meaning primarily the peasantry, because they had a basically conservative attitude toward their ancient traditions, were more resistant to conversion to Catholicism. Moreover, it appears that the Orthodox rite exercised so much influence over the Szeckler population that in 1234 Pope Gregory IXth thought it necessary to intervene to halt the continuing loss of Catholic faithful to the Orthodox church. This he did "in the interests of those Hungarians and Germans in the Kingdom of Hungary who, together with the Wallachians, despised the Catholic bishop of Cimania and received the Holy Communion from the fraudulent bishops who served according to the Greek rites."

Toward the end of the 13th century, the bishops began oppressing the Orthodox believers, whom they considered schismatic and heretical. The Buda Synod, which took place in the year 1299, decided among other things that the Romanians would not be allowed to build their own churches or other religious buildings or to take part in religious services in the existing churches.

In the year 1248, King Sigismund had already decided that "all noblemen and *kneazes* who allow Orthodox priests on their estates will be stripped of their possessions. Orthodox priests lead the people into heresy, and if they baptize a child according to the Orthodox rite, their possessions shall be confiscated."

Under these circumstances, it is easy to understand how many Romanians abandoned the beliefs of their ancestors. This facilitated the spread of Magyarism, since religion was in those days the central element in the making of nations. It is important to remember that the first king of Hungary, Stephen the Holy, received his title and his crown from Pope Sylvester.

After the Hungarians were defeated by the Turks at Mohacs in the year 1526, Buda was turned into a Turkish *pashalik*, or dependency, and Transylvania became an autonomous principality. During the reign of the Transylvania princes, who had broken with Catholicism in favor of Calvinism, the oppression of the Orthodox became even fiercer. Orthodox Romanians, no matter how small their number, were still considered heretics, but this time not by the Catholics but by the Calvinist "heretics."

In the year 1566, the Transylvania Diet at Sibiu decreed that "these Romanian bishops, priests, or monks who do not assent to abandon their heresy and continue to lead the people to their doom, must be expelled from the country." The subsequent union with the Roman church did not put an end to the persecution of the Orthodox Romanians. Oppression and persecution naturally resulted in important divisions among the Romanian inhabitants of the Szeckler region.

There are no statistics for those ancient times. Those which do exist start with the 18th century; from these we find that, while in 1700 the Romanians still represented 30 percent of the entire population of the Szeckler region, over the next 200 years they dropped to 5 percent.

In the year 1743, in 100 villages of the Szeckler county of Trei-Scaune, Romanians could still be found in 94 villages. Today, in 26 villages of that county, there is not a single Romanian, while in another 46 villages there has been a marked decrease in the Romanian population compared to that in the year 1743. In 22 villages, however, both sectors of the population had increased at approximately the same rate.

From the statistics compiled in 1733, 1750, 1760, and 1805, it is apparent that the "Szeckler bloc" contained numerous Romanian enclaves. In less than 170 years, entire villages were completely Szecklerized, so that villages which had once been conspicuously Romanian in appearance underwent a radical change.

The Szecklerization continued during World War I when the small number of Romanians who had managed to survive the forced Magyarization were obliged to adopt either the Catholic or the Calvinist faith. It is interesting to note that the process of Szecklerization continued during the first years of the establishment of Romanian rule. This was due to a number of phenomena, including mixed marriages and the limitation of baptismal ceremonies to the recognized churches. "Even under Romanian rule," wrote Sabin Opreanu in 1927, "The Romanians could not cope with the pressures of the Szeckler masses."

Although the process of Szecklerization had basically deprived the entire territory of its once heavily Romanian elements, in order to make the Hungarian nature of the "bloc" even more decisive, the Hungarians systematically left the Romanians out of their statistics. Their method was quite simple. Every man who could speak Hungarian was listed as Hungarian. But it was only natural that, after a thousand years of living together with the Szecklers, the Romanian population could also speak Hungarian. This strategem was really extremely naive. The real state of affairs could be gauged from the fact that the religion of the citizen was entered immediately after his nationality. The Romanians—and only the Romanians—belonged to the Orthodox or Greek Catholic church, while the Szecklers and the Hungarians were almost exclusively Catholic or Calvinist. Thus, in the nationality column only a very small number of inhabitants were listed as Romanian. However, in columns that gave the number of adherents to religions which were exclusively Romanian—i.e., the Orthodox and Greek Catholic religions—the numbers increased considerably. In the Szeckler county of Odor Hei, for instance, the census for the year 1910 listed only 2,840 Romanians. Actually, the number was much larger—if one looks at the entry referring to Hungarian subjects by religion, it becomes apparent that there were some 5,500 Romanians.

An even more dramatic case which demonstrates the mystification practiced by the Magyar authorities has to do with the village of Micfalau in Trei-Scaune county. In the census of 1910, only six Romanian inhabitants are listed in this village. However, the same statistics listed 918 Orthodox and Greek Catholic believers. For anyone who was aware of the real state of affairs, this was the figure that represented the real number of Romanians in the village of Micfalau. But for those who were not aware of the details or the Magyar practice of mystification, the Hungarian statistics were impressive.

The last century witnessed a campaign of forced denationalization by a variety of violent methods, which Hungarian authorities plied in the Szeckler region much more vigorously than in the rest of the territory. But while the Romanians, thanks to their numerical superiority, could hold out more effectively against the attacks they had to face in the other regions of Transylvania, in the Szeckler region denationalization had a highly destructive effect on the Romanian community. It took on the aspect of cultural genocide and, to a certain degree, of genocide in the physical sense.

A Hungarian writer, Geza Kosztenszky, had no scruples about affirming in public, and this with amazing frankness, the goal of Hungarian policy with regard to its minorities.

"Let us leave out," he said in his brochure *Our National Policy*, "the conventional lie according to which we do not want to kill the non-Magyar nationalities. *Yes, we want to exterminate them, and we have to exterminate them!*"

This is the kind of government which some of Lord Rothermere's partisans offer as an example of "tolerance."

Hungary's minister of foreign affairs at the time, Hyeronimy, immediately congratulated the author of these lines, and, in doing so declared himself a supporter of the most brutal denationalization tendencies that had been displayed by nationalistic writers in Hungary.

The Hungarians reached their goal and exceeded it.

There are, however, traces of the past which will never disappear but continue to exist as a permanent source of indictment in spite of all that has been done to encourage delusion. It is living evidence of the not so remote past. Indeed, there are in the Szeckler villages many small churches, now deserted, both Orthodox and Greek Catholic. Sometimes they stand, one beside the other, like "two orphan sisters" now abandoned because the Romanians disappeared from those villages a long time ago. But, by their mere presence, these abandoned holy places speak in vivid color about a past which has been recorded by history, a past which, despite their desperate attempts, the Hungarian chauvinists were never able to destroy.

The Use of the Schools to Denationalize the Romanians

Thus far we have dealt with the contribution made by religion to the process of denationalization of the Romanians who inhabited the territory of Transylvania. The church was assisted in this process by its inseparable companion, the schools. The first schools in Transylvania were confessional schools. It stands to reason that if the Orthodox church itself underwent such violent attack, the Orthodox schools were very limited in number. Generally, Romanian children had to attend Hungarian schools, where they did not hear a single word of Romanian spoken, except during the twice-weekly catechism classes.

In the entire Szeckler region, there were 27 Romanian schools compared with 438 Magyar schools of all kinds. Such was the situation in the field of elementary education. What this means is that there was one Romanian school for every 16 Hungarian schools, which exceeded even the overwhelming disproportion—1 to 7—between the Romanian and the Szeckler populace.

The situation in the field of higher education was simply tragic. In the entire Szeckler region, there was not a single Romanian secondary or professional school before World War I. In comparison, the Hungarians had 10 high schools, 15 civil schools, 4 professional schools, 20 schools for apprentices, and 25 agricultural schools—that is, a total of 74 secondary schools or schools of higher education. But there was not a single Romanian school. In fact, those students who were Romanian were deprived of the right to attend all schools of higher education if they did not belong to one of the Magyar religions.

The Hungarian school system was directed toward a well-determined goal. It sought to turn the polynational Hungarian state into a monolithic one, no matter if it had to resort to the violation of human conscience in order to reach that goal. Under such circumstances, when Count Albert Apponyi in his bulky propagandistic book *Justice for Hungary*, charged that the Romanian people in Transylvania lacked education, his characterization has to be put down as an outrageous act of cynicism. Because it is cynical to refuse a minority the right to be educated in its own language, and then accuse it of illiteracy!

Compelled to attend Hungarian elementary schools since there were no Romanian schools, obliged to speak the Magyar language on all occasions, surrounded on all sides by compact masses of Szecklers, subjected to all kinds of pressures and interference on the part of the state administration, Romanians in the Szeckler region lost their ability to communicate in the Romanian language. Ironically, many of them spoke about their Romanian nationality in Hungarian—for example, they would say *En Olah Vagyok* ("I am Romanian!").

Count Apponyi, it should be mentioned here, contributed to the undermining of Romanian culture by the laws he decreed. He said that there was no need for another culture to exist in Hungary, that the Magyar culture was that of the intellectual elite, "the cream of society." This elite, he said, must at all costs belong to the Hungarians.

The conceit which is characteristic of Hungarian nature was now replaced by a utilitarianism that was not quite so vainglorious. What the Hungarian leaders were interested in was that the so-called Hungarian "intelligentsia" should use the Magyar language and adhere to the Magyar religion, no matter if individual members of this intelligentsia were of Romanian, Czech, Slovenian, or German origin. Thus, the Hungarian intelligentsia was only Magyar in name. In fact, it constituted a melting pot of intellectuals representing the various nationalities which formed the mixed edifice of the Hungarian kingdom.

It is, of course, extremely difficult to recognize in a Hungarian of the 20th century the descendant of a Romanian who was denationalized at the beginning of the 19th century, or the descendant of Slavs who had been Magyarized for a period of centuries. In the same way, it would be very difficult for the traveler who visits the famous San Marco Square in Venice to be able to recognize the ancient plain crossed by the Danario River in those places where today the Doge's Palace, the San Marco Basilica, the clock tower, and the famous *campanile* rise majestically. But, historically, the ancient plain and the Danario River are facts that cannot be destroyed.

The authentic Romanian nature of the region in southeastern Transylvania which is today settled by the Szecklers was suppressed by the Hungarians by methods of the most despotic kind. Does that write "finis" to the Romanian history of the region?

Twenty-five years ago the ancient past succeeded in coming back to life under the granite tombstone where it lay. The stone had been put in position, thanks to the diabolical skills displayed over a thousand years by the one-time rulers of this former Roman province. It appears that justice can prevail—but only with difficulty. The triumph of truth over the deception of immediate appearances has been made possible only by great efforts and sacrifices.

By a variety of means, the Hungarians have demonstrated their wish to keep alive a problem which supposedly had been definitively settled after the First World War. How did they do this?

They did so with the help of a skillful and sustained propaganda, by means of an unremitting agitation addressed to world public opinion, and by means of conveniently noisy manifestations of sympathy toward the country the propagandists were addressing. ("We are of a Gepidae origin, thus, a Germanic one," Karacsonyi said in Germany; "We are England's friends," declared the authors of *Justice for Hungary* in Great Britain.)

They did it by employing all kinds of insinuations addressed to "the man on the street" and by means of lectures
given by Mr. This or Mr. That—"the great friend of the Magyar
people"—in Paris and London and Berlin, and of late in the
large cities of the United States. They were abetted, too, by
Lord Rothermere's far-reaching action, as well as by concessions of all kinds made by Count Bethlen to the great financial
interests in the city (the case of the big Hungarian banks, the
Commercial Bank in Budapest and the Hungarian Loan Bank).
There were other means by which they applied pressures in
favor of their objective, but these were the principal means
they used. Posing as "defenders of European culture and civilization," Hungarian propagandists persisted in placing special emphasis on the "oppression exercised by the Romanians
through the school system." When we come to analyze the
Magyar educational policy, a contrast will be made between
the school system in Romanian Transylvania during the two
decades of Romanian administration and the school system in
Hungarian Transylvania. Before doing so, however, let us analyze one of the other means employed by the Hungarians to
achieve their Machiavellian objectives: the radical transfor-
mation of the characteristic ethnic aspects of the territory on
the eastern side of Transylvania.

Magyarization Supported by
the Hungarian Administration

During the 19th century, the Hungarian administration
gave solid support to the efforts by the church and the school
system to Magyarize the Romanians within the Szeckler territory. When the government bodies themselves, that is, the
administration, took on the task of denationalizing the Romanians, the effect was instantly perceptible. Indeed, the
administration had at its disposal a multitude of means to
compel citizens to display a certain attitude, even when their
conscience rebelled against it. For example, the need for the
imperative necessities of every-day life is stronger than the
voice of conscience. The Hungarian administration knew how
to employ these necessities, conditioning their availability on
the "voluntary" loss of nationality.

If a Romanian in the Szeckler region wanted to buy a piece
of land, the greedy Szeckler institution known as "Szeckely

Kirendelcseg" intervened so that the land was purchased by the Szecklers.

If a Romanian wanted to become a worker in a national enterprise, he had first to adopt the Magyar religion.

Count Zenthal and Count Bernath, of the village of Miklosoara, forbade the Romanians to work on their estates unless they first changed their religious beliefs. The immediate result of this prohibition was that 48 Romanian families adopted Magyarism.

One could go on and on surveying the means employed by the imagination of the Hungarian leaders for the purpose of reducing the number of Romanians in southeastern Transylvania and establishing a strong Magyar majority there. It is true that the majority were apparently Magyar, but this also served as a potent instrument of revisionist propaganda.

The Army as an Instrument of Denationalization

The Hungarian army also played an important role in the process of denationalizing the Romanians in the Szeckler region. The only Romanians in all of Transylvania who were required to perform their military service in the Hungarian regiments were those who lived within the Szeckler region. The other Romanians served in their respective regiments where the language used was almost invariably German. In order to reenlist in the army or military police force, it was a prior condition that the subject had to give up his religion; for Romanians, simple Hungarian citizenship was not enough. One could list innumerable cases of this kind. We shall mention two cases, of a very large number which came to our attention, for the purpose of illustrating the radical changes a Romanian had to undergo when he reenlisted in the army.

In order to become first sergeants in the military police, two Orthodox Romanians, Petru and Niculae Barsan from Aita Seaca in Trei-Scaune county, had to dress in Hungarian clothes, had to change their religion from the Orthodox to the Protestant rite, and had to give their names a Hungarian sound, which they did by converting them to Peter and Miklos Berszany.

Another Romanian, Mihail Suciu from Valea Zalagului, converted from the Orthodox religion to the Roman Catholic religion and adopted a Szeckler name, Szocs Mihali.

This is the reality beneath the surface of what passes for integral Magyarism. These are the geniune Szecklers, "the most noble branch of the Hungarian people"—Petru and Niculae Barsan and Mihail Suciu!

In less than fifty years, wrote the Hungarian writer Paul Balogh, 200 Romanian villages disappeared thanks to the various pressures of Magyarization. After that time, the pace of the imposed denationalization did not diminish; on the contrary, it reached even more alarming proportions.

The Romanian Basis of What Was Ostensibly a Magyar Population Bloc

For the reasons set forth, the Magyarization of the Romanian population in southeastern Transylvania is not a product of a natural process but is, on the contrary, the consequence of the forced denationalization of the Romanian populace in that area. This elementary truth was given far too little consideration at the time the Romanian lands were being mutilated and the Magyars were penetrating to the heart of areas previously held by the Romanians, at a distance of only a few kilometers from Brasov.

One or two generations after the Szecklerization of the area, the Szecklerized Romanian who had reached a higher level in the social hierarchy generally denied his origin. Sometimes, however, he did not, as was the case of the famous Hungarian general of Romanian origin, Janos Czecz, who played a prominent role in the Hungarian revolution of 1848, serving as Chief of Staff to the leader of the revolution, Louis Kossuth.

A situation was created in which it would have been impossible by means of documents and simple assertions, to establish the Romanian genealogy of each Szecklerized family for a period of time going back more than two generations. In order to establish a clear-cut difference between the essential elements of the Szeckler bloc, one has to resort to a scientific method.

It would be absurd to assert that the Szeckler Magyar bloc, which had a lot to do with the injustice perpetrated at the Vienna conference, is completely the product of the denationalization of the Romanians. From a Romanian standpoint, it would also be unjust not to recognize that the Romanians had participated in large numbers in the social life of the Szeckler region and that they had played an important role in creating the compact Magyar mass in this region.

As Professor Iuliu Moldovan of Cluj put the matter, "in a conscious attempt at denationalization, the Szecklers increased their numerical strength with Romanian blood."

For this reason researchers had to resort to scientific investigation of ethnic origin, based on the serological composition of blood. This experiment involved a number of blood tests unparalleled in the history of medicine. Drs. Romneteanu and David, who embarked on this vast task of research, made 10,600 serological tests of Szeckler subjects and 3,856 on Romanians. The investigators reached the following conclusions: the blood index of the Romanians in the Szeckler region is identical to that of the Romanians on the other side of the Carpathians and, even more important, in almost all cases under observation, it was identical to that of the Szecklers—while completely different from that of the Hungarians proper. These results helped us in reaching the conclusion that the Szecklerization of the Romanians was begun as early as the 12th century A.D.

What is now a historical fact was probably not foreseen by the Hungarians when they embarked on the nefarious task of turning what had been a genuine Romanian land into a distinctly Magyar one.

Since the entire structure erected by Magyar propaganda after Transylvania was rejoined to Romania is based primarily on the argument of the solid "Magyar bloc" in the four Szeckler counties (in addition to combating this rectification, some of the most zealous propagandists even wanted to add a "corridor" to connect Hungary with the Carpathians), we shall devote a bit more space to this important problem.

It goes without saying that the fact that the Romanian element mingled with the Hungarian element in the Szeckler region was not without perceptible consequences. The complete Szecklerization of the Romanian element took place slowly, over the centuries. In time, it became apparent that this integrated element was exercising a remarkable influence over the integrators. This phenomenon becomes easy to understand if we look back over the history of the Romanian people. The fact is that all of the peoples who had long contacts with the Romanians and lived alongside them peacefully were gradually integrated by the Romanians. Their ability to assimilate other ethnic elements was thus demonstrated to be of a very high order. But when the Hungarians, by violent means, denationalized the Romanians and compelled them to lose themselves in the Szeckler masses, Romanian civilization and customs still proved to be formidable forces. The result was an extensive Romanianization of the customs, habits, and way of living of the people who ostensibly absorbed them.

Within the thicket of Magyarism here and there one could still find clearings of denationalized Romanianism. The Szecklers observe some holidays which are characteristically kept by Orthodox Romanians. They observe fasts which accord with the Romanian religious fasts. And they adopted certain customs which are living evidence of the influence of the Romanian element on these Szeckler masses. For example, they ring the church bells in summertime when heavy clouds gather, foretelling the imminence of a hailstorm. They have evening sittings of village girls and women to work on communal projects. They have their own chorals. Their *viclein* (a popular drama dealing with the birth of Christ) is an exact translation of a similar Romanian drama. And on May Day, they place birch branches at the gates of young girls and aspiring young men.

Such customs, which constitute in the final analysis the character of a nation and contribute to the differentiation of character between nations—customs which have been kept for centuries and which have become part of the nature of the people—could not have been so generously assimilated by another people if there had not been a comingling of the two peoples on a large scale.

Moreover, the Szecklers adopted the Romanian folksongs and ballads. These folk products are in fact exact imitations of similar products in Romanian folklore.

Of course, peoples who cohabit a region together are prone to borrow from each other. But here we do not witness a process that moves in both directions—that is, from the Szecklers to the Romanians and from the Romanians back to the Szecklers. The Romanians did not adopt Szeckler habits, customs, and mores—it was the Szecklers who adopted the Romanian ones. This phenomenon can only be explained on the basis of the continuing presence of the Romanian element within the Szeckler society.

Another clear proof of the Romanian origin of important elements of Szeckler culture of today is offered by the names of places—valleys, hills, meadows, plains, and towns—in this region. We mention among others such toponymic names as: Desis, Coasta, Frumoasa, Fantana, Zapada, Lunca, Vadu, Murgu, Izvor, which are of indisputable Romanian origin.

The influx of Romanians into what later became the Szeckler region resulted in widespread use of Romanian words of Latin origin. In many cases, the word was borrowed directly from the Romanian. Other words passed through a Slavic channel before they entered popular usage.

Is there any field of activity in which the ancient Romanian influence is not reflected? In architecture, there are the wooden buildings which are exact replicas of similar buildings characteristic of the Romanians. Then there is the sculpture in geometrical motifs, clearly different from the Hungarian and Transylvanian Saxon motifs. Then there are the musical motifs which, in themselves, bring the Szeckler people much closer to the Romanians than to the Hungarians of the steppes. Finally, the Szeckler folk dances and costumes exhibit many Romanian elements which obviously played a role in the development of the Szeckler national character. There are so many deep evidences of Romanian influence within the Magyar bloc in southeastern Transylvania which can only be discovered by the keen eye of the investigator. As a matter of fact, until very recently the Szecklers felt themselves to be much closer to the Romanians than to the Hungarians, whom, in fact, they looked upon as foreigners. Mihai Szoke, who is described by Silviu Dragomir as "a scholar who had made admirable studies regarding the Szeckler problems," sadly admitted before World War I that the Szecklers were more familiar with the city of Bucharest than they were with Budapest and that they called Moldavia "the inner country" (*belfold*). He also quoted the words of a Szeckler mother whose daughter was leaving for a job in Moldavia: "I prefer her to go to Moldavia, not Budapest, because at least she will not be in a foreign country there."

It is beyond any doubt that these incidents were not inspired by isolated sympathy for the neighboring Romanian people. On the contrary, such expressions bear testimony to the deeply rooted sentiments which bind the Szeckler people to the Romanian people. It is, indeed, "the voice of blood," to use the expression in a figurative sense.

The tendency to migrate to Moldavia, where a big colony of *ciangai* (Szeckler immigrants) grew up, cannot be viewed as an accidental occurrence. It is part of the many manifestations which, together, brought the Szecklers closer to the Romanians than to the Hungarians.

Said one Szeckler writer: "We are not witnessing any ephemeral incident, but are in the presence of a well-defined historical process." He added the observation that "for some centuries, perhaps as much as 700 years, the Hungarian population in the southeastern Carpathians has unwittingly pressed outward toward Moldavia."

If the Szecklers had felt themselves to be genuine Hungarians, it goes without saying that we would not have been witnesses to so many clearly anti-Hungarian manifestations. Neither would we have read in an ancient Szeckler chronicle, written by the chronicler Cserey, in the 17th century, that "Transylvania's misfortune has always come from Hungary and the Hungarians."

Against this background, can anyone consider the Szecklers' separation from Hungary an historical injustice?

Injustice, indeed, there was—but the real victims of injustice were the Romanian people when the so-called Magyar bloc in 1940, which was set on uniting with Hungary (it was in fact a bloc of denationalized Romanians and Szecklers), tore Transylvania to pieces. In this way, they brought about a state of affairs which obviously could not endure because it was in violation of the most elementary logic. The only possible solution—and one that is imperiously called for by the entire situation—was the return of the *status quo ante*.

Today, propagandist tracts published by the Hungarians, including statistics, combine the Szecklers with the Hungarians. This is obviously done for political reasons, out of a desire to support territorial demands by pointing to the large number of co-nationals living outside Hungary proper.

But if we study the documents of Hungarian history, from the very beginning up to the 15th century, we learn that the Hungarians have always considered the Szecklers a distinct nation, most of the time with special interests and sometimes with opposing interests. The Hungarian-Szeckler solidarity, to the extent that it existed, had a well-defined character. In essence, it constituted a unity of the privileged classes against the Romanian natives, who lived in a status of permanent servitude.

When the first Transylvanian diet convened in 1291 A.D.,

it consisted of the nobility (in the eyes of the reigning dynasty of that time, the nobility was virtually synonymous with the Hungarians), the Transylvanian Saxons, the Szecklers and the Wallachians (*nobililus, saxonibus, syculis et olachis*).

In those far-off days, the Romanians had not yet been pushed down to the inferior status that was to be their lot during the following centuries. The Transylvanian diet document dates back to the 13th century when the rights of the remaining natives were still accorded precedence and were respected.

In the various armies recruited in Transylvanian territory during the 13th century, the Szeckler troops are mentioned as distinct from the Hungarian troops. In a fundamental document dealing with Transylvania's system of government—the famous "Union of the Three Nations," which was concluded in 1438 A.D. (the Transylvanian writer Gh. Moroianu described it as "the most atrocious conspiracy in history")—the Szecklers are once again described as a nation distinct from the Hungarian nation. The contracting parties to the "Union of the Three Nations" were the Hungarians, the Transylvanian Saxons, and the Szecklers. The caption *Unio trio nationum* in itself clearly shows that, in the opinion of the times, what was involved was three separate nations, cohabiting on the territory of the one-time province of Dacia.

Instead of listing all the evidence supporting this basic truth—today an indisputable one—it would suffice to list all the documents bearing on Transylvania's history in general. From this there clearly emerges the conclusion that the Hungarians and the Szecklers are two completely different nations, united only by a common language, but separated by all those things that separate one nation from another.

We shall confine ourselves only to the latest Magyar document relating to Transylvania: the written statement of the Hungarian delegation to the World War I peace conference in Paris. In this statement it is written that "the Szecklers are of an Avar origin." Obviously, this means that they were not considered Hungarians proper. In the same document, one can also read that the Transylvanian Saxons "agreed during the Middle Ages, with the other two nations, with which they cohabited on Transylvanian soil, the Hungarians and the Szecklers, on something akin to a social contract, each nation being master in its own territory." Could anything be clearer? As a matter of fact, these quotations are from what the Hungarians themselves called "the unique thesaurus of Hungarian science." To dispute the quotations would be tantamount to doing injury to the prestige which Magyar science is obviously entitled to—which, of course, is not part of our intention. Therefore, according to what principle could the Hungarians demand the return of the Szecklers to their "motherland"?

According to the principle of language? But if we did this, then part of Belgium and part of Switzerland would have to be incorporated into France; Zurich and Bern, Switzerland would have to be annexed to Germany; and large parts of the southern Balkan peninsula would have to be restored to Romania.

When a political edifice is supported by such flimsy pillars, it is inevitable that some day it will undergo a fatal collapse. In the lives of peoples, as in the lives of individual men, fraud and injustice can lead only to provisional stability. In the end, justice will always triumph—even if it takes 1,000 years.

But not all provisional conditions last 1,000 years!

Imperialistic Designs

The Hungarian people have never been numerous. We do not fault them for this. In fact, we are inclined to believe that it is not a disadvantage for any people, nor is the fact of being numerous a quality deserving of special praise. It is quality rather than quantity that determines value. It is a shortcoming, however, to seek to compensate for lack of national quantity by finding additional space. The possibilities of expansion are not unlimited; in fact, they have a limit which cannot be exceeded. This is a universally valid law, with both the vegetable and the animal kingdom. It is the law which governs the life of peoples as well as that of the individual. But the Hungarians, unfortunately, did not want to take this law into consideration.

Despite their relatively small numbers, the Hungarian people set their minds on achieving dominion over a maximum of territories. Perhaps they were inspired, or obsessed, by the quasi-mythical illusion of Saint Stephen's empire. Moreover, there was an interval in Hungarian history when Hungary's kings nurtured the hope of universal domination, of bringing the old Holy Roman Empire back to life under their protection. Indeed, the Hungarian people still speak proudly about the reign of King Ludovic the Great, of the Angevin family, who, at the end of the 14th century gave the Hungarian crown actual or formal domination over Northern Banat, Croatia, Dalmatia, Bosnia, Serbia, Bulgaria, Wallachia, and Moldavia. Although this was not a territorial conquest, he also negotiated a personal alliance with Poland.

The Dream Unravels

But no matter how beautiful a dream may be, it remains but a dream. And so, one day Hungary's vast kingdom started to disintegrate.

The kingdom's boundaries started closing in; its outline began to shrink. In 1920 Hungary became again what it had been at the very beginning and what it should have remained in its own interests. It became an almost pure Hungarian state with its area reduced to 92,000 square kilometers. But even on this restricted territory, the Hungarians were not able to achieve a homogenous national state. Of the 8,688,319 inhabitants in 1930, minorities (Germans, Slovaks, Romanians, Croats, Serbs, Jews, and others) accounted for 1,500,000, and only 7,200,000 were pure Hungarians.

But in the minds of their leaders the moment of glory achieved in the Middle Ages was deeply implanted. They began again to dream the dream that previously had possessed them. They dreamed of a central European empire under the protection of the 8,000,000 Hungarians—a population which could be contained by an area of a city like London.

If the Hungarians had been contented with a homogenous national state on a territory which was naturally theirs—the Alfold, sung of by the poets—they could truly have contributed a larger share to the world's spirituality than what they actually did contribute to the patrimony of European cultures.

But Arpad's successors dreamed of political glories which exceeded their powers and, above all, the possibility of conquest. In this way, they wasted their efforts in negative actions by seeking the destruction of the fundamental national elements on the territories they dominated. They engendered antagonisms among the people who cohabited these territories by striving to paralyze all efforts at national awakening.

The German Colonists

The second element which had to submit to the well-conceived Hungarian plans were the German minority. The suc-

cessive leaders of the Hungarian kingdom were faithful followers
of the Hungarians' first king, Stephen the Holy, whose motto
was: *Uniusque linguae, uniusque moris regnum imbecile et
fragile est* ("A country in which a single language is spoken
and which has a single character, is weak and feeble"). St.
Stephen's motto speaks for itself about the real nature of the
problem which tormented Hungary's leaders through the Middle Ages. The Hungarian people were very few. In order to
have a country they could call their own, they had to appeal
to other nations to join them.

By the grace and will of St. Stephen's successors, the motto
quoted above was also put into operation in Transylvania, despite the fact that the people in this province spoke a single
language, Romanian, and displayed a single character, resulting from the inter-mixture of the Dacians with the Romans.
These elements should have been enough to ensure a normal
evolution of the problem. Thus, Romanian Transylvania became colonizing territory, not only for the Szecklers but also
for the German settlers—Transylvanian Saxons, Swabians,
Teutonic Knights, and others—whose aid was enlisted to support Hungarian domination over large provinces which the
Hungarians could not have preserved by themselves.

The Germans began colonizing Transylvania at the time
of Stephen the Holy, who was himself married to a princess of
German origin. The process of colonization was intensified under King Geiza II (1141-1161 A.D.), during the 12th century.
According to Nicolae Iorga, what persuaded the western Germans to leave their native country and settle in Transylvania
was the extremely difficult economic plight of their homeland,
which was badly overpopulated in terms of the arable soil available to it.

The German colonists settled down in those regions where
the population was sparser and which gave promise of a more
comfortable living. Without a doubt this is the meaning of those
"deserted places"—in reality, thinly populated places—which
are mentioned in the "Acts of Privilege" of King Andrei II and
King Geiza II.

The first groups of Germans, who were natives of Fran-
conia, Lorraine, and Luxembourg, set up their settlements in
the Bistrita, Somes, Tirnave, and Sibiu counties. In the year
1211 A.D., King Andrei II called upon the Teutonic knights,
who were then crusading in the Holy Land, to come and

populate Tara Barsei. As generally happened with colonists, they were granted certain privileges, which are listed in the Act of 1211 A.D. and which were renewed by decree in 1222 A.D.

In this latter Act we find for the first time a reference to the country of the Wallachians, which the colonists apparently had the right to cross without paying any taxes. The Szecklers are also mentioned here as a separate nation, distinct from the Hungarian nation—who, as a matter of fact, did not live in Transylvania at all at that time. Indeed, other documents of the period dealing with the peoples of Transylvania do not say a word about the existence of Hungarians in this province.

The Transylvanian Saxons who in the year 1224 A.D. were officially recognized by Hungarians as a distinct people had over the previous century grown to significance as a community and are also mentioned in other documents of the time. The Romanians and Szecklers, too, are frequently mentioned among the peoples residing in Transylvania.

Again let us emphasize that there is absolutely nothing in the literature of that period or about that period that suggests a Hungarian presence. Among other documents, we may quote the ordinances of the Tatar Khan Cadan, governing the kinds of currency in legal circulation in Transylvania. In dealing with the Transylvanian population, the ordinances make mention of the Romanians, the Szecklers, and the Transylvanian Saxons—but they do not say one word about a Hungarian presence in Transylvania.

It appears that from the moment they set foot on Transylvanian soil, the German colonists, as natives of the western part of Europe, gave solid evidence of their will to independence. By the Hungarians this was deemed as "treason to the Hungarian crown." Because of this, the Teutonic knights, only a few years after their arrival in Barsa county, were forced to abandon their settlements and move to Poland, and finally to Prussia.

Many German colonists were farmers or agricultural workers, but the great majority were laborers who worked in the salt mines, silver mines, and gold mines, and skilled craftsmen who could work with any tool. There were also among them a goodly number of successful merchants.

To the skilled craftsmen and merchants, we owe the establishment of the first urban settlements in Transylvania.

Indeed, they were also responsible for many urban settlements in Hungary itself. This is something that Hungarians freely admit. "Many of our towns," says the Hungarian writer Isztvan Kniezsa, "are of German origin."

Newcomers to Transylvanian territory, like the Hungarians and the Szecklers, the German colonists felt themselves under pressure to make common front with the other two peoples who were also considered undesirable newcomers. The objective of this united front of newcomers was to subordinate the native masses, so that they became slaves and serfs in the land where they had once been the masters.

The Union of Three Nations

Their relegation to an inferior status moved the Romanian people to revolt. Their first uprising took place in the year 1437 A.D. The consequence of this revolt, which was quickly suppressed, was that the condition of the native Romanian population, instead of improving, became more distressing. In fact, the revolt led to a coalition of the privileged classes in Transylvania against the ancient native Romanian population, for the purpose of suppressing any future Romanian attempt to better their lot by revolting. The leaders of this first Romanian revolt in Transylvania were hanged, while the Transylvania peasantry had to pay a heavy blood tribute on the altar of liberty. The coalition of the three nations who imposed their rule on the Romanian populace—"the diabolical alliance," as it is called by Moroianu—was formally constituted in the year 1438 A.D. That moment in history marks the beginning of the long ordeal of the native Romanian population, a nightmare which was not to come to an end until 1918—that is, 480 years later—and which, for a large part of the population, was to be repeated in 1940.

An observation must be made at this point. From the fact alone that the three groups of newcomers in Transylvania were obliged to make common cause against the native Romanian population, one is able to judge the dimension of the force which the Romanians represented even in those far-off days. The Hungarians by themselves did not possess the strength needed to suppress the Romanian will to freedom. To achieve their objective, they had to join with the forces of the two other national groups which had moved into Transylvania. This is a matter which should be given greater attention, especially by those who have been told repeatedly that the question of the Transylvanian Romanians really involves a limited number of "intruders," whose pretensions and territorial claims are completely without warrant. (Most instructive on this point are the statements made by Regent Horthy immediately after his triumphal entry into Transylvania, following its reincorporation into the Hungarian empire.)

The three-nation alliance sought to exclude the Romanians from public life. To this end, the three nations concluded another pact—as well-meaning as the first one—the so-called "Pact of the Four Religions." According to this agreement, the four religions—to which the Romanians did not belong—were decreed as official religions, while the Orthodox religion of the native Romanians—who had been Christianized many centuries before the Hungarians—was considered a tolerated one.

To belong to the Lutheran, United, Protestant, or Roman Catholic churches in Transylvania, meant to belong to the privileged class. The Orthodox believers were reduced to an inferior condition and treated over the centuries as a "tolerated" people.

This is how the Romanian people, Transylvania's oldest native population, were, as a result of the Hungarian invasion, reduced to the status of a tolerated minority in their own country, and how the Christian Orthodox religion—the oldest form of Christianity, which had flourished in the former Roman province of Dacia—was reduced to a tolerated rite.

The situation of the native Romanian population in Transylvania becomes even more tragic when we consider that their status was inferior not only to the Hungarians—who, as invaders, had managed to make themselves the official masters of the territory—but even in comparison with the Szecklers and the Transylvanian Saxons who were more recent colonists. Kniezsa has written that it reflects glory on the Hungarian people that the quality of the "three nations" and of the "four religions" was respected. In fact, the pacts of the three nations and the four religions constitute an indictment against the Hungarians for the injustice these pacts did to millions of native Romanians.

The Transylvanian Saxons, taking advantage of the privileges granted to them, and making good use of the qualities characteristic of their race—in particular, discipline and a capacity for work—managed in a short period of time to acquire great strength and influence in the regions which had been bestowed on them. During the 18th century, and even during the first half of the 19th century, most Transylvanian towns still bore the stamp of a distinct Germanic character.

The Transylvanian Saxons: An Isolating Element

During the second half of the 19th century, the Hungarians took a number of frightened actions to cope with the amazing progress made by the German urban element as well as by the Romanian element in the countryside which gave evidence of a strengthened national consciousness. The Hungarians embarked on an energetic program of forced Magyarization. The results of this program in the Szeckler region have already been examined. In addition, the program succeeded in replacing the German element with an ostensibly Hungarian one in many towns in Transylvania.

What the Hungarians had decided was that the role of the Transylvanian Saxons was to serve as "an isolating element among the Romanian masses," as Professor Silviu Dragomir puts the matter. Indeed, the Transylvanian Saxons were gathered in masses in a triangle formed by Bistrita, Brasov, and Orastie counties, separating the compact masses of Romanians which surrounded them on all sides. Inside this triangle, the Hungarian element was almost nonexistent. The Romanian populace, however, deeply rooted in Transylvanian soil, also managed to hold out in those regions where the Germans were concentrated. They held out in small ethnic islands which the Transylvanian Saxons were unable to denationalize.

The Hungarian ethnographer, Daner, made no secret of the role that Budapest had delegated to the Saxon colonists in Transylvania. Indeed, this is what he wrote on the eve of Hungary's entrance in World War I in 1914:

> The Transylvanian Saxons constitute a vast network. Its fabric is weak here and there, and prone to break. But the network is much stronger where there is a need to seek a counterbalance to the large number of Romanians by invoking the help of other national groups . . . Thus, the Saxons give important assistance to the Hungarians in maintaining their national unity.

This, therefore, is how Transylvania really appeared after

centuries of Hungarian domination—"compact masses of Romanians," surrounded on all sides by peoples who were not native to the region, who worked with each other in hindering the free and normal development of the native Romanian population.

The figures quoted by Daner for the purpose of illustrating the advantages which accrued to the Hungarians from the presence of the Transylvanian Saxons, testify eloquently at the same time to the disastrous results that the colonizing activities of the Transylvanian Saxons and the Szecklers had for the Romanians in Transylvania. In the Szeckler regions bordering on the Romanian regions in other Transylvanian counties, the Romanian population increased by 5 percent from the year 1900 to 1910. In the Odorhei County, on the other hand, which was completely isolated from the Romanian centers of population and which was close to the Transylvanian Saxon area, the Romanian population increased by only 3 percent during the same interval.

In short, over a period of ten years, the Romanian population in the areas that had been colonized by the Szecklers and the Transylvanian Saxons grew by only 5 percent and 3 percent respectively—while in the kingdom of Romania, the Romanian population witnessed a massive growth because of its high birth rate. Because of their inflexibility, statistics sometimes reveal major tragedies. The tragedy of the Transylvanian Romanians is thus dramatically revealed by the tiny coefficients for the Romanian birthrate in the Szeckler and Saxon regions of Transylvania. Behind these coefficients there lurks the reality of Hungarian oppression—all the Machiavellian calculations of the "isolating strata," all the bitterness of the forced denationalization which over the years was the lot of the Romanian populace in Transylvania.

Comment becomes superfluous in the presence of these distressingly significant statistics. Count Apponyi in his work, *Justice for Hungary*, spoke of "the providential mission which the Hungarian race carried out in the most endangered region of the continent." This statement should be perceived in the light of these statistics.

Vanity is the only really "great" thing that is possessed in abundance by the small Hungarian people, who speak about having a "providential mission" vouchsafed to only a few truly great peoples in this world. What was the Hungarian people's

historic mission? Anyone who takes a good look at the ethnographic map of Hungary before World War I will realize how
many nations were swallowed up by Magyar imperialism and
the eight million Hungarians—a race which could be amply
accommodated within the confines of one of the larger cities
of the world, such as London or New York. In Transylvania,
in particular, despite all their efforts, the Hungarians did not
manage to achieve a truly dominant position.

The Swabians

The Hungarian effort to assert themselves in Transylvania
was, as we have pointed out, assisted by the Szecklers in the
eastern part of the province and by the Transylvanian Saxons
in the southern part. Beginning with the 18th century, however, the Hungarians also received important assistance from
the Swabian colonists in the northwest and the southwest.

As has been mentioned previously, the Hungarians realized that they could not prevent the natural development of
the native Romanian population, except with the help of the
Szecklers and the Transylvanian Saxons. But this assistance
turned out to be insufficient. Beginning with the 18th century,
the Hungarians started colonizing the Banat and Arad regions,
as well as those of Satu-Mare and Salaj, with Swabian Germans—an ethnic group which registered 255,349 people in the
Romanian census of 1930.

Unlike the Szecklers, who were concentrated in a single
region and who, because of this, were able to preserve their
national unity, the Swabians were spread over a large area
and there was a corresponding lack of cohesion among them.
The Hungarians took advantage of this lack of cohesion in
order to Magyarize the Swabians incrementally. As for the
methods used, the Hungarians have always been past masters
in the art of denationalization. For each nationality they de-
vised a method which corresponded to the stamina and mentality of the nationality in question. The Swabians, because of
their meager numbers and their lack of national solidarity (an
element that determines the basic strength of a people), were
Magyarized more by diplomatic skills than by violent methods.
But along the way the Hungarians took advantage of the various needs of the Swabian minority.

Professor F. Krauter, writing about these methods says:

"Because of the lack of land, the Swabians had to send their children to school. All careers were open to Swabian youth. Provided that they attended Hungarian schools, they could ascend to the highest steps of the social hierarchy." This, of course, involved abandoning their mother tongue and becoming, in time, "artificial Magyars"—which, for the purpose of Hungarian statistics, was the same as the real thing.

Bit by bit the Swabian German language was forced out of the secondary schools and churches, in this way speeding up the denationalization of the German minority in the 18th century. The consequences of this denationalization were so significant that the German writer, Lutz Karodi, asserted in a book printed in Berlin in the year 1930, "If it had not been for the peace treaty [the Versailles Treaty], in less than thirty years the Swabians would have been completely Magyarized." Moreover, under Romanian rule, the Transylvanian Hungarians, taking advantage of the tolerance which was characteristic of successive Romanian governments, sought to influence the normal development of the Swabian minority by trying to win them over to the side of Magyarism. For example, during the census of 1930 Hungarian propagandists traveled widely in the Swabian villages and market towns seeking to persuade the Swabians to declare themselves to be Hungarian. Thanks to the pressures of various kinds exercised by these propagandists, the 1930 census recorded only 31,007 Swabians in the Satu-Mare and Salaj counties. This contrasted with statistics compiled by Albin Sherbauer immediately after World War I, which showed 51,200 Swabians in the same counties. What this means—which is clearly impossible—is that the number of Swabians decreased by almost 50 percent in a decade.

In a nutshell, the Swabians were the victims of the same policy of Magyarization which had previously been used against the Romanians. Thanks to this policy, hundreds of thousands of Romanians and thousands of Swabians ostensibly became Hungarians, while, in fact, they were really Magyarized Romanians and Swabians—which, of course, is not quite the same thing.

The Real Cost to the Non-Magyar Nationalities

Unfortunately, there are no statistics which reflect the real losses of the Romanian population in Transylvania—that is, there are no statistics which record, in addition to the actual decrease of the Romanian population in different regions, the lack of population growth in comparison to the Romanian birth rate in those regions not under Hungarian influence. If such a work were ever written, everyone would see how little Turanian blood flows in the veins of Arpad's alleged descendants who live in the territory of the onetime province of Dacia.

The Germans were not at all impressed by the various philo-Germanic manifestations by the Budapest government in the immediate post-World War I period. Instead, they sought to discover what losses their co-nationals had suffered in Hungary, which had lost some of its territory after the war. In an investigation published by *Deutsche Allgemeine Zeitung* in January 1933, this prominent newspaper drew a comparison between the data contained in the Hungarian statistics of 1920 and those for 1930. While the Hungarian population had recorded an increase of 845,000 people, the German minority for the same period showed a decrease of 72,000 people.

"It is impossible," said the author, "that the Germans suffered a decrease of 15 percent of their number. These figures are so alarming and frightening that a thorough investigation is necessary."

In his work *Das Deutschtum in Rumpfungarn* ("The German Nationality in Reduced Hungary"), Dr. Jacob Bleyer, a former German minister for minorities, compared the various Hungarian statistics and reached the conclusion that in the time interval between 1880 and 1910 the German minority in Hungary had lost 53,348 souls, while the Hungarian population had recorded a natural growth corresponding to their mean birth rate. "In fact," said Bleyer, "the German population did not suffer a decrease of 53,000, but of approximately 315,000 if one takes into consideration the fact that the German population outside Hungary had recorded a growth of 43 percent during the same period."

With good reason Bleyer asked, "Can it be that the German mothers did not give birth to a single child in these 30 years?"

The Hungarian propagandists, for their part, were apparently unimpressed by the overwhelming evidence which was being amassed against them. They continued to claim that "Hungary is a country of classic political and religious liberties" and that "the Hungarians are the most tolerant people in the world." That great propaganda master, Dr. Goebbels, could have learned much from the Magyar propagandists.

The Goal of Colonization

After surveying the basic historical facts concerning the three non-Hungarian minority nationalities in Transylvania, the goal of the colonizing process carried out by the Magyars over the years appears in its true light.

Having found in Transylvania a very large native Romanian population and realizing that their inferior numbers would prevent them from achieving a dominant position in the province, the Hungarians sought to counterbalance the force represented by the Transylvanian Romanians by colonizing the territory of the province with foreign peoples, primarily Szecklers, Transylvanian Saxons, and Swabians.

Even though they played different roles at the beginning of the colonizing process, all three elements—the Szecklers, the Transylvanian Saxons, and the Swabians—became, with the passage of time, effective weapons in the hands of the Budapest leaders, who sought to denationalize the Romanian minority and hinder its normal development.

After some time, in order to give Transylvania a homogenous national Magyar appearance, even the elements which had been used to colonize Transylvania became themselves the targets of forced denationalization. In the absence of anything better, the Hungarians had to content themselves with artificial Hungarians because of the lack of real ones.

The Transylvanian Saxons were able to offer resistance against the forced denationalization offensive thanks in the first instance to the assistance they received from the Germans in Hitler's Reich who were interested in the fate of their kindred all over Europe—for example, Austria, Czechoslovakia, and Poland. Second, they manifested an indestructible national solidarity.

By way of contrast, the Swabian Germans fell victim to the denationalization process, and they swelled the ranks of the "new" Hungarians. Unable to Magyarize the Transylvanian Saxons, the Hungarians obliged them to serve their main goal—that is, the denationalization of the autochtonous Romanian population—by interposing their communities among the compact masses of Romanians. In this way they were separated and could be governed according to the age-old principle of divide and rule.

In the difficult war of denationalization initiated by the Hungarians—a war characterized by a total inequality of forces between the governed and the governors—the Romanians inevitably lost ground over the centuries. But the Romanian people were able to maintain their principal position with a stubbornness which was unique in history. This accounts for the miracle of the history of the Romanian people—for the perseverance which helped them to maintain their essential position despite the most ferocious attacks.

It is a surprising fact that the more violent the offensive action unleashed by the Hungarians against the Transylvanian Romanians, the more deeply the Romanians sank their roots in their ancestral land beyond the Carpathians. Intolerance and violence have always been bad counselors.

The Achilles heel of the Magyar minority policy has always consisted of an intolerance which estranged them not only from the potential friendship and support of the oppressed nationality, but also from the sympathy of the civilized world. The description of the Hungarian people presented in an article dealing with Hungary in the great French encyclopedia, *Larousse*, is characteristic on this point—and, of course, nobody could accuse *Larousse* of Hungarophobia. This is what *Larousse* said:

> The Hungarians have always shown too little respect for other nationalities and behaved with too little tolerance toward the other races with whom they lived together; that is why these nationalities have always looked for an opportunity to revenge themselves.

But the oppressed nationalities at the end of their ordeal did not make an effort to take revenge. The Romanian revolution of December 1, 1918, and the uprisings of the other nationalities during the same year did not terminate in bloodshed. Instead, the oppressed peoples returned to their national life, rejoicing in the fact that the chains of their age-old bondage had at last been broken.

3. REVOLT AND REPRESSION

*From the Union of Fagaras County
to the Great Union*

One of the factors which undoubtedly contributed to the unyielding permanence of Transylvanian Romanianism was the large numbers of Romanians in two counties on the other side of the Carpathians, Moldavia and Wallachia.

At the beginning of the 14th century, the union of the *knezats* and *voivodates* of the so-called "Romanian country" (Wallachia) was an accomplished fact. In the year 1330 A.D., Tihomir's son, Basarab, defeated the Hungarians at Posada, thus achieving his country's independence. This battle is compared by Professor Gheorghe Bratianu with the battles of Morgarten and Sempach, which led to Switzerland's independence.

Wallachia's princes often extended their rule over the regions beyond the Carpathians. The process started with Prince Vlaicu, who annexed to his country certain tracts of Romanian land in Transylvania, primarily Fagaras County. The process continued with Mircea the Elder, who, taking account of the possessions he had accumulated, called himself "Prince, by the grace of God, and sole master of Ungro-Wallachia, of the land beyond the Carpathians up to the Tatar land; *Hertzog* (Duke) of Almas and Fagaras; Prince of Banat to the west." The process culminated with Michael the Brave who, after defeating Andrei Bathory's army at Selimbar, near Sibiu, triumphantly entered Alba-Julia, the Transylvanian principality's capital, on November 1, 1599.

In the northern region of the eastern range of the Carpathians, the Romanian *knezats* were united by the Maramures Princes, Bogdan and Dragos, who, according to Iorga, "gave new meaning to the life of the peasants they found in the valleys of Moldavia, turning a rural democracy into a military state."

In the 15th and 16th centuries A.D., Stephen the Great, who must be ranked one of the most brilliant princes produced by the country (he was also called "Christ's athlete" after his successes against the Turks), and Petru Rares, one of Stephen's successors, also annexed to Moldavia the Transylvanian lands of Balta Fortress and Ciceu.

It is true that these territorial conquests did not last very long, with the exception of Almas and Fagaras Counties, which were under the rule of the Wallachian princes for more than 100 years (1366 to 1478 A.D.). But their mere existence demonstrates that the unity of all Romanians has been a constant concern of the leaders responsible for the destiny of the Romanian people on both sides of the Carpathians.

For the Romanian people in Transylvania, the growing interest displayed by the Romanians on the other side of the Carpathians represented a very real help in their fight against Magyarization. It gave them the necessary staying power to hold out for centuries and not to despair of the achievement of the ideal of a united Romania.

The Romanians Rebel

The Romanian people were oppressed by the feudal regime which existed in Transylvania. The "legal" state was composed of three privileged national groupings which, together, by the irony of fate, did not succeed in matching the numbers of the native Romanians, who existed as a "tolerated minority."

According to the modern conception of the state, the state system which was created by the Hungarians in the Middle Ages is almost inconceivable. It was a system in which the feudal regime inventively surpassed the feudal regimes in other western countries. The nation was not constituted according to blood criteria but, as a modern Hungarian writer put it, "according to affinities," thus idealizing a difference which was in fact extremely prosaic.

The Hungarian nation did not exist at the time of the conquest of Pannonia. The Hungarian tribes grew into a nation as the result of related origin, language, traditions, and ideals. For all practical purposes, the Hungarian nation was restricted to the nobility. "The essence of the Hungarian nation," writes Tibor Joo, "is represented by the members of the Holy Crown, that is, the nobility. The common people, townsmen and serfs, are not members of the Magyar nation. They lead an autonomous ethnic life."

"The greatest misfortune of our time," points out Joo, "comes from the fact that the Hungarian state system was replaced by the modern concept of the nation state, based on an ethnic element." Both Joo and the other contemporary Hungarian writers who belonged to the same school speak about the Hungarian feudal system—with a nation in which membership was restricted to the "privileged"—as an ideal worthy of imitation.

It is obvious that, within the framework of a state and nation organized in this way, the existing gap between the Hungarians in Transylvania and the Romanians in the same province was bound to get wider and wider.

Almost all the Romanians were peasants. They could never aspire to the advantages which the Hungarian nation obviously had within the state. Of course, this was a misfortune from the immediate standpoint of the Romanians, who had to endure the bitterness of their lowly status. But, for the Romanian cause, their nonintegration into the Hungarian nation happily resulted in keeping the Romanian national conscience awake and alert for the benefit of unborn generations who had to endure the yoke of the Magyar "nobility."

Since, within the structure of the Hungarian state, the social element was closely connected with the national element, it is obvious that all of the uprisings against the injustices of Hungarian rule were triggered by both social and national causes. By the nature of things, both causes, the social and the national, were inseparably intertwined in repeated bitter revolts. The Szeckler peasants also had to suffer because of this state of affairs, but for them the question did not go beyond the limits of social pressures.

The Romanian subjects, on the other hand, had to endure oppression in the double capacity of members of an inferior class and members of a foreign nationality.

Nothing can better aid us in obtaining an accurate picture of the plight of the Romanian subjects within the Hungarian state than the description offered by the Austrian observer Hacquet, who traveled in Transylvania at the end of the 18th century. It is to be noted that the description which Hacquet offers of the situation of the Transylvanian Romanians is also valid for the years that followed, with the qualification that their plight became much more difficult with the passage of time. Hacquet wrote:

> This nation [the Romanian nation], forgotten and op-
> pressed, has the worst plots of ground, the most desolate
> and infertile in the whole country. But even these plots
> are taken away from them as soon as they have cleared
> and leveled the land to grow corn. Every Transylvanian
> Saxon and every Hungarian can take possession of these
> plots, even if the Romanians had been the owners for
> hundreds of years, driving the Romanians and their fam-
> ilies into the mountains where there is nothing but rocks,
> or even causing them to leave the country. The Romanians
> are not allowed to come closer than are the gypsies to
> Saxon or Hungarian villages. They have to stop like out-
> laws about half the distance of a rifle shot from the fence
> of wild roses surrounding the Saxon and Hungarian vil-
> lages [legal boundaries in one's own country!].

This is the real status which the Magyar nobility had reserved for the millions of Romanian peasants who fell under
their sway. Hungarian propagandists in western Europe and
in the United States did not say a word about this when they
sang hymns in praise of the civilizing mission of the Magyar
people in central Europe.

From time to time, however, a document emerges like that
written by Hacquet, who was an Austrian geologist, which has
the effect of raising the veil that for centuries has covered the
sacrilegious crimes committed by the Magyar rulers on Transylvania's Romanian soil.

Two Italians, Massaro and Burgi, who had become ac-
quainted with the methods of government employed by the
Magyars in the 16th century, left similar descriptions for generations to come of how the Magyars became the rulers of this
region, which meant nothing to them—except that it provided
them with a place that they could rob and pillage at will. Massaro declares: "There is no injustice or sacrilege that they [the
Hungarian leaders] will not commit if they are offered money."
Burgi is even more outspoken: "If Hungary could be saved from
the whirlpool of the Turkish menace for a price of three florins,
you will not be able to find three people in the country ready
to make this sacrifice."

The peasantry, who had been driven to extremity, rose in rebellion for the first time in the year 1437 A.D., as we have mentioned before. The immediate result of this uprising was that the three privileged nations closed ranks and set up the well-known Union of the Three Nations, which, for roughly 500 years, suppressed all strivings for liberty.

The suppression of the emancipation movement became particularly bloody at the beginning of the 16th century. In the year 1514 A.D., the Romanian peasants made common cause with the Hungarian peasants, who were also groaning under the yoke of the Hungarian nobility—who felt that they alone truly represented the Magyar nation. This uprising, bloodily suppressed, went down in history as the rebellion of "George Dozsa's crusaders." About this uprising and its suppression, the writer, C. Sassu, had this to say:

> The revenge which followed the revolutionary uprising surpassed all imagination, unleashing the full fury of those who, for the moment, had felt themselves to be in jeopardy. The horror of contemporary witnesses who had become accustomed to all kinds of cruelties during the time of the transition which marked the beginning of the 16th century, was very great. A legend even began to circulate about Voivode Zapolya, who was reported to have lost his sight during religious services, in the presence of the Holy Sacraments. This heavenly punishment was reversed only two years later in response to the pious prayers of his mother and his sister.

After the suppression of the revolt, a new era—a more bitter one—commenced for the Romanian nation. The Transylvanian Diet passed legislation binding the peasants forever to the plots of land they were working. At the same time, the peasants were forbidden to carry weapons any longer. A peasant who was found to possess a rifle in the face of this law was punished by having his right hand cut off. So that the Transylvanian peasantry should never in the future dare to rise up against their oppressors, Voivode Zapolya's clerk, Stefan Verboeczi, drew up an entire new code of law, regulating the relations between the oppressors and the oppressed. Through these laws he widened the gap between the nobility—the only class which possessed rights—and the lower orders which seemed doomed to carry the yoke of bitter oppression forever.

The reactionary Tri-partite Codex (*Codex Tripartitum*) of 1558 A.D. represented the revenge of the Hungarian nobles against the Romanian laboring population, just as the association of the three privileged nations imposed the revenge of the same Hungarian nobles after the first Romanian uprising in the 15th century. But the more bitter the oppression, the stronger the reaction.

The peasant uprisings (*tumultus rusticorum*) came one after another. To the various types of persecutions described in the preceding pages, there was added during the 16th and 17th centuries the element of religious persecution. This was stirred up by the Calvinist princes of Transylvania, because the Romanians had refused to give up the Christian-Orthodox religion of their ancestors. The *approbatae et compilatae* laws, which were passed by the Transylvanian Diet in 1653 A.D., provide the most faithful index to the oppression to which the Transylvanian Romanians were subjected by the Calvinist princes and their swarms of nobles. Here is one of the most infamous stipulations in the collection of laws concerned with the Romanians in Transylvania:

"The Romanians are only tolerated in this country, and that only temporarily (*pro tempore*), for as long as the princes and the nobles wish it to be so (*usque bene placitum principum et reguicolarum*)."

These words by themselves are enough to illustrate the tragic situation of the Romanian peasantry in "the classical country of tolerance." The Romanian peasants were at the complete mercy of the Hungarian nobles.

Unable to convert the Romanians to Calvinism by methods of persuasion, the Transylvanian princes resorted to a series of cruel measures which will stain their coats of arms forever—as though they were not already sufficiently stained at the time.

Thus, the Romanians were forbidden to carry weapons, to possess horses, to wear boots and cloth trousers and fine linen shirts—and, last but not least, to wear hats that cost more than one florin.

Toward the end of the 17th century, as a result of the religious union of the Transylvanian Romanians with the Church of Rome (1697 A.D.), the situation of the Romanian masses seemed somewhat improved, since the Austrian emperors tried to bring about the conversion of the Romanians to

Greek Catholicism by more humane means. Under this approach, the peasants who joined the United Church (Greek Catholic) were to enjoy a special status and were no longer considered "tolerated"—an insulting and demeaning term.

But the promises of the Hapsburgs were far more generous than they were realistic. Many of these promises were never realized because the Imperial Court was against them. But most of the promises failed of realization because they were systematically sabotaged by the Magyar nobility.

Inocentiu Micu-Klein

Inocentiu Micu-Klein was a Greek-Catholic bishop who was one of the most fervent supporters of the Romanian cause in Transylvania during the first part of the 18th century. He sent no less than twenty-four petitions to Vienna asking for the fulfillment of the emperor's promises. His petitions made the point that subjects who have obligations should also have rights. (*Qui sentit onus, sentiat et commodum*—literally, "He who bears the burden, let him also enjoy the benefits.")

But the three privileged nations in Transylvania did not speak the same language. In fact, they bitterly opposed any improvement in the lot of the Romanian peasants.

Alone, in the Transylvanian diet in 1744—an assembly whose hostility came close to violence—Micu-Klein forthrightly and uncompromisingly defended the rights of the Romanians. He referred to them as "the most numerous nation in Transylvania"—a statement which is in harmony with all the other evidence we have adduced concerning the numbers of Romanians in Transylvania at the time.

The nobility, in their elegant contempt for the laboring masses in the fields, the mines, and the quarries, dealt with them in these terms: "There is no Romanian nation. There are only Wallachian plebians." But the bishop was not at all impressed with the arrogance of the nobility. He kept on defending the Romanians, who, he said, "are oppressed by a bondage more cruel than the Egyptian bondage," described in the Bible. The representative of the nobility retorted that the Romanians are wanderers. To this Micu-Klein replied, "What else can they be if they are oppressed to death?"

The Transylvanian Saxons sided with the nobles. They said to Micu-Klein, "But the Romanians are thieves and outlaws!" To this Micu-Klein answered bluntly, "You should not be surprised at this, since these unfortunate people possess nothing except what they wear on their own backs."

The Hungarian nobility managed to get rid of this inconvenient opponent, who had the courage to claim for the Romanians (in their own country!) the same rights as those enjoyed by the illustrious members of the Holy Crown.

Micu-Klein was summoned to Vienna to be placed on trial. He was never to return to Transylvania where, in his own see, the town of Blaj, he had set up a small "Rome of the Romanians."

The status of the Romanian peasantry in Transylvania is apparent from the description written by the Austrian geologist, Hacquet, which we have quoted above.

A letter from the Empress Maria Theresa, dated 1773—the year when the future emperor, Joseph II, was scheduled to visit Transylvania—throws even more light on the state of affairs. Maria Theresa demanded of Transylvania's governor that he "clear the roads of the corpses of those killed by hanging, impaling, or quartering, which the Hungarians, to the travelers' horror, have let rot on purpose alongside these roads." But Transylvania was not honored by the visit of an imperial guest every year. From the empress' description, one can easily imagine the sinister aspect which the Transylvanian roads must have presented, strewn as they were with the corpses of Romanian serfs.

Horia, Closca and Crisan

The ceaseless agitation which existed within the ranks of the Romanian peasantry culminated in 1784 A.D. in the revolts of Horia, Closca, and Crisan.

As we have pointed out, the liberal measures decreed by Emperor Joseph II favored the Romanians in Transylvania, but they came up against the stubborn opposition of the Magyar nobility, who refused to give up any of the privileges they had bestowed on themselves. The only recourse for the Romanians was represented by the claims they presented to the Imperial Court in Vienna. Without means, their delegations had to walk all the way from Transylvania to Vienna.

It took them four weeks to reach Vienna, and another four weeks for their return trip. Returning home, they found that they had to face the same inflexiblity and violence with which their demands had been opposed at earlier dates by the Magyar nobility. In 1779, 1780, and 1782, Romanian delegations set out from Transylvania to Vienna. As a result of their experience on these pilgrimages, they gradually became aware of the superiority of their numbers over all the other nations in Transylvania, as well as of their precedence on the soil of the former province of Dacia. All of this gave rise to a nationalist effervescence. This effervescence manifested itself in a sporadic manner, but it was nonetheless symptomatic.

The Romanians in Hunedoara addressed themselves in these terms to the county prefect: "We cannot help wondering why it is that you, the Hungarians, in addition to forcing us to bear the yoke of serfdom, place so many pressures on us Romanians. We have been and we still are more numerous than you are. What is even more important, we have existed for a much longer time in this country, since we are the descendants of the ancient Dacians."

Oppression and exploitation can produce the most audacious action. A short while before Horia's revolt, Florea Cosma, a Romanian from Garbau, spoke to Count Szent Paul in these candid and forthright terms: "This country is ours. Hungary is yours. Before not too long we shall drive you out of here." We do not know what Cosma's fate was after speaking these words. But that they did not go unpunished is a reasonable surmise, given the attitude of the Magyar nobility toward the native population.

Rettegi, a writer contemporaneous to the period we are discussing, had no qualms about admitting that he "was afraid of these Romanians because they are ten times more numerous than the Hungarians in Transylvania." Rettegi also expressed fear that the Romanians would display a growing awareness of their Dacian-Roman origin. Obviously, this was bound to happen sooner or later as historical knowledge broke through the heavy clouds of ignorance.

In the light of these facts, one can only regard as ridiculous statements like that of the Hungarian writer Kazsonyi, that "Dacian-Romanism is only an invention of the Imperial Court in Vienna for use against the unity of the Hungarian people." That is what Kazsonyi had to say in his book, *La Parent'e des Peuples Danubiennes.*

The Dacian-Roman concept—that is, the concept that the

Romanians were the direct descendants of the Dacian-Romans—was a theory which had already gathered much momentum and which sooner or later, like all universal truths, was to come to enjoy general acceptance.

The Horia uprising, named after its principal leader, was on a massive scale which threatened the strong position of the Hungarian nobility. One can easily understand, therefore, why the Hungarian nobility made the most strenuous efforts to crush the uprising. The uprising, led by Horia and his two comrades, Closca and Crisan, began on October 31, 1784. By the end of the same year, it had been completely crushed. The leaders of the uprising managed to hide themselves temporarily, but their chief assistants in the various regions of Transylvania, where the uprising had reached very serious proportions, were put into prison and sentenced to death.

A Verdict Unique in History

The verdict pronounced by the criminal court under the chairmanship of a gentleman named Andrei Forrai, a knight of the Order of St. Stephen and an official of Arad, surpassed in its cruelty the most terrible verdicts handed down by the courts of the Inquisition in the Middle Ages. We shall list some of the sentences handed down against the Transylvanian Romanians by the Magyar nobility in order to bring to life the hatred which the Hungarians felt for the native Romanians of the area.

The sentence handed down in November 1784 against the leaders of the uprising involved twenty-two convictions. Some of the condemned men were sentenced to have "their hands cut off, then be beheaded and quartered." Others were condemned "to be beheaded by broad sword and then quartered." Some of the Romanian rebels were condemned to death by strangulation. Father George of Corbesti was condemned "to have his hands cut off and then to be beheaded." The mayor of the village of Ilteu and George Hotarasu were "to be beheaded by broad sword and their corpses quartered." Two of the accused were sentenced to be hanged in front of the entire population of the village. Finally, one of the convicted men was condemned to undergo quartering without being granted the "favor" of first being beheaded—in other words, he was to be quartered alive.

Even the horrors imagined by Octave Mirabeau in *The*

Garden of Ordeals, pale in the face of such tortures—which, indeed, constitute an indelible stain on the coats of arms of the Magyar nobility.

How can these sentences, unique in the annals of modern justice, be reconciled with "the historic civilizing mission of the Hungarian people in the Danubian area"—a mission emphasized in all Magyar propaganda materials distributed abroad?

To complete this tragic story, the leaders of the movement, Horia, Closca, and Crisan, were also caught after a period in hiding. The first two were sentenced to be quartered. Crisan committed suicide in prison, but "dead as he was," his body was still subjected to the punishment of quartering.

The visits of Joseph II to Transylvania as well as the reception Horia had received at the Imperial Court had caused the Romanians to believe that the leaders of the Romanian peasant uprising were carrying out the emperor's tacit will.

But the Imperial Court in Vienna, which at the beginning had appeared to encourage the Romanians to demand fairer treatment of the Hungarians, also sided with the Hungarian nobility when it appeared that the uprising had become a threat to the status quo.

A Western Philosopher Protests

The terrible tortures to which the leaders of the uprising were subjected made a profound impression on European public opinion. Horia's face had become familiar throughout western Europe thanks to the numerous engravings which appeared in major western publications at the time. In effect, these engravings immortalized him. But nothing illustrates more dramatically the horror created in western European countries by the bloody suppression of the Transylvanian revolt than does a letter written at the time by a philosopher in Dublin, Ireland. The letter was addressed to Emperor Joseph II of Austria a short while after the death sentences against the leaders of the Transylvanian uprising had been carried out. Although the writer of the letter asked to remain anonymous, the letter does betray that he was of French origin.

The letter is a scathing accusation which, unfortunately for the Romanian people, is essentially valid for the entire period of Hungarian domination in Transylvania.

"I am the first," says the author of this passionate indictment, "to defend the cause of the Romanians who, in the suppression of the insurrection, were the victims of force. I repeat: The Romanian people have the right to rise up in arms so long as they are compelled to live in serfdom and misery. To punish them for exercising this right means to punish them for being human beings."

In those days, as they were to do during the following centuries, the Hungarians attempted to distort the truth by portraying the role of the Transylvanian Romanians in a false light. But the anonymous philosopher in Dublin was not impressed by scribblers who sought to justify the deeds of the "illustrious noblemen responsible for suppression of the Romanians of Transylvania and the administration which aided them in this suppression." The preceding passage is quoted from the letter of the Dublin philosopher, who characterized them as "monsters who prostitute their pens for the purpose of enhancing the misery of the people."

"If you are convinced," continued this anonymous defender of the Romanian people, "that justice is on the Romanian side, then you must lose no time to give them back their liberty and their land . . . But, if you think you must side with the nobility and you do not wish to return to the Romanian people what is theirs, then there is only one way to do justice to everybody: Leave the country to its own destiny and let the slaves rise up in arms against their oppressors." (The phrase "return what is theirs" constitutes a tacit recognition of the precedence of Romanian property rights in Transylvania.)

This moving plea for Romanian liberty provides dramatic proof of the echoing reaction which the uprising led by Horia, Closca, and Crisan had in the civilized countries of Europe.

The Hungarians apparently believed that the tortures which they inflicted on the leaders of the movement would destroy forever any attempt by the Romanians to regain their liberty and their land. The Magyar nobility deliberately sought to crush the rebellion in a manner that would terrorize the peasantry. The means used to achieve this kind of oppression surpassed the verdict itself in cruelty. Indeed, they were comparable only with the methods of cannibals, seeking to terrorize the white settlers. Thus, Crisan's body was quartered and exposed successively at Abrud, Buciumi, Brad and Mihaileni, while his head was stuck on a pike in front of his house in Carpinis.

Brutal repressions often produce results different from the anticipated ones. That this is so was proved again by a statement written by the Hungarian nobility in Transylvania immediately after they had crushed the revolt of the Romanian peasants. They were obliged to admit that in Transylvania there are "as many Horias as there are villages." In the perspective of history we can state more accurately that there were as many Horias as there were Transylvanian peasants.

From "King" Horia to King Ferdinand

The Romanian people were never able to forget the odious attempt of the Hungarian nobility of that time to ridicule their struggle for freedom and land by crowning Horia with a cardboard crown bearing the inscription "King of Dacia"; indeed, for centuries after the death of Horia, they sought to achieve the revival of Dacia within the natural boundaries established by the ethnic Romanian population.

Documents of the time establish that the title "King of Dacia" was not conferred on Horia by the Transylvanian Romanians or by Horia himself. It was invented by the Hungarians with a view to nullifying the sympathy which Emperor Joseph felt for his Romanian subjects. In fact, in the year that he was slain, a Magyar publication in the German language sarcastically referred to Horia as *Seine Majestät Horia* ("his majesty, Horia").

History has its own laws, which cannot be grasped by contemporaries, but can only be understood in the perspective of centuries. There exists an invisible interdependence between historical facts which causes us to ascribe such facts to an "inherent justice," when in reality they have to do with causal relationships.

Horia was not king of Dacia, but he prepared the way for another leader of the Romanian people to rise to this honored position. The peasant rebellion of 1784 was only an episode in the revival of Romanian consciousness in Transylvania. One of the late results of this revived consciousness was the crowning of King Ferdinand of Romania at Alba-Julia in 1922. This time, however, the crown of Dacia was not a cardboard one. One of the first acts of King Ferdinand was to remake the ancient boundaries.

Two Documents of the 18th Century

In concluding this chapter, which deals with the Romanian revolt of 1784—a revolt which has echoed over the centuries in the history of the Transylvanian Romanians—we shall quote two documents of the time which fully support our assertions.

The first document is a written statement addressed by the Hungarian nobility to Count Jankovitsch, the special envoy of Emperor Joseph. In it the Magyar nobles try to justify the bloody repression of the Romanian peasant uprising.

"Our ancestors who came from Scythia," said the Hungarian nobles, "conquered this holy motherland with blood and arms. After subjecting and turning into serfs the ancestors of the Romanians who today rose against us, they governed their new subjects peacefully, but kept them under severe discipline without altering their way of life."

The notions of tolerance, intolerance, discipline, and harshness have for the Hungarians a meaning completely different from that which they have for other peoples.

The significance of the phrase "severe discipline" is to be found in a letter written by the Emperor Joseph. "The Hungarian," wrote the emperor, "does not care about what is just or what is unjust. A serf is his master's slave. These miserable Romanian subjects, who are without question the oldest and most numerous inhabitants of Transylvania, are maltreated by everybody, Hungarians and Transylvanian Saxons. They are overwhelmed by injustice. I am surprised that there are still Romanians in Transylvania, that they have not all run away."

In the light of these lines, written by the Austrian emperor himself, further comment becomes unnecessary. The reader himself will substitute the concepts of intolerance and oppression for the phrase "severe discipline" used by the Magyar nobility in their statement.

From these two documents it also emerges that in the 18th century—that is, when political considerations had not yet taken over in the field of history—the fact of the Dacian-Roman continuity in Transylvanian history was definitely sanctioned by authority.

The Hungarians assert this continuity quite clearly in stating that their ancestors conquered the land from the forefathers of the Romanian people—the same Romanian people who rose up in arms against the Magyar tyranny.

The emperor himself confirmed this continuity in words which require no comment: "The Romanians are, without any question, the oldest and most numerous inhabitants of Transylvania."

Such formal acknowledgements do not have the quality of surprise. For the Hungarians, might made right—but this is only a reflection of the mentality of the time. The Romanians had been defeated in battle by the ancestors of the Magyar nobility. The factor of precedence was of secondary importance—certainly not important enough to alter a situation which had as its moral basis the successful exercise of force by the Magyar nobility.

As for Emperor Joseph, the acknowledgement that one of the nationalities which was subject to the imperial crown had territorial precedence over another nationality which was subject to the same crown, exercised no influence on the dependent relations of either nationality toward the emperor. However, the 19th century saw an advance in the principles of international law, according to which the rights of nations were no longer dependent on force but on the natural connection between the territory and the people who occupy it.

International acceptance of this idea inevitably had to result in the acknowledgement of age-old Romanian rights over Transylvania.

Magyar Distortions

In order to contain the natural progress of the concept of Dacian-Romanian continuity, the Hungarian historians and, in particular, the pseudo-historians, embarked on a campaign that distorted Romanian history and denied the most elementary truths. Until the 18th century, the idea of Dacian-Romanian continuity on the territory of Transylvania was unanimously acknowledged, and the Romanians were considered to be the oldest inhabitants of the area. During the 19th and 20th centuries, however, both Magyar and Transylvanian Saxon historiography executed a *volte-face* on this matter, denying the truth, which was evident.

In a summary of Romanian history recently published by the Magyar English language publication, *The Hungarian Quarterly*, the Hungarian writer Zombor Szasz attempts to present the theory that the concept of Dacian-Roman continuity was a "Romanian invention started by the Transylvanian writers Gheorghe Sincai, Petru Maior (*The History of the Beginnings of the Romanians in Dacia*) and Samuel Klein (*Elemente linguae dacoromanum sive valachicae*—'Elements of the Daco-Romanian or Wallachian Language')." This theory, apparently, first saw the light during studies of the resemblance between the Romanian and Latin languages carried out in Roman schools.

Moreover, Szasz, who wrote for readers abroad, apparently believing them to be totally ignorant regarding the life and problems of the peoples of the Carpathian-Danubian area, asserts that the concept of the Dacian-Roman continuity was more of a political dogma than a scientific theory. This dogma, Szasz concludes, was intended to give strength to the movement for Romanian independence and ultimately to ensure the achievement of Romanian aspirations for national unity.

So that the English reader of Szasz' article may be properly informed, let it be said that Szasz, a Hungarian writer who pretends to be a Romanian historian, forgets all about the old Hungarian chronicles and the other recent proofs which give Romanian claims the most authentic scientific character.

For this reason we address a question to Szasz: "Are you motivated by the achievement of Romanian unity or, to use your own words, by the endeavor to disprove the Dacian-Roman origin of the Romanians in Transylvania as well as their precedence in the former Dacian territory?"

But Szasz, apparently believing that he is the first to publish a synthesis of Romanian history in English, takes great liberty with that notion of the truth which is supposed to be the guiding principle of every honest historical work. There are two ways to mislead somebody. One can deliberately omit information which would settle the question at issue (distortion of truth by omission); or one can openly distort the facts (the active method). Szasz, like the entire modern school of pseudo-historians, is animated by a single passion: shaping in the minds of the foreign readers a completely false picture of the evolution of the Romanian nation. For this reason, he makes use of both methods.

We have seen that Szasz is an expert when it comes to ignoring everything that is opposed to Hungarian policy in Transylvania. He is also a master in the second method of distorting the truth. For example, he ascribes to Romanian historians the statement that after the Magyar invasion (and, of course, "after the immigration of the Romanians to Transylvania"), "the Romanians and Hungarians joined forces and together built a new state."

This is utterly false. None of the Romanian historians has ever made such a statement, not even C. C. Giurescu whose work, *History of the Romanians*, inspired Szasz' writings. On the contrary, the entire history of the Romanian people in Transylvania constitutes a dramatic protest against the total ousting of the native Romanian element from the leadership of Transylvania.

Supplex Libellus Valachorum

We have seen how the three privileged nations, the Hungarians, the Transylvanian Saxons, and the Szecklers, who came into Transylvania as visitors and then became its masters, appropriated for themselves the right to shape the destinies of the country, excluding the Romanians from any participation in public affairs. In 1791 Emperor Joseph II died. On the eve of his death, he revoked all those measures he had taken to improve the lot of the Romanians. Emperor Leopold II ascended to the throne. The Romanian people, influenced by the French revolution which paid tribute to the principles of *Liberté, egalité, fraternité*, sent the emperor a written statement known in the history of Transylvania as the *Supplex Libellus Valachorum*. This name was given to the document by the three nations which enjoyed a comfortable life, thanks to the labor of the humble petitioners.

This written statement was the first large-scale political action of the Transylvanian Romanians. Its emphasis was essentially nationalist. Horia's revolution had begun to bear fruit. Although humble in its choice of words, it was in fact a firm and explicit assertion. It constitutes a strong affirmation of Romanian national rights in Transylvania. It conveys an awareness of power, but at the same time, of the historic mission of the Romanian people in Transylvania. The meaning of this political petition was explained very simply by Nicolae Iorga: "The petition was the affirmation of just rights."

The authors of this political petition were the bishops of the two Romanian churches in Transylvania. "Although we are more numerous than all the other nations in the principality taken together," said the petition, "we are the most miserable and lowly."

The Romanians were aware of their numerical superiority, and, at the same time, they were aware of their Dacian-Roman origin which, according to the principle of precedence, gave them certain rights in the area. Consequently, the petitioners asked not that the ancient rights of which they had been deprived be *granted* to them, but that they be *given back* to them. At the same time, the petition asked that the state cease regarding its Romanian subjects as a "tolerated" or "accepted" minority and that the political rights of which they had been deprived be reinstated.

Was Dacian-Roman continuity a political invention? Were the Romanian people united in mind and sentiment with the Hungarian people, in helping the Magyar nobility to build up the Hungarian state? Can it be that the Hungarian historians—the real historians—found nothing to object to in these historical monstrosities, launched by politicians who, overnight, had become great scholars in a field of activity in which Hungary already had so many celebrities? Can it be that modern Hungarian historiography is based on the calculation that scholars in other countries—to whom the aberrations which abound in their so-called historical works were so transparently addressed—were not able to tell the difference between history and propaganda?

Anyone who sought to familiarize himself with the history of the gigantic battles which the Romanians in Transylvania had to fight before they were granted the most elementary civil and political rights, would have arrived at completely different conclusions from those formulated by the politicians and so-called historians in Budapest.

The Transylvanian Romanians have always considered themselves the descendants of the Dacian-Romans, and they were considered as such by all the other peoples in Europe. If they did not voice this belief publicly, despite the fact that nobody has ever denied their Dacian-Roman origin, it was because the conditions of life imposed on them by the clique of Magyar nobles in Transylvania had prevented them from doing so.

The Situation of the Romanian Peasantry

Until not so long ago the Romanians in Transylvania simply "lay" (the word belongs to Vicar I. Pora of Nasaud) in a status of inferiority equalled only by the living conditions of the pariahs in India.

When the Romanians began their struggle in the political arena with a view to regaining their ancient liberties and territories, they were, as the Vicar of Nasaud put it, suffering under the yoke of oppression. This struggle was to culminate in the Act of Union on December 1, 1918. Unfortunately, the Act did not obviate the need for further struggle.

The implications of the Budapest historians, that the Romanians were working side by side with the Hungarians in a joint effort to build up the Hungarian state, had a well-defined goal. This was to instill in the minds of the foreign historical investigators some confusing facts regarding the real situation of the Romanian peasantry in Transylvania—and this, precisely at the moment when this peasantry was asserting for the first time its right to a national life of its own. Szasz' subtle assertions are definitively disproved both by the documents of the time and by the whole historical evolution of the Transylvanian Romanians.

Until late in the 19th century, the Romanian peasantry in Transylvania had to bear the yoke of terrible feudal oppression. It was not merely that, in terms of rights, they had never been the equals of the Magyar nobility, but that they were treated like pariahs on the land where once they had been masters.

Liberty, but not for the Romanians

The feudal constitution which was operative in the province of Transylvania brought with it an oppressive system which nipped in the bud any attempt to shake off the Magyar yoke. The situation of the Romanian peasant in Transylvania was in every respect much worse than that of the Hungarian peasant in the Hungarian kingdom proper, although the latter lived a hard enough life.

In 1566, the Magyar nobility had granted the Hungarian peasants the right of free migration on the territory of the Hungarian kingdom—that is, the right to move from one place to another and back again, if this was deemed necessary. This right, whose denial today is regarded as a defiance of the most elementary humanitarian consideration and of individual rights, was refused to the Transylvanian Romanians until

1791. In that year, under the pressure of the revival of Romanian national consciousness, and also under the influence of the great achievements of the French revolution of 1789, the Transylvanian Diet finally abolished "perpetual servitude"—that is, serfdom.

But within Hungary's feudal regime, tolerance had a special meaning. Although the perpetual servitude of the Romanian peasants had been formally abolished, the fate of the Transylvanian peasantry did not improve, even with the liberty to migrate. It was characteristic of the Magyars of that time that they knew how to take away with one hand what they had given with the other. In principle, the Romanian peasant had the right to leave his Hungarian master at will and move to another state. In practice, this liberty was annulled by a condition reminiscent of the bargain driven by Shylock in *The Merchant of Venice*.

The Romanian was allowed to leave a master whose "severe discipline" he found unbearable only if he could find another man to take over the miserable life he was leading. Moreover, his replacement had to be as able as he was "to bear his public obligations, and to work in the same conditions."

Further, in order to make the elementary human right of migration unattainable, the Romanian peasant also had to pay the Magyar nobleman compensation for "the damages, brought about by his leaving, to the public and private economy." The consequence of refusal to pay this compensation was characteristic of the Hungarian feudal system. A man who would not pay his compensation was condemned to receive twenty-four blows of the cudgel every day—while a woman, being more delicate, was given only twenty-four strokes of the whip.

To this objective prohibition on migrating from the land he was working, must be added the prohibition on the right of Romanians to purchase even the smallest plot of land. Finally, in order to form a picture of what Romanian life was like under the constitution (the famous constitution which has been held up for others!), there was the anarchy which governed relations between the Magyar nobleman and the Romanian serf. These relations, arbitrarily determined by the nobleman, featured such refinements as daily blows of the cudgel for the smallest infraction.

How much credence can we give to Hungarian historical works when a writer like Denes A. Janossy compared the constitution which governed the lives of the Romanian peasants with the Magna Charta in England, which was the source document of civil liberties in that country? How much credence can we give when a politician like Zombor Szasz has the brazenness to characterize the problem in these words: "They [the Romanians] complain of a lack of liberty and equality in a state whose liberal institutions offer sufficient guarantees of both." [In the face of statements like this, there are still people who say that the Magyar historians do not have a sense of humor!—*Author.*]

An enormous gap separated the Hungarian nobility from the Romanian peasantry. The rough, inhuman treatment which the Romanian peasants had to bear for centuries, the conditions of bondage in which they lived and from which they could not hope to escape except by their own means, account for—they even justify—the violence of the Romanian response when the time came to settle accounts.

When, in 1831, the first movements started and then spread among the oppressed peasantry of the Slavic countries, they had a strong echo within the ranks of the Transylvanian peasantry.

Meanwhile, liberal intellectuals in Hungary, inspired by the constitutions of western countries, had started stirring against what Kossuth called the "chauvinistic despotism of the Austrian government." The Hungarian nation was asking for its right to a free, unfettered life. The cause of the Hungarian peasantry found partisans in the ranks of the liberal parties. From the tribune of the Austrian Parliament, Baron Kemeny Denes, the chief of the Liberal Party, described the miserable condition of the Hungarian peasantry in these heartrending words:

> The peasants have been robbed of all their human rights, indeed, of their human condition—and then they have been given tasks which not only ask too much of the land they toil on, but which exceed their physical powers. While the nobleman lives a comfortable life doing nothing, the peasant breaks his back in the field.
> Take care! God cannot abide such a state of things for long!

If this was the situation of the Hungarian peasantry, one

can readily imagine what the plight of the Romanian peasantry was like in those days.

The Romanian intellectuals kept the Romanian popular masses well informed on the progress made by the great movements for national liberation which had started in the West and which were now being witnessed in central Europe.

The demands of the Romanian peasantry had always come up against the intransigence of the Magyar nobility, who were refractory to any improvement in the lot of their subjects. Now, inspired by the peasant movements in other countries, the Romanians started nurturing hopes of liberty. But they were greatly disappointed when they saw that the movement of Lajos Kossuth, despite his generous rhetoric, not only did not embrace the special cause of the Romanians, but, on the contrary, excluded it from their program.

At that point, it became possible to see clearly the nexus between the national cause and the social cause of the Transylvanian peasantry. Kossuth and his entire movement apparently did not consider the Romanian peasantry a social class which had the same right as the Hungarian peasantry to be defended against the tyranny of the nobility. Instead, they looked upon the Romanian peasantry as a separate nation which, if allowed to better their fate, could become aware of their natural rights. This, of course, would have been highly dangerous for the oppressor class, the Hungarian noblemen.

Thus was born the antagonism between what Kossuth was claiming for the Hungarian nation itself and what he denied to the Romanian nation. Faced with two virtually identical situations, the Hungarian revolutionary movement recommended two completely different attitudes. It was not chauvinism or irredentism when Bzeredy exclaimed in the Austrian Diet that "the Hungarians also have their force", or when he said on another occasion to the Diet, "let us help the people to rise up!" Nor was it irredentism when the great Hungarian politician, Szecheny, declared that "the Hungarian nation is chosen by God to dominate all the peoples around it." Nor was it irredentism when a poet like Vorosmarty wrote: "Any Hungarian man who walks this earth and has the sky over his head, should at the same time be a man and a Hungarian." But apparently it was considered irredentism when the Romanians dared to demand "the acknowledgement of their natural rights, based on equity and justice."

4. HUNGARIAN LIBERAL AND CONSERVATIVE ATTITUDES TOWARD THE ROMANIANS

The Machiavellianism of Kossuth's Revolutionaries

When the winds generated by the Paris revolution of 1848 reached Vienna and Budapest, Kossuth asked England and France to assist the movement for the liberation of the Hungarian people from the Hapsburg tyranny.

Nothing could have been more natural than this. But at the same time, nothing could have been stranger or more audacious than when the same Hungarian revolutionaries asked the western nations to intervene for the purpose of restraining the movement for Romanian independence which had become increasingly conspicuous in the Romanian principalities. "If the situation were changed [in the Romanian principalities]," said Kossuth, "it could bring about an incalculable moral effect on the Romanians in Hungary."

In short, the leader of the Magyar revolution was outlining for his friends in the West the danger which the Romanian independence movement represented for Europe. At the same time he was telling them of the immense advantages that would accrue to the West from Hungarian liberation—a liberation that could be achieved only as the result of a movement similar to the Romanian liberation movement.

Kossuth and his representatives made a superhuman effort to persuade the British, in particular, how much they stood to gain from an economic standpoint if Hungary achieved independence. The revolutionaries did their utmost to realize their dream of seeing Hungarian ships, flying the Hungarian flag, docked in Liverpool and Marseilles.

In the thick of the revolution, a spokesman, A. de Gerando,

made the following statement in France: "The Hungarians of all races [*sic*!], that is, all the nationalities in Hungary's territory, are unanimous on the defense of the interests of the common motherland [*sic*!] against the Hapsburgs."

This is propaganda pure and simple. And, like all propaganda, it involves deliberate distortions and the negation of the most elementary realities.

Machiavelli's principles have never been better illustrated. In order to achieve their goal—that is, the liberation of the Hungarian people from the yoke of Austria—the Hungarian revolutionaries were prepared to use all means, even the most revolting and cynical ones.

The Hungarian Liberals and Conservatives: Solidarity against the Romanians

Even when they ostensibly spoke in favor of the Romanian people, the representatives of Magyar liberalism did so in the expectation that they might then more easily Magyarize the Romanian masses. Indeed, they made no secret of this goal.

"The abolition of privileges," said the liberal Hungarian economist Heteny at a moment when great liberal reforms were being carried out in the rest of Europe, "will represent for the Romanian people their best opportunity to achieve educational rights as well as the right to purchase land. This will lead in the end to the complete Magyarization of the Romanian element."

However, the persistence of a feudal mentality within the ranks of the Magyar nobility in Transylvania was enough to frustrate all attempts at liberalization. That is why even Heteny had to place his plan for the emancipation of the Romanian people [read, "emancipation-Magyarization of the Romanian peasantry"] in a very remote future. Said this leader of Magyar liberalism: "Who would care to bear witness to the sudden ruin of ancient families for the sake of a new idea?"

Professor Silviu Dragomir admirably characterizes the situation of the Hungarian theoreticians of the time, confronted with the problem of the Transylvanian Romanians. "They were wavering," he said, "between a cynical refusal and a calculated hesitation."

Whenever the Romanian demands were mentioned, all the existing differences between the Hungarian political parties and all the doctrinal differences between all the political-economic doctrines of the time disappeared, as if by magic. These demands, indeed, always succeeded in bringing about the complete solidarity of the most deadly political adversaries.

But of all the political parties, the conservatives proved particularly refractory to the idea of liberty for the Romanians.

"If serfdom is abolished," said a representative of the conservatives, "it will require only one generation for both the Hungarians and Szecklers in Transylvania to be destroyed, yielding their places to the Romanian and Transylvanian-Saxon nations." To this the conservatives added: "The Romanians, poor people who hardly manage to satisfy their hunger with corn flour once a day, will become the masters of the pure Hungarians and the Szecklers; and, since they are now more numerous than we are, they will impose their own nationalism on us. This is something God must protect us from." Apart from its political significance, this statement helps to reveal the true status of minorities in the Hungarian "minorities paradise" in central Europe.

For all these reasons, the Romanians had to be kept in a perpetual state of misery, extreme poverty and ignorance, so they would not be able to add to their power through numbers. Their status could be improved only if they first gave up their Romanian nationality. This was the essence of the Machiavellianism of Hungarian minorities policy. Thus, Magyar policy wavered between two options. First, there were people like Heteny who asserted that "first you plant the tree, then you gather the crop"—that is, first, the Romanians had to be emancipated and only then should one proceed to their Magyarization. Second, there was the opinion of the Magyar conservatives who took the stand that the Romanians should be completely Magyarized first, and only then should they be granted their liberty—liberty which they had a right to, according to all divine and human laws.

But even among liberals there were intractable enemies of the Romanian cause, nor was there any concept of progress where the Romanian nation was concerned. Thus, one of the most outstanding representatives of Hungarian liberalism, Baron Nicolae Wesseleny, wrote to Kossuth about the problem of Romanianism:

We should not forget that the Hungarian nobility is the

basis of our nationality. It is true that the Hungarian
nobility has committed many errors. But it is also true
that the Hungarian nation exists by itself and only for
itself. If the thousands of noblemen were to lose their
wealth, the entire nation would suffer because most of the
millions of people who will take their place are not of
Magyar origin.

This was the crux of the matter. It was a fight between
millions of Romanian landless peasants against thousands of
Hungarian land owners for control of an area that had been
Romanian in the beginning. Initially, there had been only
hundreds of thousands of Romanians. However, as a result of
a high birth rate, they had become millions—and these millions
had been subjected by a few hundred families of nomadic
knights, who had increased their numbers by no more than a
few thousand.

But Wesseleny's letter to Kossuth is also worth mentioning
because of another conclusion which derives from it. This conclusion had the effect of upsetting the entire structure of Hungarian propaganda in foreign countries for decades to come. In
essence, this propaganda sought to contrast Hungarian "tolerance" for their subjected nationalities to the Romanian "intolerance" during the two decades of Romanian rule in
Transylvania.

The Romanians Equal Zero

We quote from Wesseleny's writing a fragment which is
worthy of appearance on the frontispiece of a universal history
of intolerance:

That a limited number of Hungarians succeeded in dominating, thanks to their nationalism and their language,
an overwhelming majority of the other races was possible
only thanks to the fact that this imposing majority for us
is equal to zero (*Hogy halunk ama nagy tobbseg ew zero*)
and that only the nobility has real value. But most of the
noblemen are Hungarian and that is why it is not absurd
to admit that their nationality and language are dominant factors. This state of affairs will change, however,
when the millions of non-Hungarians are no longer simply

a numerical majority but, in addition, a majority of the citizens who enjoy full rights.

Such was the status to which the masses of Romanians had been reduced by the Hungarian nobility—a nobility which, on the eve of great changes in Europe, continued to live, in their castles in Transylvania, a feudal type of life characteristic of the lords of the Middle Ages, dividing their time between hunting parties, love affairs, and feasts.

A numerical majority without rights, equal in value, in terms of its influence and state rights, to zero—this was the end result of the age-old policy of repression and intolerance.

The Romanians had hoped that Kossuth's generally liberal movement, which had spoken in generous terms about the aspirations of the people, could help them to achieve their own principal goal. However, the leader of the Hungarian revolution of 1848 came out strongly against Romanian emancipation, abruptly bringing to an end the interminable political philosophical discussions that had been stimulated by the situation of the Romanian serfs. Kossuth's viewpoint was quite explicit: the Romanians should stop considering themselves a distinct nation, after which they could be granted an acceptable social and economic situation.

"The Romanians' desire to have a political existence of their own," said Kossuth, "is unattainable because it would lead to the destruction of the unity of the Hungarian state." [As though the Hungarian revolution had as its goal something other than the breaking up of the Hapsburg state!] "If need be," he continued, "the sword will decide."

The method advocated in theory had to be put into practice. To this end, Kossuth resorted to radical stratagems. Within the framework of the constitutional autonomy of Transylvania, Romanian nationalism in a short time would have become an element that had to be reckoned with, and none of the artificial barriers raised by the Hungarians would have been able to contain it. United with Hungary, Transylvania stood in danger of losing the independent character which it had enjoyed throughout its history. It would have become, in the hands of the Hungarian leaders, a vast proving ground where they could exercise their methods of forced denationalization.

Transylvania: An Independent Province for Centuries

In fact, the struggle against the Romanian nationality had become a struggle between the principle of retaining Transylvania's autonomy and the opposing principle, which sought to join the province to the Crown of St. Stephen. Union with Hungary would have connoted a real revolution in the history of Transylvania, because, from the moment when the Hungarians imposed their rule over the territory of the onetime province of Dacia until the middle of the 19th century, Transylvania had not for a moment ceased being a territory regarded as distinct from the kingdom of Hungary.

Transylvania had maintained this independence, even during the period of Turkish rule which had covered a part of Hungary proper as well as Transylvania. While Buda, in 1529, and Hungary proper, in 1541, had been converted into Turkish *pashaliks*, Transylvania had been recognized as a separate province, the principality of Transylvania, completely independent of the Hungarian kingdom and paying direct tribute to the Sublime Porte [the government of the Ottoman Empire].

In the year 1688, Turkish sovereignty, which had not in any way hindered the autonomous development of Transylvania, came to an end. It was followed by the domination of the Hapsburg monarchy which, from the beginning, had to contend with a strong opposition in the Transylvanian Diet.

Cserey, a Szeckler chronicler who was contemporary to the period we are discussing, characterized the change of sovereignty in these words: "Poor Transylvania exchanged the wooden yoke of the Turks for the iron yoke of the Hapsburgs!" The Transylvanians sought to oppose violations of their ancient rights. It came to the point where the emperor's envoy, the Jesuit Anton Dunod, shouted in the Diet at the outraged deputies: "His Majesty will protect you, with or without your consent!"

The emperor's army spread terror among the Transylvanian population. Transylvania had no alternative but to submit. On May 9, 1688, councillors representing Prince Mihail Apafi signed at Sibiu a declaration of Transylvanian obedience to the Hapsburg crown.

Transylvania remained under the suzerainty of Hungary for centuries after its initial conquest. However, it did not become administratively a part of Hungary until the year 1867, when, by vote of the Hungarian Diet, it was physically incorporated into Hungary—against the popular will of its Romanian residents. This remained its status until December 1, 1918, when it separated from Hungary and joined the Romanian kingdom, pursuant to the unanimous will of the Romanian people.

In the year 1790, the emperor of Austria, whose connection with Transylvania was based on a personal union, insisted on reconfirming Transylvania's independence and on its complete separation from Hungary, in terms which are not subject to misinterpretation: "Transylvania," he said, "is a self-determined principality, independent from all other countries and having its own constitution and laws."

The independence of Transylvania can be traced back to the ancient traditions of the autonomous Roman province of Dacia which, after the fall of Rome, had become the *voivodate* "over the mountains" (*Transilvae*—literally, "over the woods"), and finally the principality of Transylvania.

Its independence, however, had been exploited for the benefit of a clique of Magyar noblemen who, even in modern times, abusively oppressed the great masses of Transylvanian Romanians, whose permanent presence constituted the factor primarily responsible in determining the province's autonomy. When the time arrived for the Romanian masses to demand the benefits of independence, the Hungarians proclaimed Transylvania's union with Hungary. In doing this, they delivered a mortal blow to Romanianism, which, until that point, had appeared to be on the way to a vigorous self-assertion. At the end of May 1848, the Budapest government arranged a special session of the Transylvanian Diet to proclaim the union of Transylvania with Hungary.

Union or Death!

The Hungarian propagandists launched the motto "Union or Death" in the expectation that it would capture the excited spirits of youth and would have a stirring effect on the general population. If, according to the Magyar concept, failure of the union meant the death of privileges, the success of the union meant the death of Romanianism. Indeed, among the 446 deputies in the Hungarian Parliament, there was not a single representative of the Romanians in Transylvania.

According to statistics adduced by the Hungarian writer Fenyes (quoted by the Hungarophile writer, A. de Gerando), there were at that time 2,311,000 Romanians in Hungary and 4,870,000 Hungarians. If there had been a just distribution of

representation, the Romanians should have had approximately
50 percent of the representation enjoyed by the Hungarians.
But the liberals in Budapest granted the Romanians zero opportunity to manifest their popular will, thus effectively nullifying the possibility of a Romanian national political
manifestation. In short, Kossuth's revolution identified itself
with the political mentality which had for centuries characterized the Hungarian government.

In the face of the unsympathetic attitude displayed by
Kossuth, the Transylvanian Romanians had no other recourse
than to offer opposition—the stubborn opposition of the peasant
masses, deeply rooted in the land on which they were living,
the angry opposition of peoples who could no longer tolerate
the situation in which they had been placed.

Simion Barnutiu's Proclamation

Simion Barnutiu, a leader of the Transylvanian Romanians, on March 25, 1848, issued a proclamation to the Romanian
people which constituted a signal for struggle against the
union:

> The Hungarians asked Transylvania to accept the
> union. This is a question of life or death, so every Ro-
> manian must open his eyes. He must make good use of
> the opportunity, because he can either win everything or
> lose everything. If he loses, he is bound to lose even that
> which has been his so far—his nationality. Listen, des-
> cendants of the Romans, to the answer you have to give
> the Hungarians and the Transylvanian Saxons: "We will
> not accept the union until the Romanian nation has re-
> turned to it the political status of which the Hungarians,
> the Szecklers, and the Transylvanian Saxons have de-
> spoiled us.

Influenced by the great spirit of the changes which were
taking place in Europe at that time, the proclamation ended
with this impressive peroration:

> Every town and every village is vibrating with the
> sound of joy because today is the day on which the dead
> have risen. We, the millions of political dead, we have not

been a nation. Today is the day of our resurrection. Let us topple the tombstones from our graves, let us shake off the centuries-old chains which have bound the Romanian nation, so that it can raise itself from the dust and live in peace.

The Assembly at Blaj: May 1848

In May, 1848, two leaders of the Romanian church, Bishop Jean Lemenyi and Andrei Saguna, convoked a giant meeting on the plains surrounding the town of Blaj for the purpose of asserting Romanian national consciousness and protesting against the proposed union.

The meeting was an impressive manifestation because of the large number (over 40,000) of delegates and peasants who came from the most remote corners of Transylvania, and also because of the importance of the decisions taken on this occasion. For the first time in the political history of Transylvania, the Transylvanian Romanians were gathered together with those on the other side of the Carpathians. Indeed, this giant manifestation of Romanian nationalism in Transylvania also featured some of the outstanding personalities in the Romanian principalities—among them Alexandru Ioan Cuza, the future prince of the principalities; Vasile Alecsandri, the bard of Latinity; Alecu Russo, Eliade Radulescu, and many other representatives of Romanian political and cultural life of the time.

With overwhelming unanimity the Romanians who took part in the manifestation decided to demand and fight for their recognition as an independent nation, coequal with the other three privileged nations of Transylvania, the Szecklers, the Hungarians, and the Transylvanian Saxons—all of the latter, originally foreign peoples on Transylvanian soil who had arrogated to themselves the exclusive right to dispose of Transylvania's destiny.

"The decisions of this gathering," said Moga, "remained permanent demands, until 1918, of the Transylvanian Romanians in their struggle for independence."

The Romanian National Party in Transylvania, which fought for three-quarters of a century to achieve the just demands of its people, owes its existence to the historic decisions in 1848 of the great assembly on "Liberty Plain."

In order to prove how little the Hungarian leaders understood about developments in the Romanian community in Transylvania, it is sufficient to quote from a letter addressed by Baron Iosika to Baron Wesseleny, describing the great Romanian manifestation at Blaj. "The gathering," he wrote, "was ridiculous and stupid." Of course, Iosika found it ridiculous because of the hopes which the Romanians obviously nurtured that their political demonstration would have an effect. And he found it stupid because the Romanian serfs dared to demand that they be treated as equals of the Magyar nobility—from whom, because the Magyars had willed it this way, they were separated by an abyss.

At the time of the assembly in Blaj, as has been pointed out, Romanian sentiment was virtually unanimous in opposing the union. Indeed, the Romanian leaders from both Transylvania and the principalities were already turning over in their minds some thoughts about a different kind of union. The difference was that this time they were thinking about a natural union—which had to happen one day—uniting the destiny of the Romanian people on both sides of the Carpathians.

The idea of creating a Dacian Romania had attracted more and more support, while calls for dismemberment of the Hapsburg monarchy were more and more manifest.

"Transylvania," said a priest in Madarasul de Cimpie after the great meeting at Blaj, "is no longer Transylvania, but Romania."

Summing up the impact of the May 1848 actions, the great Romanian patriot, Nicolae Balcescu, said: "The day of May 3, 1848 [the day on which the Blaj Assembly convened], is a luminous day, which speaks to us of liberty and Romanian glory."

The Revolution of 1848

As was to be expected, the Hungarians were not indifferent to the continuing restlessness of the Romanian populace. They embarked on countermeasures intended to put a stop to the movement for Romanian national revival. This resulted in a stepped-up persecution of the Romanian intellectuals. In addition, the houses of the peasant delegates to the Blaj assembly were burned down, and the priests were put into prison, or hanged or shot. Fires alternated with massacres and other excesses. The Romanian peasantry took up arms by way of manifesting their readiness to resist. In September of 1848, the Romanians organized a second gathering on Liberty Plain near Blaj. This gathering was attended by 6,000 armed Romanians from the Apuseni Mountains, under the leadership of the lawyer Avram Iancu, the future hero of the bitter resistance in the Abrud Mountains.

Meanwhile, the union had been approved by the Diet and accepted by the emperor. Acceptance was more or less extorted from the emperor by his Hungarian subjects. When the law imposing union was handed down to the Emperor Franz Joseph for promulgation, he asked the Hungarian government to give him some time to meditate on the measures which were to be taken to implement it. To Count Bathyany, the Hungarian minister, Franz Joseph said: *Aber lieber Herr Graf, können sie mir doch ein wenig Bedenkzeit geben,* that is, "Dear Count, give me a little time to think it over." But, yielding to pressures, the emperor signed the law—which was to write finis to the recognition of the Romanians as an autonomous nation on the ancient Roman land of Dacia—without brooding excessively over the consequence of his action.

The Hungarians encountered stubborn Romanian resistance in implementing this law and taking over the state administration. Indeed, the Romanian people could not be induced to surrender the one thing which centuries of Hungarian terror had still not been able to take away from them—their sense of national unity.

The ensuing oppression, which was carried out by subordinate bodies in accordance with instructions received from Budapest, aggravated the discontent and disturbances among the Romanian peasantry.

In this situation—brought about in the first place by the stubbornness of the Hungarian nobility and the hostile attitude of Kossuth's so-called revolutionaries, and, in the second place by the awareness of the inferior status of the Romanian peasantry—a single spark was sufficient to start a conflagration.

The Hungarians once more struck back with their customary harshness. There is in the soul of the Hungarian people a centuries-old hatred against the Romanian element in Transylvania. For this hatred there is absolutely no justification, since the Magyar element enjoyed the advantages of oppressors and exploiters. In fact, the existence of this hatred can only be accounted for by the inability of the Magyars to transform the soul of Transylvania.

One can denationalize individual elements within a people—but one can never denationalize an entire nation.

The catastrophic costs of the revolution of 1848 in Transylvania faithfully reflect the image of the terror unleashed by the Hungarians against the Romanian people, who were fighting for their sacred right to national liberation. Two hundred and thirty villages were razed to the ground. In the suppression of the revolution, 40,000 people were killed. The damages came to the immense total—for those days—of 30 million gold florins.

In comparison, the revolution of 1848 in France took only 15,000 victims. The Hungarian repression of the Romanian uprising was so bloody that a Romanian historian could with good reason declare that the revolution in Transylvania "had taken on almost apocalyptic proportions."

The Austrian army and the armed Romanians under Baron Puchner defeated the Szecklers. Kossuth's army, under the Polish General Ben, managed to conquer Brasov and Sibiu, so that Transylvania was, for a time, in their hands.

Avram Iancu

The Romanian peasant troops withdrew to the center of Transylvania where, under Avram Iancu's leadership—he had been made an *ad hoc* Captain of the army—they mounted a resistance, unique in history, to the Magyar troops in the Apuseni Mountains.

Avram Iancu and his peasant troops fought against the cannons of the armies of Hatvany and Vasary with weapons which they had made themselves or which they had come by with difficulty—rifles, bows and arrows, pikes, and—cherrywood cannons. Iancu, "the king of the mountains," relying on his own obstinacy and the justice of his cause, simply strengthened his resolve.

While Kossuth's army was fighting to keep millions of Romanians in bondage, the Romanians were fighting for the principle of liberty which reputedly was the foundation of Kossuth's revolution.

"We are free men," said Iancu, whose fierce fight in the Abrud Mountains created a legend. "It is for our freedom that we have resorted to arms. It is for this that we have shed our blood."

Before being executed, the prefect Boteanu, one of Iancu's

lieutenants, showed the courage to hurl in the faces of his torturers the opinion of the Romanian people concerning the concept of liberty which animated the Hungarians. "Your liberty," he shouted, "is nothing but flattery, cheating, and empty words!"

Horia and the uprising of 1784 and Iancu and his revolution of 1848 represent two notches cut in the log of the Romanian national revival, two stages in the difficult struggles the Transylvanian Romanians had to wage for the most elementary of all claims: equality in rights as well as in obligations with the other peoples with whom they shared the territory of Transylvania.

Contemporary Hungarian writers put down as "irredentism" the natural movements of the Romanian "minority-majority" for freedom from Magyar bondage.

The British writer, Arthur Seton-Watson (*Scotus Viator*), who has on various occasions unmasked the oppressive methods used "throughout their history by the Hungarians toward the cohabitants of their territory who were of a different origin from theirs," borrowed the term "irredentism" from Magyar propaganda. He did so, however, with that humor specific to the British, and he challenged the imputation of irredentism, using the word consistently between quotation marks.

As a matter of fact, this so-called irredentism was nothing more than the cry of revolt of millions of people, native to the area, against the feudal methods inherited from the Middle Ages and introduced by several thousand privileged Magyar noblemen, who were seeking to perpetuate them forever.

Instead of changing with the times, instead of adapting itself to the natural evolution of the political system, the Magyar policy clung to the retention of the many inequalities and to the oppression which this necessitated. In the light of the spiritual conquests of the 19th century, such a policy had become anachronistic and intolerable.

The most trivial improvements in the welfare of the Romanian people had to be drawn by force from the Magyar nobility. Alternatively, whenever they decided of their own accord to improve the situation of the minorities in Hungary they did so only under the pressure of circumstances, and only when it was already too late. The events that took place between 1848 and 1849 constitute unchallengeable evidence of this historic truth. When Kossuth's armies were defeated, the leader of the so-called Hungarian revolution finally realized what an important source of support he had lost in the battle for national liberation by his two-faced policy toward the Romanians.

Kossuth's Regrets

After the disaster of Villagos on July 29, 1849, Kossuth, who up until that time had stubbornly denied that the Romanian nation had any claim to national rights, decided to change his intolerant attitude toward the Romanians with a view to patching up a friendship with the Romanian masses against the Austrians. At the 11th hour, he finally decreed a law which granted to the Romanian nation in Romanian Transylvania the right to freedom and to conditions equal to those of the other nations who lived in the area. When Iancu learned about the text of the law, he was still continuing his heroic resistance in the Abrud Mountains. But it was already too late. Kossuth was no longer master of the situation. The Austrian-Russian troops scored one victory after another. Kossuth abdicated, escaping to Varna and then, via Great Britain, to the United States.

The changes which Kossuth's elitist conceptions underwent during the years of exile and meditation, far away from the tumult which is inherent in politics, are extremely edifying.

The central idea which had inspired the policy of the Hungarian revolutionary leader at the time when he appeared to be the architect of Hungary's political destiny, consisted simply of enshrining the preeminence of the Hungarian nation in all those provinces where the Hungarians were politically dominant.

Some rights and liberties were granted to the other peoples—provided they gave up their nationality. This was tantamount to a refusal to do justice to the Romanians, a nation to whom nationalist ideas were as important as they were to the Hungarians.

During the years of the revolution, Kossuth was adamant on this point. "We shall sweep away the Romanians and the Transylvanian Saxons from the face of the earth," he said at that time, "if they rise against the Magyar motherland." Kossuth realized—too late—that the achievement of the homogeneous Magyar state based on the Crown of St. Stephen was a utopian goal. He admitted that Hungary was a polynational state, and from this conceptual premise he drew all the logical consequences.

Thus, Kossuth dreamt about the achievement of a Danubian confederation, with the participation of the four states within the Danubian area: Croatia, Hungary, Serbia, and Romania. This plan was elaborated in 1862. How distant was this plan of the great Hungarian patriot from the narrow, chauvinistic one he had sponsored only three years before, which had spoken of a homogeneous Hungary, achieved through the destruction of all other nationalities!

Unfortunately, the mentality of Kossuth's conationals had not evolved in the same direction, but had remained stuck in the rigid pattern of outdated ideas: a homogeneous Magyar state, set up by the forced denationalization, if necessary, of the Romanians, Slovaks, Croats, and other peoples. As though vigorous peoples, inspired by an awareness of their ancient nationality, could be wiped off the map by mere legal measures or by oppressive means!

Moga wrote that Kossuth's new concept had produced consternation among the Hungarians. They must feel the same consternation today when they read the letters-from-exile of the great patriot leader and when they examine the map drawn up by Jaszi Oszkar, based on the data contained in those letters and published in the American magazine, *Foreign Affairs.*

After outlining the ethnographic history of the various peoples in Hungary, Kossuth assigned to the Romanian ethnic element a territory not only as large as the one fixed by the Trianon Treaty but even larger.

When the great Kossuth himself recognized Romanian rights to the entire territory of Transylvania, within the same limits established by the peace treaty of 1920, how can one take seriously assertions like those contained in the propaganda book, *Justice for Hungary,* which said: "The Trianon Treaty was not based on common sense, but on the greed of neighboring nations and on the ignorance of the great powers, which gave ground under the pressure of Czech, Romanian, and Serbian imperialism."?

How can one consider such statements other than as the intemperate outbursts of a chauvinistic politician, who, in his contempt for truth of crystal clarity, keeps on making the most bizarre misstatements?

After the failure of the Magyar revolution, Emperor Franz

Joseph established an absolutist regime over all of the Austrian empire. The first consequence of this regime was that all the nations living under the monarchy were deprived of their rights. Thus Franz Joseph had achieved an equality between his Romanian and his Hungarian subjects, but this was an equality based on the lack of rights.

5. THE FIGHT FOR PARLIAMENTARY REPRESENTATION

The Absolutist Regime

The Austrian regime was for the Hungarians a belated reward for the capacity for harshness and severity of which they had given proof in their relations with the Romanians. But the Romanians had not been fighting for centuries so that they could be satisfied with this downgrading of the Hungarians. Nor had Avram Iancu resisted a much more numerous enemy in the Abrud Mountains in 1848 for the sake of the medal which the emperor had bestowed on him.

In all historical works targeted at readers abroad, the Hungarian publicists sought to emphasize the demoralizing effects which the measures taken by the absolutist regimes had had on the Romanian people—as though the regime installed by the Hungarian revolution had been of a nature to fill the hearts of the Romanians with enthusiasm and hope! No matter how hurtful the new autocratic regime was to the expectations of the Romanian people, it was infinitely milder than the terror of the near past. Within absolutist Austria, the Romanians at least had hopes for a better future. Within a military Hungary, conversely, the future of the Romanian nation in Transylvania was transparently clear, and this situation gave birth to the most bitter desperation.

Gyorgy Majlath, a representative of the Hungarian people in the Imperial Senate in 1860, declared in firm terms: "The Hungarians are faithful to the idea of a uniform kingdom, with a single nation of Hungarian nationality—all other citizens, regardless of their language, having to consider themselves Magyars."

This, therefore, was the real goal of the Hungarian revolution and not the ideal of liberty in the general sense, as Magyar historians later sought to convey.

In the light of this truth, today an axiomatic one, Hungarian attempts abroad to appear as champions of human freedom were childish in the extreme.

To anyone who has followed the extraordinary efforts made by the Hungarians to maintain their medieval privileges even during the modern era—scorning the most elementary rights of the peoples who shared the area with them and flying in the face of the progress made in the social-political realms in other European countries—it is nothing short of flabbergasting when the Hungarians dare to assert that "the whole of Europe felt admiration for the stubborn struggle the Hungarians were waging for the abolition of their own privileges." (See Pál Török, in *Der Vergangenheit des Ungarischen Staatslebens*—"The History of Hungarian State Life.")

Not only did the Hungarian nobility do nothing to reduce or abolish the gap which separated them from the mass of Hungarian peasants, but, on the contrary, they did their best to thwart the liberal measures the Imperial government sought to take.

Nicolae Balcescu had been right when he stated that "the Hungarians during their history learned nothing and forgot nothing."

After the defeats at Magenta and Solferino and the loss of Lombardy, the Austrians decided to abandon the absolutist regime in favor of a regime based on constitutional rights.

The Constitutional Regime

All this time, with unrivaled obstinacy, the Hungarians gave evidence of their determination to persevere in their oppressive and intolerant policy toward the Romanians. With diabolical stubbornness, they sabotaged all the liberal measures decreed by Emperor Franz Joseph, and they did not desist from their efforts until their viewpoint had triumphed.

After consulting the authorized representatives of all his provinces, the emperor decided to adopt the so-called system of "historico-political individuality" as a means of governing his various provinces. Under this system, the provinces had the right to legislate, although they lacked the other attributes of sovereignty. Over the provincial Diets, by the decree of October 20, 1860, the emperor set up a supraprovincial central parliament. At the same time, he firmly demanded of Council President Rechburg that he make a break with the past by replacing the anachronistic feudal constitution of the great Duchy of Transylvania with a modern constitution that did not enshrine the privileges of the nobility, the forced labor of the serfs, and the inequalities between nations. The emperor also distinctly expressed the wish that "the nations which thus far have been excluded from exercising their political rights should be represented in the Transylvanian Assembly."

After centuries of despair, a ray of hope finally broke through to the Romanians on the other side of the Carpathians.

It is highly interesting to note the attitude displayed by the Romanian masses toward their former oppressors on the day when their right to a free life, after long centuries of bondage, was finally recognized. Instead of giving unrestrained expression to their passions, which had built up over centuries of oppression, they reached out their hands in a demonstration of brotherly understanding.

At the conference of the Transylvanian Romanians in Sibiu, the voice of wisdom could be heard. The Romanians spoke of "good relations between all the nations of the motherland," of "cooperation for the common welfare," of "national equality, fraternity, and liberty." This attitude was characteristic of the Romanian people.

Adamant in affirming and achieving his own rights, the Romanian is never intolerant or vindictive toward his former oppressors. At a time when others would think of revenge, the Romanian adopts a Christian attitude—the true Christian attitude of forgiveness.

To this display of understanding on the part of the oldest and most numerous Transylvanian population, the Hungarians answered with hostility. They did not understand—not even at the eleventh hour—that the justice granted to the Romanians was not a favor, but the fulfillment of a natural evolution which could not have been stopped by anything or anybody.

Kemeny, the Chancellor of the Assembly, by means against which the Romanians have always protested, succeeded in leading the Transylvanian representation to the mixed conference which assembled at the beginning of 1861. The 539,218 Hungarians and Szecklers had 24 deputies, while the Roman-

ians, although they counted 1,353,550, had only 8 representatives—a quota equal to that of the representatives of the
Transylvanian Saxons, who numbered only 196,375 of the total
population.

Although they were still unequally represented, the Romanians had, for the first time in their history, the opportunity
to assert themselves as a nation alongside the other three privileged nations, who, over the centuries, had monopolized the
right to conduct the political life of Transylvania.

It was the beginning of a new era in the life of the Romanian people on the other side of the Carpathians.

The Hungarians, through a surprising maneuver, managed to prevent the fruition of the beautiful but short-lived
dreams of the Romanian people. At the mixed conference, the
Hungarian representatives, taking advantage of their overwhelming majority, ruled that the conference was without purpose. They justified their attitude by saying that the Diet in
Cluj in the year 1848 had confirmed the decision of the Diet
in Bratislava, declaring Transylvania united with Hungary.
They declared obstinately that not even the Austrian emperor
had the power to reconsider this historic act.

But Franz Joseph did not intend to yield to the Magyar
pressure, knowing that only through the honest cooperation of
all the nationalities in the empire could the polynational monarchy maintain its unity. Accordingly, the emperor summoned
the Diet of Transylvania to meet on November 4, 1861, ignoring
the decisions by the conference of Alba-Julia. On the Diet's
agenda, among other weighty problems, was "the political and
religious equality of the Romanian people."

The Hungarians Grow Stronger

As a result of these actions, the Hungarians embarked on
bitter opposition to Franz Joseph. By hook or by crook, they
were bent on preserving their privileges by keeping a people
of 1,400,000 Transylvanian inhabitants in bondage.

The chancellor sent in his resignation, and the chancery
refused to publish the emperor's edict. The legal reason adduced
by the Hungarians was the bilateral character of Transylvania's union with Hungary, against which the emperor's
unilateral desire to ignore the act of union became inoperative.
This argument had only apparent legitimacy. In fact, it was

completely false, since its premise was inexactly stated. Transylvania—the real Transylvania—had never signed an act of union with Hungary. The truth was that only the Hungarians in Transylvania had voted for the union—which, of course, was not the same thing as Transylvania manifesting its desire to unite its destiny to that of the country of Arpad. And who in the Hungary of that time would be interested in framing arguments adverse to this proposition?

The stubborn opposition unleashed by the Hungarians had the practical result of imposing a two-year delay on the summoning of the Transylvanian Diet. But the persistent protests of the Transylvanian Romanians were finally successful in overcoming the Hungarian opposition, and the Transylvanian Diet was summoned into session in the month of July 1863.

Aware of the importance of the occasion, the Transylvanian Romanians conducted themselves in an exemplary manner throughout the election. No potential Romanian vote was overlooked—and none of the Romanian votes accrued to the benefit of the opposition party.

"The Romanians," said Pacatian, "went to the voting places as though they were going to church."

"Transylvania," said Moga, "has passed this political examination cum laude." It was the first "political examination" they had experienced in their long history under the domination of the Hungarian nobility.

Because of electoral conditions imposed on the voting in Transylvania, the province's representation in the Diet was still far from a pro rata basis. Nevertheless, in comparison to the past, the election was amazingly successful. The Romanians elected 46 deputies, the Hungarians and the Szecklers together, 43, and the Transylvanian Saxons and the Swabians, 32. Adding the allocation of seats reserved for the emperor, we come up with the following figures for the final distribution of the deputies' seats: Romanians, 56; Hungarians and Szecklers, 54; Transylvanian Saxons, 44.

The result was enough to spread panic within the ranks of the Magyars in Transylvania. In freely manifesting the popular will, Transylvania had ceased to be a colony of the Magyar nobility. Indeed, many noblemen, seeing their centuries-old status endangered, made preparations to leave for Hungary. This is yet another evidence of the shallowness of the ties which bound the Magyar nobility to the land of Transylvania. The nobility had profiteered from the riches of Transylvania—but a change of political climate was enough to start them packing their bags.

The exemplary solidarity and conduct of the Romanian people in the electoral campaign of 1863 frightened the Hungarian nobility because they had consistently underestimated the possibilities of political action by the Transylvanian peasant masses. Even the great Hungarian patriot Szechenyi, had erred in mistaking the patriarchal peace which characterized the life of the Transylvanian peasants for a lack of interest in the larger problems affecting their future. In fact, the Romanian peasant masses always possessed a national consciousness; all that was lacking for its manifestation was favorable political conditions.

If the Hungarian nobility had been able to foresee the political future, if they had been able to foresee the outcome of the elections for the Transylvanian Diet, it stands to reason that they would have thought of rapprochement and peaceful cooperation with the Romanian peasant masses. But in politics there exists an element of historical fatalism which makes one persist in the mistakes of the past even when everything indicates that one is walking into the arms of disaster.

The Hungarians sabotaged the Transylvanian Diet which convened in Sibiu by refusing to take part in its sessions. However, the Diet, which claimed to represent the great majority of the Transylvanian population, approved an article of law on September 10, 1863, which decreed "equal rights for the Romanian nation in Transylvania." This law—the first in Transylvanian history which was printed in parallel texts in Romanian, German, and Hungarian—was approved by Franz Joseph on October 26, 1863. (An interesting detail: the Emperor Franz Joseph signed the Romanian text with his name spelled in Romanian—Franciscu Josifu).

This date would have become a historic landmark in Transylvanian history if the Hungarian nobility had not sought to sabotage the effect of the law respecting equal rights for the Romanians. Indeed, the law of 1863 represented a genuine revolution in the outlook of the Hapsburg rulers whose mentality until then had been shaped by the influence of the Hungarian nobility. After centuries of brutal injustice, this new outlook granted political equality with the three privileged nations to the Romanian people.

Paragraph 3 of the law said: "The four nations acknowledged by this law, that is, the Magyar, the Szeckler, the Transylvanian Saxon, and the Romanian nations have completely equal rights and may make use of these political rights in accordance with the Transylvanian constitution."

It was a belated correction of the mistakes of the past.

The Magyar commitment to sabotaging the law of 1863 was not at all surprising. It formed an integral part of the generally retrograde mentality of the leading clique of Magyar noblemen. The only thing that was surprising was the attitude of Franz Joseph. Although, when he spoke about the Romanian people he referred to them as "my brave Romanians," when he was called upon to translate the law into concrete action, he permitted its implementation to be postponed *sine die.*

The attitude of Franz Joseph was dictated by political circumstances, both external and internal. Initially, Franz Joseph was inclined to favor little reforms affecting the status of the millions of Romanians in Transylvania. The Romanian revolution of 1848 had shown the monarchy the scope and power of Romanian nationalism in Transylvania. After the absolutist period under Bach, the constitutional epoch initiated by Schmerling had given the Romanians the possibility of again voicing the demands which they had so firmly expressed in the program approved by the Blaj assembly on May 15, 1848. Aware of its rights and of the power which these rights conferred to turn them to good political account, the Romanians had become a threat to the shabby edifice of Franz Joseph's monarchy.

Abroad, the union of principalities under Prince Cuza was a first step toward the great union which was yet to come.

In the face of this double threat which, as Prokesch-Osten put it, had frightened Austria to the marrow, Franz Joseph deemed it more prudent to have the Romanians on his side than to have them against him. That is why he decreed the liberal law of 1863.

The Hungarian nobility did not abandon their Machiavellian plan. Deak and Eotvos, the Hungarian moderate leaders, were able to win the support of the Empress Elizabeth for their cause. They were able to get the Court talking about the advantages of Austro-Hungarian cooperation. This was to be the beginning of a larger action which was carried out at a later date.

The Hungarian nobles continued to plot against the Romanian people, with the goal—of which they made no secret—of securing Emperor Franz Joseph's recognition of Transylvania's union with Hungary, basing themselves on the imaginary principle of "the right of continuity."

Austria's Chancellor Schmerling, who had favored and had even embarked on a policy of concessions that would have had the effect of equalizing the status of the peoples of the Austro-Hungarian monarchy, was obliged to leave his post in July 1865.

In the summer of the same year, Bishop Saguna, returning from an audience with the emperor, sadly declared that the atmosphere at the Imperial Court appeared favorable to an agreement with the Hungarians, the price of this agreement being the sacrifice of the legitimate rights of the Romanian people.

The events which followed fully confirmed the pessimistic predictions of this great Romanian. In September 1865, the Transylvanian Diet, which had been elected with the participation of all the Transylvanian nations, was dissolved, and a new Diet, elected according to the old Hungarian criteria, was convened at Cluj.

Magyar Plots and Schemes

In the perspective of history, the method used by the Hungarian nobles to stifle the voice of the Transylvanian people seemed to us even more odious than has heretofore been indicated. During the free elections of 1863, the Hungarians had been able to elect only a minority of the deputies. In the new elections, they were able to manage things so that they had a massive majority. This majority expressed the will of the Transylvanian Hungarians—but not that of Transylvania itself. In the new Diet, the Romanians, who represented the very heart of Transylvania, seated only nineteen deputies.

Saguna protested in vain, in the name of the millions of Transylvanian Romanians, against this obvious violation of the will of the Transylvanian people. Under pressure of events abroad, including one defeat after another for the Austro-Hungarian monarchy (Koniggratz-Sadova), the emperor finally had to yield to Magyar pressures in order to preserve the unity of the empire. The Diet in Cluj once again voted, on December

25, 1865, to affirm Transylvania's union with Hungary. In consequence, the emperor incorporated the Diet into the Hungarian Diet in Budapest.

The Moor had done his duty; the Moor was free to go now.

In 1867, the clique of Magyar nobles at the Imperial Court intensified their pressures on the emperor so that, *nolens volens*, he decided to revoke all the liberal laws the Diet had voted for at Sibiu.

In this way, the Transylvanian Romanians, who had succeeded in regaining assurance of their liberties after bitter struggles over many centuries, again became victims of the ancient bondage which had been imposed on them by an unrelenting enemy.

"The cup [of liberty]," said Seton-Watson, "was snatched away the very moment it touched the Romanians' lips."

Among the arguments the Hungarians used with the Emperor in persuading him to sign the decree voiding the emancipation of the Transylvanian Romanians, was that it would constitute a deadly danger for the monarchy if a Dacian-Romania, within the boundaries of the ancient province of Dacia, were ever achieved.

Romanian Hopes

The union of the Romanian principalities and the advent to the throne of the united sister countries of Prince Carol of Hohenzollern constituted the first stages of the predestined union of all of Romania.

The sufferings of the Transylvanian Romanians did much to bring to fruition a concept of a unitarian Romania, with the Carpathians as its axis.

Historians, men of letters, and journalists had confirmed for the mass of the Romanian people the common origin of the Romanians on both sides of the Carpathian range, and their passionate natures extrapolated from the act of union the most daring plans for the future.

The inspired lines of Andrei Muresanu, "Awake thou Romanian soul," were stimulating everybody.

The politicians on the other side of the Carpathians firmly formulated the principle that the Romanian subjects of the kingdom had a right to manifest an interest in the fate of their co-nationals over the mountains.

Ion Bratianu gave expression to this concept in a metaphor which afterward became famous:

> When a sister of mine is married, I have no right to poke my nose into her business. I have no right to do anything that would make her husband suspect me of intending to create an issue between them. But if her husband—my brother-in-law—beats her up or treats her like a slave, knowing that noble blood flows in her veins, if he picks up a knife with the intention of stabbing her, don't I have the right to raise my voice to prevent him from committing the crime?

The principal guidelines followed by Romanian foreign policy in Romania's relations with the Austro-Hungarian monarchy were from the very beginning clearly defined.

On the one hand there was a firm declaration that Romania would not interfere in the internal affairs of the neighboring monarchy. On the other hand it was made clear that the Romanians in the principalities would consider themselves in solidarity with those in Transylvania whenever the national existence of the latter was in jeopardy.

King Carol himself had embraced this viewpoint. In an audience with the French ambassador in Bucharest, Carol Hohenzollern declared that he did not mean to encourage an anti-Hungarian attitude among the Romanian people on the other side of the Carpathians. But his statement contained the firm addendum that "the Romanians in the principalities cannot remain indifferent to the plight of millions of their conationals [in Transylvania]."

Confronted by this unity of national opinion on both sides of the Carpathian mountains, the contrary maneuvers of the Hungarian nobles were of little avail.

It was in vain that they sought to terminate cooperative relations between the Romanians in Transylvania and those in the principalities. It was in vain that the Hungarian nobility forbade the import and distribution on Transylvania's territory of anything printed in the Romanian principalities. Truth was marching on, and nothing could stop it.

The objectives of the Romanian people had been clearly expressed, in a manner that left no room for doubt. They demanded the recognition of their nationality within the Austro-

Hungarian monarchy, and equal treatment with other nations in their relations with the state.

But the Hungarian chancellors at the court of Franz Joseph depicted the resulting situation in such dark colors from the standpoint of the monarchy's future that Franz Joseph yielded to the Magyar viewpoint on the need to keep the Romanian nation in Transylvania in a position of obvious inferiority—with the transparent goal of ultimately obliging the Romanians to accept their Magyarization.

How wrong this policy was could be seen in 1918 when the oppressed nationalities found, in their inferior status itself, the necessary strength to do battle for equal rights.

Transylvania had been united by force, but it was losing its age-old independence. This was not all. By the strength of circumstances, Romanian nationalism had received a grievously wounding blow within a polynational Hungarian state. Far surpassing all other nationalities in Transylvania, the Hungarians concluded, the Romanians represented only a small proportion—some 15 percent—when their number was equated against the population of the entire Hungarian kingdom.

The goal, of the union with Hungary, therefore, was a good deal more than a mere administrative device. It took on the aspect of a Machiavellian maneuver whose purpose it was to weaken the Romanian element in Transylvania.

The Dual Monarchy

Within the framework of the dual monarchy established in 1867, this maneuver was meant to trigger radical effects. Only three weeks after Franz Joseph was crowned king of Hungary as a result of the pact concluded between Vienna and Budapest, the Hungarian kingdom stood fully equal in rights with Austria as part of the Austro-Hungarian empire. It is an interesting footnote that the crown used in the coronation ceremony was the crown of the Romanian Matei Corvin.

Thus, Hungary had at last become a sovereign state, enjoying complete independence for all practical purposes in a number of areas. The Magyar cause had triumphed. The Hungarians were treading on air.

Completely dependent on the Hungarians from this moment on, the Romanian people over the next half century were to witness a considerable deterioration in their situation. The plight of the Romanians had also been cruel when they were directly dependent on Austria's emperor. Any informed person can easily imagine what it meant to remain Romanian in a Transylvania directly governed by the Magyar nobility.

On the day the dual monarchy was installed, the Hungarian nobility embarked on the most frenetic campaign of denationalization witnessed by contemporary history. Their principal efforts were concentrated against the Romanians. "The Magyar oligarchy," says Bertrand de Jouvenel, "which is proud to have won its independence from Vienna, now Magyarizes the Slav and Romanian populations which were their subjects." In consolidating their state goals through the dual monarchy (see Horvath, Szekfu, and others), the Hungarian nobility put aside the modest ideal of national liberty which they had sponsored, and became instead the aggressive supporters of an imperialist ideal, tied to the myth of St. Stephen's Crown. This goal could not be achieved if the nations which inhabited Transylvania together with the Hungarians were not destroyed, in particular, the numerous and vigorous Romanian nation which was descended from Trajan's legionaries and Decebalus's Dacians.

First, they began to stir up a campaign against the subject nationalities—which, in fact, were only demanding the liberties the Hungarian people had also been fighting for. Chauvinistic writers, in the forefront of whom were Vajda and Bela Grunwald, said that the mere fact that the subject nationalities existed constituted a definite danger for Hungary; while the Hungarian historian Paul Hunfalvy, himself a Magyarized German, compared the Romanians of Transylvania with the "redskins" in North America, and simply threatened them with extermination.

When one of the few Romanian delegates in the Budapest Parliament ventured to speak out in support of his suppressed conationals, the Hungarian political right abused him with expressions such as, "Go to Bucharest!" or "Let them emigrate!" In other words, they were asking the Romanian people, who had deep and ancient roots in Transylvania, to emigrate from the land of their forefathers, leaving behind as almighty masters the uninvited visitors who had come from beyond the Ural Mountains.

It is easy to understand, therefore, why all hopes for a

better future for the Romanians in Transylvania were directed toward the Romanians in the United Principalities beyond the Carpathians, where the foundation of a resurrected Romanianism was being laid.

Moderate liberals among the Hungarians, notable among whom were Deak and Baron Eotvos, were accused of weakness and lack of patriotism for opposing the berserk methods of the Hungarian chauvinists, who had perhaps become overexcited about the dream of a Magyar empire, coinciding with the empire once governed by the crown of St. Stephen.

The basic principles of the Liberal Party were in fact the same as those of the ultrachauvinists; only the methods were different. While Deak and Eotvos sponsored the policy of moderation, the Magyar chauvinists supported the use of violent means. But both spoke about the need to convert the ethnically variegated Hungarian state into a homogeneous state where there would only be one nation—the Magyars. In any case, the attitude of the Hungarian liberals is worthy of mention, since it helps to define more starkly the extremist mentality they opposed.

Baron Wesseleny's Prophetic Vision

On August 24, 1868, old Baron Wesseleny—about whom Alexandru Vaida-Voevod once said, "Although blind, his mind could see better than could the old and modern chauvinists"—uttered the following prophetic words from the tribune of the House:

> The matter I am going to talk about is of the utmost importance. It has to do with the pacification and reconciliation of the various peoples living in our country. I cast a glance, with the eyes of my soul, to the cloudy future of my country—and the future looks darker than the never-ending night in which I now live. I can see a single light, and even that looks dim enough. That light is the peace and understanding which is still capable of saving us.

Wesseleny said that "the three privileged nations and the four churches which are acknowledged by the state represent the seven capital sins of Hungary." And he declared, in ringing terms, that "to openly unite us with the nationalities is the only way open to us."

The Hungarian nobility had two paths open to them. The first was that of reason and consideration; the second was that of passion and intolerance. They chose the latter. The future showed that Baron Wesseleny had been right.

Violence had never been a good counsellor, while all things based on intolerance have broken down like so many sand castles at the first breath of wind.

The policy inaugurated by the Hungarian nobility in 1867 and continued until 1918 has been described by one of the world's great reference books, *The Italian Encyclopedia*, in the following terms: "From 1867 until 1918, despite a law that had granted rights to its various nationalities (1868), Transylvania was subjected to a determined policy of Magyarization (*una risolute politica di magiarizazzione*)."

The Italian Encyclopedia, incidentally, could scarcely be accused of Magyaro-phobia.

If the Hungarian nobles had been able to curb their exaggerated ambitions, and if they had looked upon the dual monarchy as a first step toward regional federalism, the entire historical evolution of central Europe would, of course, have been completely different. This is a point on which all contemporary writers are agreed. The Transylvanian Romanian writer, Alexandru Roman, managing editor of the newspaper, *The Federation*, declared with prophetic foresight in 1868: "If the dual monarchy does not lead the way to federation, then it is a *unio duorum natiorum contra plures* ('union of two nations against many'), which will inevitably lead to the empire's collapse." In the same year, the Romanian nationalist Soimescu, wrote: "The arrogance of the Magyar nation will lead to Austria's destruction."

Confronted with the immense problems issuing from the reorganization of the state, the Transylvanian Romanians reacted in a puzzled manner. They groped in the darkness for a long time, not knowing which path led to the triumph of their just national claims.

Some of them, like the great patriot, Saguna, were for pursuing a more moderate policy in the hope that it would result in at least a minimum of positive achievement. Saguna's entire doctrine was summed up in the maxim, "Do it—and keep silent about it."

Political Abstentionism

There were others, still, who favored a policy of "total passivity," in this way overlooking all that had been done in Transylvania against the will of the Transylvanian peoples. A series of gatherings was convened at Miercurea, Inidioara, and other places. At these gatherings, the Romanians of Transylvania proper finally decided in favor of an attitude of total passivity (Miercurea—March 7-8, 1869). They decided, in a "desperate resolution" (Nicolae Iorga), to witness political events which concerned them directly, without attempting to prevent them or even attempting to condemn them.

The Romanians in Hungary and Banat, during the same year, embarked on a policy of active participation in Parliament for the purpose of defending their interests.

Alexandru Mocsonyi, a passionate champion of the Romanian cause, said in an appeal for unity: "Only a nation which knows how to fight for its freedom will ever fully enjoy it."

The violence with which the Magyar representatives greeted every Romanian interpellation in the Budapest Parliament had the effect of stimulating the handful of Romanian delegates instead of intimidating them. They continued to assert themselves as the representatives of a distinct nation, challenging the passionate chauvinism of the Hungarian deputies and demanding that, after centuries of injustice, the Romanians be acknowledged to be equal in rights as well as in duties.

"We demand to be regarded as a nation," said one of the deputies, "for we have the same rights as the Magyar nation."

"We are here, on our land," added Vincentiu Babes, in this way pointing to both the precedence of the Romanian populace in Transylvania and to its permanent presence there.

Acting with boundless arrogance, the Hungarian deputies contented themselves with brutal replies—a frank admission of their helplessness in the face of reason.

"You are a savage race of swineherds!" they said in answer to the Romanian deputies. This was an imprudent reply; indeed, it was twice imprudent. In calling the Romanians swineherds, the Hungarian deputies forgot that the greatest warrior in Hungarian history, Ioan Huniade, had been a Romanian. They also forgot—and this time bad faith may have been at work—that, of all the European peoples, the people which had always shown the greatest interest in pig breeding had been the Hungarians. This is confirmed by all the contemporary

Hungarian writers and all Hungarian statistics, going back to the earliest days.

The Hungarian professor, Bela Hayuko, in a study dealing with the livestock of Hungary which was printed in the volume *Das Antlitz Einer Nation,* informs us that "pig breeding has been known to the Hungarian people from the oldest times." We also learned from the writings of Anonymous that when the Hungarians arrived in what is today Hungary, they brought with them herds of swine. Today, in those Hungarian regions where there exist large forests of oak trees and bogs, the breeding of pigs has increased tremendously (*Ein gewaltige Aufschwung*).

The debasing epithets which the Hungarian deputies in the Budapest Parliament hurled at the Romanian deputies demonstrated the profound contempt felt by the Magyar nobility (a mixture of races unique in Europe) for the Romanian people—a peasant people whose misery and social inferiority was directly attributable to their oppression by the Magyar nobility.

The Austro-Hungarian ambassador in Bucharest, Prince Furstenberg, relates that Tisza even refused to answer the Romanian delegates when they greeted him politely.

The policy of abstention and passivity, which was favored by the great majority of Romanian people, made it possible for the Hungarian nobility to go ahead with their plans for Magyarizing the other peoples of Transylvania. At the same time, Emperor Franz Joseph was influenced to such a degree by his counselors that, whenever he received a Romanian delegation, he addressed them in a reproachful tone and scolded them for not being tolerant enough of Hungarian policy—and he was speaking of a people who had turned passivity and docility into a political dogma.

It is, of course, possible that the abstentionist policy of the Romanians in Transylvania was a direct result of the Hungarian electoral system, which was characterized by the Hungarians themselves (Pester Lloyd) as a "real hullabaloo, risen to the rank of law."

Romanian participation in the Transylvanian elections was hampered by an infinite number of fault-finding conditions, intended to mystify the electorate. Thus, if, in the Szeckler region, four to five thousand votes were sufficient to elect a deputy, in the Romanian region, sometimes 40,000—or even 50,000—voters were assigned to a single electoral district.

Under these circumstances, Coloman Tisza, the leader of the so-called Liberal Party, secure in the knowledge that he had on his side the Austro-Hungarian minister for external affairs, the Hungarian Andrassy, was able to govern like a despot for fifteen years, from 1875 to 1890. There are dictatorships which publicly admit the authoritarian nature of their government and justify it on the grounds of imperious necessity. The Hungarian nobility, on the contrary, governed their country by the most despotic means while they posed abroad as champions of freedom. The hypocrisy of their methods from 1848 on was repeated in every stage of Magyar history.

Thus, in 1868 the Hungarian Parliament passed a nationalities law ostensibly based on liberal principles and couched in the most explicit terms. The introduction of this law may be considered an example of rhetorical generosity toward the nationalities. As always, the rhetoric was too good to be true. It was all dust thrown in the eyes of the people. The "liberal and generous" nationalities law was never put into practice. Some of the provisions in this law were simply annulled. Others remained dead letters from the beginning.

But what was particularly revolting was the cynicism with which the Hungarians boasted about the unrivaled generosity of provisions which had ceased to enjoy any legal force and had, therefore, to be considered nonexistent.

Arthur Seton-Watson, an acknowledged expert on the Austro-Hungarian monarchy, in his *History of the Romanians*, lists a number of examples of the Hungarian nationalities law which reflect the flagrant inconsistency between the theoretical methods advocated by Hungarian law and those methods that were actually put into practice.

The contradiction was particularly manifest in the field of education. The authors of the law had used eloquent words in proclaiming "the necessity to grant all citizens, irrespective of nationality, the possibility of being educated in their native tongues." But on the heels of this law, the Hungarians embarked on a campaign of Magyarization in the schools which jeopardized the very existence of Romanianism. The schools increasingly became instruments of Magyarization.

In the beginning, Magyarization affected only the secondary schools. Toward the end, however, it was also extended to the elementary schools. In 1879, Minister Trefort, a Magyarized Dutchman, proposed in Parliament a law dealing with the

Magyarization of the elementary school. But the Romanians in every province under Hungarian rule closed their ranks against the increasingly unyielding attitude of their Magyar governors.

"We are here—and we shall stay here, like an eternal rock, as a people destined to live here by God himself," declared Ioan Hodos, in his response to the Hungarian Parliament when it voted the law calling for the speedier denationalization of millions of the Romanian peasants in Transylvania.

The Memorandum Era

At the Sibiu conference in 1881, the Romanian National Party in Transylvania revised its program to make Transylvania's independence its number one demand. Simultaneously, the party decided that, as between the revolutionary method of achieving national rights and the moderate method, they would choose the latter, in the belief that one day their claims would find an echo in the heart of Emperor Franz Joseph.

The conference also decided to draw up a written statement in French for the purpose of letting the peoples of the West find out about "the terrible sufferings endured by the Romanians in Transylvania, as well as the persecutions they are subject to today." The memorandum, which came out in Paris in 1883, had a very strong impact in France, Great Britain, Italy, and Belgium. It was the first document to appear outside the borders of the Austro-Hungarian monarchy that dealt with the inhuman treatment the Transylvanian Romanians had suffered for centuries. For the first time, the western nations had been asked to take a stand in support of the charges brought by the Romanian people against the feudal methods legitimized by the Hungarian government in Budapest—methods which, in the words of Arthur Seton-Watson, "the Hungarians intended to perpetuate in Transylvania, despite the natural evolution of political institutions in western countries."

A few years later, the students at the universities of Jassy and Bucharest, in their turn, published a lengthy memorandum addressed to people abroad, in which they described in detail the stages of the tragedy experienced by the Romanian people in the former province of Dacia after they had fallen under Hungarian rule.

The memorandum resulted in a great wave of sympathy

for the cause of the Romanian people in Transylvania. This was so particularly in France. The general association of French students considered the memorandum and issued a statement which quoted the famous words of Montesquieu: "There exists a criminal code for nations as well as individuals." The French press, in its turn, spoke bitterly about the feudal methods of governing employed by the Magyar noblemen.

In Belgium, Professor Louis van Keymeilen of Anvers wrote an impressive article, published in the magazine *Le Precurseur*, which finished with these words: "Western Europe must not forget that the Romanian people stand as front-line sentries of civilization in eastern Europe, and because of this we in Europe cannot be indifferent to what is going on at the present time in the foothills of the Carpathians."

The Hungarians quickly published a reply to this Romanian memorandum, invoking their "democratic" laws, their "liberal" constitution, and all the other tired arguments repeatedly used by Magyar propaganda abroad. The answer was also replete with insults addressed to the Romanian people in Transylvania.

The Reply

The Romanian students in Transylvania could not remain indifferent to the cynical manner in which the Hungarian reply distorted the real state of affairs. They published a reply to the Hungarian "reply" in Romanian, English, French, and Italian.

"This reply," says George Moroianu, "was written with admirable political good sense, and it made use of a unique method of documentation, based on the laws and statistical data of the Hungarian state."

The reply was indeed an act of exceptional courage if one considers the mentality of the governing circles in Transylvania.

"The publication of this reply," continued Moroianu, "produced an enormous sensation in Hungary, since neither the Magyar press nor the Hungarian government had expected this courageous action by the young people of Romania, in defiance of the fury and revenge of the authorities."

When a judicial investigation was opened against the authors of the reply, all the Romanian students in the Hungarian universities declared themselves in solidarity with its contents.

The Conviction of Aurel Popovici

Since it was the Hungarian intention to avoid a political scandal, they limited the judicial investigation to a single one of the memorandum's authors, Dr. Aurel Popovici.

Guarded by bayonets, Popovici was transported like a common thief from Predeal to Cluj, where he was sentenced by a chauvinistic jury to serve four years in prison and to pay a fine of 5,000 florins, which was an enormous sum in those days.

The man sentenced by the jury in Cluj was later to become the closest advisor of the Archduke Ferdinand, the presumptive heir to the Austro-Hungarian throne, and the victim of the Sarajevo tragedy.

To form an opinion as to how the west regarded the state of affairs in Hungary at the time, and of the agitation triggered in the west by the trial of Aurel Popovici, it suffices to quote two items from the western press.

"This trial," wrote Felix Lesseur in *La Republique Francaise* (Jules Meline's newspaper) of September 2, 1893, "will remain one of the darkest examples in European history of the tyranny and brutality of which a people are capable when they have set their minds on oppressing other people."

In another item, the same journalist describes the never-ending trials of the Romanian leaders in Transylvania as "Hungarian judicial farces."

On the same day, the newspaper *Il Foro Romagnolo* of Ravenna, wrote: "The sacrifice of these generous-spirited champions [i.e., the Romanian patriots] will contribute substantially to a change in the state of affairs in St. Stephen's kingdom—this monstrous edifice where justice and morality are strangled by a cruel despotic hegemony."

The conviction of Popovici could not discourage the Romanians. On the contrary, it made them even more determined to continue their war with greater vigor. The Romanians decided to appeal to the good will of the emperor, and to this end they drafted a memorandum to be presented to the emperor by 300 representatives of the Romanians in Transylvania.

The 300 representatives, headed by the lawyer Ioan Ratiu of Turda, left for Vienna. But, yielding to Magyar pressure, the emperor refused to receive the delegation. Nevertheless, the envelope containing the Romanian memorandum reached the emperor. Without opening it, he sent it to the Hungarian minister of foreign affairs, Hieronymiyi, who, in his turn, passed it on, again without opening it, to the State Archives in Budapest, where it was filed.

In this way were the just demands of the three million Romanians in Transylvania given consideration by the "liberal" Austro-Hungarian monarchy.

Thanks to one of those curious twists of fate, which often tends to be implacable, the unopened envelope containing the ignored Romanian memorandum fell into Romanian hands a quarter of a century later, when the Romanian armies triumphantly entered Budapest, the citadel of Hungarian arrogance.

On their return to Transylvania, the members of the Romanian delegation who had traveled to Vienna were the victims of many offensive incidents. Many of them were the objects of violent attacks; for example, the house of Mr. Ratiu, president of the Romanian National Party and leader of the Romanian delegation to Vienna, was badly damaged, and the Romanian leader himself, who was barely able to save his life, took refuge in Sibiu.

Their elementary right to petition the emperor for redress having been rejected—despite the fact that this right was categorically guaranteed by the constitution which the Hungarian government in Budapest was always quick to boast about—and having been denied the courtesy of having their demands at least read if they were not acted upon, the Romanians circulated the text of the memorandum abroad.

In the face of the uniquely unjust Hungarian methods, the Romanians appealed to the conscience of the world, not asking for help, but seeking to let the people in the civilized countries of Europe learn about the scandalously intolerant methods of the Magyar leaders, who posed abroad as champions of liberty.

The Memorandum Stands Trial

Yielding to pressures of chauvinistic circles, the Hungarian government embarked on a public trial of the authors of the memorandum—that is, of the entire committee of the Romanian National Party which consisted of twenty-five people. Thus, the representatives of the entire Romanian population in Transylvania were hailed before a repressive Hungarian court in Cluj.

In effect, the entire Romanian people in the one-time province of Dacia were in the dock, and the prosecutors were the descendants of the Hungarians who had invaded and occupied their province. But in this monstrous trial, the Hungarians, who began as accusers, became the real defendants in the eyes of the civilized world.

On May 25, 1894, the Magyar jurors in Cluj sentenced the Romanian leaders to terms of imprisonment ranging from eight months to five years, as well as the payment of huge fines.

The priest, Lucaciu, a stubborn defender of Romanian rights on the other side of the Carpathians, who had been sentenced several times before for his patriotic activities, was again sentenced to prison, this time for five years.

The trial itself and the severe sentences imposed on the accused Romanians triggered a wave of indignation in all the countries of the West. One has to ask, however, how the indignant judgments which were pronounced against Hungary by enlightened western spirits compared with the punishments the Romanian patriots had to endure.

6. THE RISING TIDE OF WESTERN PROTEST

The entire European press made common cause with the Romanians of Transylvania. Protest rallies were organized in Great Britain and France. Even some of the newspapers in Austria and Germany defended the Romanian cause. In the paragraphs that follow, we shall examine some of the press reaction in Germany, France, Italy, and Britain.

Germany

Neue Preussische Zeitung of May 6, 1894, wrote about the trial in Cluj, which was uniquely directed against an entire nation:

> All those who are familiar with the state of affairs in Transylvania have to admit that this trial will have only one result—that is, keeping alive the hatred of everything Magyar and jeopardizing the existence of the [Austro-Hungarian] empire itself, since everyone knows that, because of their brutal policy of Magyarization, the Hungarians today are the most hated people in eastern Europe.

It was in this vein that the German press wrote.

France

The French press warmly embraced the cause of the Romanians, a Latin people in eastern Europe, who were being tyrannically persecuted by the Hungarians. It reacted vehemently to the methods employed by the Hungarians in Transylvania for the obvious purpose of converting this Romanian province into a Hungarian one.

"The trial which is now before the jurists in Cluj and which involves twenty-five members of the Romanian National Party," wrote Henri Rochefort in *L'Intransigeant*, "really exceeds the imaginable limits of injustice." The much-feared French polemicist added these words to his judgment: "The crime of the accused is this: Oppressed, persecuted, and treated like wild animals by the Hungarians, the Romanians in Transylvania sent their representatives to their sovereign, the Emperor of Austria, to state their demands. But Hungarian vainglory does not accept the proposition that the Romanian people, oppressed and tortured by their unrelenting masters, should have petitioned for help from the supreme leader of the empire."

"This trial," wrote the newspaper *La Libre Parole*, of May 8, 1894, "represents only an episode, almost unique, of a great battle between two nationalities. The whole of Europe echoed to the agony of Kossuth and his companions, defenders of justice for the Hungarian people. But the Hungarian people, Kossuth and his comrades included, have never ceased being the most savage oppressors of the nationalities over whom they have extended their rule."

Last, but not least, the great Clemenceau, the then chief editor of the newspaper *La Justice*, in an article entitled "The Battle of the Races," presented a vivid description of the struggles of the Transylvanian Romanians against Hungarian tyranny. An acute observer of Transylvanian affairs, Clemenceau, making good use of his rhetorical talents, made a bitter accusation against the inhumanity of Hungarian rule in Transylvania.

"By arbitrary stipulations which were introduced into the electoral law," said the man who was to become the architect of World War I victory, "the Romanians no longer enjoy any political rights. The electoral census is ten times greater for the Romanians in Transylvania than for the rest of Hungary. The Romanians, who on a proportionate basis should have 75 of the total number of 417 deputies in Parliament, have in fact none."

As for the trial itself, Clemenceau described it in these strong terms: "This trial is a disgrace for the free Hungarian nation. Dr. Ratiu and his companions may be sentenced, but European opinion has already acquitted them."

In this manner the political trial by means of which the Hungarians had intended to discredit the Transylvanian Romanians turned into a bitter political lesson for the Hungarian politicians.

When the severe sentences pronounced by the chauvinist court at Cluj against the leaders of the Romanian National Party in Transylvania became known abroad, the great French historian Ernest Lavisse sent the following message of sympathy to the condemned Romanian leaders: "To those Romanians who have been unfairly accused and unfairly sentenced for insisting on the rights of the Romanian nationality, I send this message of respectful admiration and deep sympathy. I am convinced that justice and law, both brutally offended, will have their revenge. I hope that this revenge will come soon—I am convinced that it will come. Long live Romania!"

Italy

Even in Italy, which was bound to Austria-Hungary by the Triple Alliance Pact, voices were raised in its support of the Romanians who were sentenced at Cluj. The well-known archeologist, Professor Angelo de Cubernatis, wrote on July 2, 1894:

> The Hungarians did not meditate sufficiently on the course of history. They did not take into account the possibilities of a [national] revival. They entered Europe as a war-loving people, as a people of conquerors, and they managed, over centuries of barbarism and misery, to enslave the peasants who were working on their land. What the Hungarians asked for themselves is liberty. The demands which they made are worthy of our complete sympathy and of all our respect. But at the same time, they [the Hungarians] claim unheard of privileges for themselves. They desire to be absolute masters of the Romanians, and they want the Romanians to remain their servants. This is neither possible nor acceptable.

Making an excursion into the ancient history of the Romanian people in Transylvania, the illustrious Italian professor wrote:

I deem the Romanians to be the genuine Romanized descendants of the people of ancient Dacia. Rome civilized
them. They remained where they were, where the Romans
found them, and the Dacians gave the world two of the
best of the Roman emperors, Aurelian and Probus. Both
of these were Romanians from Transylvania, and through
them the Romanians really won their right to be regarded
as the sentries of the civilized world. Hungarian history
itself has glorious Romanian episodes.

De Cubernatis, in concluding his article, wrote these dramatic words: "The Hungarians should not despise the former
masters of the land [which they now occupy] in our century.
Nobody can go on terrorizing entire populations. Public opinion, which is the real tribunal of international justice, makes
tyrants wither and condemns them to isolation. And isolation
means death."

Il Diritto, a Roman newspaper, published several articles
regarding the Memorandum trial. We quote from the article
which appeared immediately after the sentencing of Dr. Ratiu
and the other Romanian patriots:

The sentence pronounced against the national representatives of the Romanians in Transylvania for drawing up
the Memorandum in defense of their people will fill the
entire civilized world with disgust . . . The Magyars are
right to care about Italy's friendship. But they shouldn't
forget that the Romanians are, like the Italians, of Latin
origin, and that, according to the natural law which governs blood relationships, they are bound to feel affection
for them.

Great Britain

In Great Britain, Lord Edmond Fitzmaurice, who served
as permanent under secretary of the foreign office in the Glad-
stone Cabinet, wrote in 1890:

The provocative attitude of the Magyar minority toward
the Romanians can, from one moment to the next, give
birth to bloody uprisings, the consequences of which are
incalculable.

He also said that:

> The Hungarians pursue a blind and violent policy against
> the nationalities which are the subjects of the Hungarian
> crown, against the Romanians in particular.

On the occasion of the trial at Cluj, there was a large rally
at Oxford University in support of the Romanians in Transylvania. This rally at the most famous of English universities
was attended by scholars, men of letters, prominent professors,
and numerous students.

W. R. Morphill, the well-known English philologist and
expert on Romania, who presided at the rally, made an impressive speech in which he asked his fellow citizens to express
their sympathy with "the cause of a nation which is full of life,
energetic, and hard working, and which only asked rights
which will make it a recognized cultural element alongside the
other nations in the great European family."

Ratiu's Declaration

We cannot end this chapter dealing with the memorable
trial that took place in the summer of 1894 in the Assizes Court
in Cluj without quoting a few fragments from the vigorous and
dignified declaration made by Ratiu, the head of the Romanian
National Party, to the Magyar jurors who were to decide the
fate of the leaders of the Transylvanian Romanians.

In the dusty archives left over from the end of the last
century in the Magyar ministry of justice, the prosecutor's
charges in effect represented the bill of indictment of those who
were brought to trial. But for history, the real bill of indictment
was represented by Ratiu's declaration:

> What compelled us to publish and spread our memoran-
> dum was the fact that both the Hungarian legislature and
> the Hungarian government convinced us that we could
> never expect justice from them. The promises which were
> made to us guaranteeing the observance of our national
> rights—promises which had been made solemnly and re-
> peatedly—have all been in vain. It is to no avail that we
> have explored all legal avenues and remedies. To no avail
> we have addressed ourselves to all the competent au-

thorities. The racial elitism of the government has launched
a war of extermination against our language and our nationality. There was only one way open to us: to appeal
to the head of state and the opinion of the civilized
world . . .

What is under discussion today before this jury is the
existence of the Romanian people itself. But the existence
of a people is not something to be discussed. It is something that asserts itself.

Deprived of the sacred right to defend themselves because
of the inquisitorial methods employed by court president Szent-
kereszty, the Romanian defendants, struggling to win the respect due to their nationality, addressed the Assizes Court,
through Ratiu's voice, with these imposing words:

Therefore, do not ask us to turn ourselves into ac-
complices in this mockery of a trial. Do not try to make
us engage in a defense which at its best is a simulacrum.
By violence and insults, you have compelled our defenders
to leave the Court. You have stirred up the press and
Magyar public opinion—of which the jury in Cluj is representative—against us and against the whole Romanian
people. We have been abused here, and our people have
always been terrorized—particularly after we denounced
to the civilized world the offenses of which we are the
victims. How can anyone speak of justice and defense in
the proper juridical meaning of these words? No—do
whatever you please. You are the masters of our physical
bodies. But what escapes your reach is our
conscience—which is the national conscience of the Romanian people.

One can easily imagine what excitement was stirred up
among the Transylvanian Romanians by the verdict of the
Assizes Court in Cluj, especially if one takes into account the
great impression this verdict created in the countries of western
Europe.

Fearing a reaction on the part of the oppressed Romanian
nation, the Hungarian authorities stepped up their oppressive
methods. They reinforced their police reserves in order to prevent or, if need be, nip in the bud any attempt on the part of
the Romanians to gain their national liberty.

The Romanians, deprived of the possibility to use Parliament to acquaint public opinion with the manifest inferiority under which great numbers of their people suffered, were limited to protesting and asking the assistance of the press in asserting their rights. This limitation was due to two causes: first of all, on the Romanian side, by a wrong policy based on passivity and abstentionism; and, secondly, on the Hungarian side, by the iron police repression, which choked off or paralyzed any attempt at collective manifestation.

But immediately after the first signs that the Romanians were becoming active in this area, the "liberal" Hungarians unleashed a violent attack, obviously meant to stifle any feeble Romanian effort to use the press. So onerous were the terms governing the existence of Romanian newspapers in Transylvania that the Romanians were compelled to print their newspapers in Arad (from an administrative standpoint, Arad belonged to Hungary and not to Transylvania), and even in Budapest.

The terror directed against those journalists who had the courage to speak openly about Romanian demands for liberty and social equality was violent—so violent that it discouraged many well-meaning intellectuals, persuading them to abandon their desire to seek the help of the press in expressing the grievances of the Romanian people.

But the terror was unable to totally stifle the Romanian cry of revolt against the injustice which had endured for centuries.

Proof of this is available from the increasingly large number of charges having to do with press and political offenses which were brought against Transylvanian Romanians, starting with the year 1844. During the decade 1884-94, 107 Romanians were sentenced to serve a total of 63 years in prison for such offenses by the Assizes Court and the other Hungarian tribunals. But the Romanian people did not give up; on the contrary, they continued to proclaim their right to freedom. Over the following decade, there were 255 such sentences, totalling 134 years of imprisonment—all this for the purpose of instilling terror and stifling revolt over the following period.

Once their passions had been unleashed, the Hungarian nobility proved unrestrainable in their nefarious, oppressive actions. The prisons were full of Romanian political prisoners, who were subject to the same treatment as the most loathsome criminals.

The French correspondent Felix Lesseur wrote an article in *La Republique Francaise* of July 22, 1893, dealing with conditions in the prison where a great Romanian patriot, [Father] Vasile Lucaciu, was serving a sentence. This is what he said:

> Dr. Lucaciu, this noble patriot whose only crime is that of fighting unremittingly for the liberties of Romanian Transylvania, and who was sentenced for this by the tribunals in Seghedin and Satu-Mare, is now serving a sentence in *carcero duro* [strict regime prison] in Satu-Mare. By a refined sense of cruelty, he was put in the same cell with a penal-law criminal who had been sentenced to 30 years imprisonment for murder.

After describing all the tortures inflicted on Father Lucaciu in his cell, Lesseur terminated his article with this expression of revulsion, which was characteristic of the reaction of the whole of civilized Europe: "This monstrosity is taking place in the heart of civilized Europe—this Europe of which the Hungarians think, on the basis of their holy mission, that it is right for them to be the master!"

From Menotti Garibaldi to Horvath

Even the most sincere friends of Hungary were unable to restrain their feelings of revolt against the barbarous acts committed in Transylvania by the descendants of Arpad.

On the occasion of the International Peace Conference in Rome (1891), Menotti Garibaldi, the son of Italy's national hero Giuseppe Garibaldi, addressed the Hungarian deputy Pulzsky, in words that retain their timeliness to this very day: "My father sympathized with the Hungarian cause and supported it, believing that the Hungarians would offer a good example of liberalism. But the Hungarians are not worthy of Italy's sympathy, since they are oppressing 3,000,000 of our brothers in a most barbarous manner."

In his polemical opuscule, in an obvious effort to upset the edifice of Seton-Watson's massive work on the history of the Romanians, Horvath, like all of his co-nationals who have considered the Transylvanian question, deliberately forgot to speak about the endless oppression which the Hungarians visited on the Transylvanian Romanians—oppressions which, it is to be noted, have been described as barbarian by Hungary's friends. With the lack of both ability and scruples characteristic of those who write propaganda, the author of this controversial work which disputes Seton-Watson has the temerity to accuse the Romanians of refusing to submit to the fate which the Hungarian nobility—who came to the territory of the former province of Dacia as invaders—had reserved for them.

The same Horvath, like so many contemporary Hungarian publicists, without taking the trouble to deny the terrible crimes the Budapest government had committed against the Transylvanian Romanians toward the end of the previous century, sought to exonerate—at least to a degree—the perpetrators of these flagrant injustices. This he did by accusing the free Romanians beyond the Carpathian Mountains of carrying on a policy which undermined the Austro-Hungarian monarchy.

The Budapest professor accused the government in Bucharest, and King Carol I, in particular, of trying to bring about the "separation of Transylvania from Hungary." They said that these concentric Romanian attacks were all directed against the Magyars, and that their object was to separate Transylvania gradually from the Hungarian crown.

Nothing could be more inaccurate, nothing more false.

The most shallow investigator who was interested in King Carol's foreign policy from 1881 (the year when the kingdom was established), until the outbreak of World War I (when King Carol died), knows that Romania's monarch, who also had the title of Prince of Hohenzollern, was very close to the Central Powers. Horvath, like all the other contemporary Hungarian writers, knew only too well that the Romanians had many times been put in a situation where they had to pretend to be disinterested in the demands of their brothers in Hungary, in order to safeguard the higher state interests of the Romanian kingdom.

In order to be able to maintain the relatively good relations they enjoyed with the Austro-Hungarian monarchy, the Romanian political leaders had to stifle what was in their hearts and speak with their minds—that is, pragmatically. Public opinion in Romania, which could not be prevented by foreign policy considerations from making common cause with the suffering Romanian masses on the other side of the mountains, was, because of this difference, many times in conflict with the governments in Bucharest.

One episode from Romanian political life at the time of the Memorandum trial is highly instructive on this point.

At the time the fury of the Hungarian government was unleashed against the Romanian nation in Hungary, the Conservative Party, under the leadership of Catargi, was in power in Romania. In line with the policy of all the governments which served under King Carol I, the Catargi government stood to one side and did not attempt to intercede in the trial which was taking place in Cluj. It also avoided expressing an opinion on the severity of the sentences pronounced by the Assizes Court in that town. The Liberal Party vehemently attacked the Conservative Party for the indifference it had shown to the fate of their co-nationals in Transylvania. But when the Liberal Party came to power, it immediately identified itself with the policy of those who had come before them, and whom they had criticized so severely at the time. Moreover, Dimitrie Sturza, the head of the Liberal Party and chairman of the Council of Ministers, was put in a situation where he had to retract, in a speech at Jassy, the accusations he had made against Austria-Hungary. This fact led the contemporary press to accuse him of complicity with the Hungarian government of Prime Minister Banffy.

7. THE PRE-WORLD WAR I YEARS

King Carol I and the Transylvanian Romanians

King Carol I was the life and soul of the policy of rapprochement with Austria-Hungary, to which he was bound by a formal treaty of military alliance. He gave further proof of his loyal attitude toward the Central Powers at the Crown Council of August 3, 1914, where, in the face of the king's expressed will, the council declared Romania neutral.

"It is said," declares Bratianu, in his work, *The Foreign Policy of King Carol I*, "that this dramatic debate [in the Crown Council] provided a real test of conscience for King Carol and that the decision of the council hastened his death."

In the light of these facts, how is it possible to maintain in good faith that Romania, and above all its Hohenzollern monarch, King Carol I, undermined the Austro-Hungarian monarchy by helping the oppressed Romanian nationality in Transylvania? To say this is an insolent negation of the truth and of the historical evidence. But has truth ever represented an obstacle for the Hungarian propagandists?

Horvath and the others *ejusdem farinae* ("of the same stripe") were quite aware that neither the King of Romania, nor the successive governments of the Romanian kingdom, nor even Romanian public opinion had ever demanded Transylvania's separation from the Austro-Hungarian monarchy and its union with Romania—this despite the fact that Romanian public opinion was passionately moved by the plight of its downtrodden Transylvanian brothers and inclined to express its warm solidarity with them.

Even Dimitrie Sturza, whose violent criticism of the Hungarians had triggered the gesture of the Budapest government, declared formally that "No reasonable man in Romania dreams of conquering Transylvania."

Because they sympathized with their brothers in Transylvania, Romanians on the other side of the mountains, who enjoyed the freedom to express their thoughts, demanded the same freedom for their brothers in Transylvania whose freedom of speech was stifled by their Hungarian rulers. They also demanded "complete equality with the Hungarian nation to appeal to the Emperor, and the cessation of the Magyarization program" [D. Sturza].

The professors in Budapest knew all these things, too, but, in order to pose as victims in the eyes of the world, they distorted the most elementary and uncomplicated events.

Hungarian Propaganda

Budapest propaganda, as a Romanian publicist, C. Graur, put the matter, is not a recent invention brought about by the consequences of World War I. Propaganda has always been a preoccupation in Budapest. Indeed, the Magyar oligarch is a born propagandist.

If the Magyar authors who are interested in the Transylvanian question (what Magyar author isn't?) had really done their best to discover the true reasons for the collapse of the Hapsburg monarchy and the breaking up of Hungary, they should not have looked for those reasons abroad, but in the history of the Hungarian people itself.

The lack of understanding of the legitimate aspirations of the nationalities which shared Transylvania with the Hungarians; the brutal methods of oppression used against the most natural and inoffensive national manifestations; the violent policy of forced assimilation including the insane campaign of Magyarization and denationalization of people who had much deeper roots in the land of Transylvania than did the Hungarians—these were the real reasons for the collapse of the polynational mixture represented by the dual monarchy.

The great French politician Gambetta stated this truth in the most explicit terms: "The Hungarians are people who, by their violent method of governing, have created the Romanian problem."

When these monstrous methods of governing became widely known in the civilized world, the Romanian question stopped being a purely local problem and became instead a European problem.

The revelations on Hungarian misrule in Transylvania produced stupefaction in the West, not only because they constituted a stain on the coats of arms of European civilization, but also because they stood in scandalous contrast with the image the West had formed about the so-called liberalism of Hungary's government.

Inside their own boundaries, the Hungarian rulers followed the most brutal policy of denationalization against the Romanians, the Slovaks, and the other nationalities—while abroad they did not shrink from comparing the liberalism of their law with that of British or American law.

In the United States, Hungarian lecturers—propagandists—were applauded for Hungary's "liberal" laws governing the treatment of other nationalities—while in Transylvania, the Hungarian noblemen were sending to prison those Romanians who dared to demand the observance of these laws, which had in fact remained a dead letter from the beginning.

So certain were the Magyars that their propaganda abroad had succeeded in establishing their fame as "champions of liberty" that, when the first articles sympathetic to the Transylvanian Romanians appeared in print, a Hungarian newspaper, commenting on the severe verdict in the Memorandum trial, regretted the passage of the days when the old and "good" habit of displaying the heads of traitors at the gates of towns was still in force. Only one month after the verdict had been handed down at the trial in Cluj, Hieronymyi, the Hungarian minister for internal affairs, dissolved the Romanian National Party, forbidding any activity under penalty of the most severe punishment. It was a new and damaging blow to the Romanian nation in Transylvania—a nation which was in its great majority peasants and which was denied the possibility of having its own representatives, voicing claims on its behalf.

Desider Banffy's Administration

Under the administration of Baron Desider Banffy, who presided over the Hungarian Council of Ministers for four years, from January 1895 to February 1899, the policy of compulsory Magyarization came to a head. Banffy made no secret of the ultra-chauvinistic principles which guided his policy.

"My chauvinistic policy," he claimed, "represents an irresistible effort to reach a well-defined goal, which we must reach at any price. This goal is the setting up of a homogeneous Hungarian state in which a single language is spoken. (*Der Aufbau des einheitlichen einsprachigen ungarischen Staates*)."

In its essence this program was tantamount to the suppression of the Romanian nation, since it meant that the Hungarians excluded the possibility of coexistence with other nationalities.

When the Hungarian prime minister declared openly for such a program of government, one can easily imagine the methods used to enforce this program.

The elections which took place under Banffy's administration became proverbial for fraud and corruption, leaving far behind them all elections of the past in this "paradise of electoral corruption." The result of the madness which had been unleashed against the subject nationalities was apparent immediately after the election. The millions of non-Magyars living in Hungary, who represented 45 percent of the entire population, managed to send only one deputy to Parliament.

As a matter of fact, the recrudescence of the oppression which was directed anew at the subject nationalities coincided with the millenary celebration of the Hungarian presence in central Europe. It became an occasion for noisy manifestations on behalf of the single-national state which governed against the expressed will of millions of non-Magyars.

This myth of a homogeneous Hungarian state, under the Crown of St. Stephen, is one which the Hungarians have always kept in mind as an ideal for which to strive. It is the most absurd idea ever to guide the actions of a government.

When they came to Europe centuries ago, the Hungarians found a lot of other nations already there. These nations had such natural stamina, their national character was so closely tied to the land they tilled, that the Hungarians were not able to assimilate them by denationalization.

The elitist self-image of the Magyars also contributed to the abyss which existed between the Hungarians and the non-Magyar peoples. Under this conception, the nation consisted of a cast of nobles, but excluded the masses who did not possess coats-of-arms—that is, it excluded virtually all the Romanians, Slovaks, and Serbs.

The principal reason why the Romanians were able to resist assimilation, despite centuries of Hungarian domination, is to be found in the extraordinary vitality of the Romanian people. These people, who were born of a mixture of Roman vigor and primitive Dacian force, had constantly renewed their vitality over the centuries by drawing on the vigorous blood of the barbarians who, in settling down among the Dacian-Roman peasant masses, were gradually assimilated by them.

There was nothing which could draw the Romanians and the Hungarians together. On the contrary, everything seemed disposed to keep them apart. On the one hand, there was the sweetness of the Latin language spoken by the Romanians; on the other hand, you had the harshness of the Finno-Ugrian language spoken by the Hungarians, full of grating double consonants (words, for example, like *csopdes, scipked, szeg,* etc.), and so different from all other European tongues. On the one hand, you had the mild and modest nature of the Romanian peasant; on the other hand, you had the vain, conceited, "superior" character of the Magyar race, about whom the British journalist, Wickham Steed, said: "The Hungarians have rarely practiced the virtue of moderation."

Such contrasts widened the gap between these two nations whom fate had brought together to live in the same land. And the harsh treatment to which the Romanians from the first were subjected by the Magyar nobility widened the gap between the two nations so much further that inevitably the day came when no bridge could be built over this chasm for the purpose of bringing the two peoples closer.

But the Hungarian nobles thought that, if they maximized the inflexibility of their treatment of the minorities, they would in a few decades be able to achieve that which they had not been able to achieve in centuries of violent rule.

Crucial Mistakes

This was an error in judgment which had important consequences for the future. The error sprang from the very nature of the Hungarian people. The purely objective manner in which the Hungarians regard the evolution of history was admirably characterized by Edouard de Laveleze in *La Revue des Deux Mondes*, in 1866. "The Magyars," he said, "can see only what corresponds to their wishes; they are blind to anything which goes against these wishes."

Nothing could be worse than to believe that you could

achieve in a century that which you had not been able to achieve by 1,000 years of oppression. During this dark period, "the Romanians were condemned to live more under the earth than above it." (These words belong to the Transylvanian writer, Liviu Rebreanu.) And this all the more so because, despite the Chinese walls built by the Magyars, the light of civilization in more recent times had reached even the most remote villages of Transylvania.

All the Hungarian leaders had repeated the same error, championing the concept that the salvation of Hungary was directly dependent on the Magyarization of the non-Magyar nationalities. This was the mentality of the entire Hungarian upper class toward the end of the 19th century, and this mentality was passed on from generation to generation. The passion and zeal with which officials put these methods into practice were tantamount to a certificate of patriotism.

Within the framework of the dual monarchy, the sacrifice of the subject nationalities on the altar of the myth of St. Stephen's Crown was the principle which guided Hungarian internal policy. The difference between the moderate Hungarians and the frankly chauvinistic ones had to do with method, not program. The former claimed that the sacrifice of the subject nationality should be accomplished by persuading them to accept this sacrifice of their own accord. The chauvinists, on the other hand, favored more violent methods. *C'était la même Jeannette, mais autrement coiffée.* ("It was the same Jeannette, but with a different coiffure.")

Coloman Szell, whose government (1899) was a model of moderation compared to that of Banffy who came before him, declared himself a convinced believer in a homogeneous Magyar state and said that "the Hungarians will never agree that their country be turned into a Swiss pseudo-confederation, and they will adamantly fight, sword in hand, against all such attempts." In 1901, under this new, more "moderate" government which had been installed in 1899, the nonabstentionist Romanians and the other non-Magyar nationalities managed to elect to Parliament the grand total of—five deputies!

The Romanians Return to the Political Arena

The year 1905 is of exceptional importance in the political evolution of the Romanians in Transylvania. After pursuing a fruitless policy of passivity and abstentionism—which, under an autocratic and despotic regime, was equivalent to political self-destruction—the Romanians made up their minds to return to the political arena in order to fight for liberty and equality alongside the other oppressed nationalities, the Serbs and the Slovaks.

Fighting side by side with the Serbs and Slovaks was to result eventually in the alliance of the three oppressed nationalities. This was the precursor of the Little Entente of later years.

However, the struggle was bound to be a very difficult one because the Hungarians were determined to put into practice "the chimera of the homogeneous all-Magyar state," as Prince Valentin Bibescu called this illogical Hungarian concept.

Magyarization by Violence

The Budapest Parliament voted for the Magyarization of Transylvanian towns and villages. They also took steps to bring about the mass Magyarization of Romanian family names. Railway stations bearing old Romanian names received new Magyar ones. All this was in order to give an eminently Hungarian appearance to towns and villages that were inhabited by Romanians.

Restrictions on "freedom" of the press were carried even further. Romanian newspapers were forbidden to circulate. No newspapers could be printed without prior approval. Whoever dared to discuss a legislative bill and take a position against it was punished—e.g., the case of editor Branik of Ujvidek. Whoever dared to comment or to say that a certain law represented a departure from the already established legal principles governing the treatment of nationalities, was simply imprisoned. Thus, three Romanian editors were sentenced, two of them to eighteen months in prison, and the other one to ten months, simply because they had criticized the famous Apponyi law which provided for the almost total Magyarization of the schools.

Any article which expressed sympathy with the oppressed nationalities was considered "propaganda against the Hungarian nation," and the authors were subject to imprisonment and heavy fines.

"Persecution," said Arthur Seton-Watson *(Scotus Viator)*

in 1907, "has been carried so far that it is almost impossible to find a Romanian newspaperman who writes for a political newspaper, and who has never been in jail, charged with a political crime."

The right of association was so limited—despite the legal provisions that were buried somewhere in the archives—that in effect it had become nonexistent. All gatherings had to be previously announced and authorized. Moreover, a Hungarian police officer had to be present at any group meeting, and he had the right to dissolve the gathering at any moment. Meetings could be forbidden for the most childish reason. Thus, when the matter of universal suffrage was up for discussion, a Romanian meeting which had this matter on its agenda was forbidden on the grounds that the organizers of the meeting had not specified that they were going to discuss the problem of universal suffrage in Hungary or in some other country.

The speakers were even forbidden to use certain words or expressions. Thus, the word "Slovak" was banned from all speeches. One could, therefore, view the highly amusing spectacle of a speech made in a meeting hall full of Slovaks in which equal rights for the "Chinese" in Hungary were championed from the platform.

But the electoral terror surpassed in violence all other forms of national oppression when the subject nationalities committed themselves to a policy of political activism. It should suffice to mention the fact that there was no secret ballot but that the voting was done in public.

Terror alternated with corruption, corruption with deception, and deception with fraud. Mass arrests of Romanian and Slovak peasants were customary happenings during the elections. There were even cases where non-Magyar voters were assassinated.

When an Englishman who was eminently temperate in his choice of words called Hungary a "paradise of electoral corruption," one can easily imagine what might happen in Hungarian elections if the goal of the Magyars was the denationalization at any cost of the subject nationalities.

Protests were the only weapon the Romanians in Transylvania had at their disposal against this relentless campaign of Magyarization. As their forebears had found in similar situations in the past, all Romanian protests had absolutely no effect on the Magyar rulers.

Only then did the Romanian leaders realize how much they had lost for the Romanian national cause in Hungary by endorsing the principle of political passivity.

In 1905 the Romanians decided to abandon the abstentionist policy, which they recognized as fruitless, and which, under an autocratic and despotic regime, was equivalent to self-destruction. They returned to the political arena alongside the other oppressed nations, the Serbs and the Slovaks, to fight for liberty and equality.

After thirty-five years of disasters for the cause of the Romanian nation in Transylvania, the basically sound principles once enunciated by the great patriot, Saguna, were once again given due consideration.

The Secret Plans of the Chauvinists

The supporters of forced Magyarization were completely chagrined by the meager results the Hungarians had achieved in Transylvania despite four decades of despotic government.

The denationalization measures were intensified, but the Romanians firmly stood their ground. The government in Budapest began to worry. It appeared that the writer Gustav Beksics had been right when he wrote in 1883 that the Magyar minority in Transylvania was in so inferior a position when compared to the Romanian element, "that it is unable to break through the impenetrable wall erected by the Romanians."

It was at that point that the first plans were made for the purpose of finding a radical solution to the Romanian problem. The most interesting plan was without question that published by Antal Huszar in 1907, entitled, *The Romanians in Hungary.* It was printed at the expense of the Hungarian government and—an important detail—it was meant to be used "in strict confidence only by certain members of the Hungarian government." All of these precautions to prevent accidental disclosure of the book's contents were justified because of the radical character of the measures of denationalization proposed by the author. None of the activities of the Transylvanian Romanians had been overlooked. The most adequate—that is, the most merciless—means of annihilation was recommended for every stronghold of Romanian resistance.

Until that time the independence of the Romanian Orthodox church had been like an impregnable fortress, always standing tall against the unremitting attacks of the Magyars. The author of the book, taking this fact into consideration, demanded simply that the church be deprived of its autonomy and that the organic ordinance governing the existence of the Church be abrogated. The Greek-Catholic church was a manifestation of Romanian separatism and, therefore, an obstacle barring the way to the unity of the Magyar state. The author of this plan, which called for the total and rapid Magyarization of the Romanian populace, proposed to the government that the Romanian church be incorporated into the Catholic church, a measure which was tantamount to eliminating Greek Catholicism.

Antal Huszar recommended confidentially to the Hungarian ministers other equally offensive measures, such as the Magyarization of all Romanian schools and increasingly severe punishments for Romanian newspaperman who offended the government. Huszar also advised the ministers to order that Romanian journalists who had been imprisoned for press offenses be required to serve the terms to which they were sentenced in criminal prisons rather than in political prisons. The author of the plan also suggested the severe scrutiny of all Romanian cultural associations (which still existed despite the terror to which their members were subject), the outlawing of the cultural society known as "Astra," the colonization of Transylvania with Magyar ethnic elements, and other similar measures.

Such was the happy regime under which the Romanians in Hungary lived at the beginning of this century. Such were the hopes they could envision for the future.

All this time, Magyar propaganda abroad was making desperate efforts to persuade the West of the good conditions existing for the Romanian nationality in the "paradise of nationalities," which is how it referred to Hungary.

Dionisie de Parmandy, for example, had the temerity to write toward the end of the last century in the newspaper *L'Indépendence Belge*, of Brussels: "Nobody in Hungary is trying to hinder the spiritual and material progress of the Romanian people, or to abolish their language, customs, and other national characteristics."

But this time all such attempts to distort the truth remained fruitless because the Romanian associations abroad saw to it that the real truth about the plight of the Romanians in Hungary were presented to the West.

Bjoernsterne Bjoernson and the Problem of the Romanians in Transylvania

That is why the great Norwegian writer Bjoernsterne Bjoernson turned down the invitation of the Hungarian committee which organized the Interparliamentary Congress that took place in Budapest in 1907. It also accounts for the exceptionally sharp tone of the letter which he addressed to the Hungarian sponsors of this occasion.

"In my youth," wrote the famous Norwegian writer, "when the Hungarian nation was oppressed, I used to love it and admire it a lot, and I shed bitter tears for it. But later, when I studied the situation more closely, I became convinced of the injustice that was being done to the other nationalities in Hungary, and I started hating Hungarian chauvinism. I am certain that there is nobody outside Hungary who does not share these feelings—and believe me, these injustices sooner or later will lead to Hungary's downfall."

What were the Romanians Fighting For?

Ignoring all the recommendations [of moderation] which they received from famous European personalities, the Hungarian rulers pursued a policy which constantly degraded the position of the subject nationalities. Apparently they had one goal, and one goal only: national unity to be accomplished through the instrument of Magyarization. Count Bethlen, who was described by Professor Silviu Dragomir as the leader of a movement intended to paralyze the cultural and economic life of Transylvania, stated in 1907: "It's now or never." During the same year, Banffy rejected any compromise on his nationalities policy because he was against any negotiated solution of the problem. "What we want," he wrote, "is a unitary national Magyar state, while they [the nationalities] want a polyglot state, with equal rights for all the nationalities."

In this sentence, written by one of the most obdurate partisans of Magyarization by violence (and, therefore, one of the greatest patriots, according to the Magyar conception), it is appropriate to underscore the goals sought by the subject nationalities, that is, equal rights in a state where the language of each nationality would be respected.

Where, therefore, is the good will of those who maintain that the Romanians in Transylvania wanted to destroy the dual monarchy of Austria-Hungary by working for a Dacian Romania, within the limits of the ancient province of Dacia?

It is an indisputable fact that, in the heart of every Romanian on both sides of the Carpathians, there existed a firm belief that the Romanian nation was destined to achieve its unity—but the achievement of this aspiration appeared so remote that it nestled in the deepest corners of the Romanian soul. It was an ideal which every civilized man carries in his soul, an ideal which said that, sooner or later, misunderstandings between nations will no longer be resolved by war. Every man carries this hope hidden deep inside him. To make it come true will require leaders with a conscious sense of mission.

It was the destiny of the Romanian people that their age-old ideal should at last come true in 1918. But until that time, Romanians on both sides of the Carpathians struggled for a common goal: to keep the Romanian spirit unbroken, stubbornly resisting the berserk attacks of the Magyars.

The tension between the two hostile camps, triggered by the mistakes of the Magyar political leaders, was getting more and more ominous. It was a gigantic contest between two nations, one of which was making a final effort, unique in history, to oppose its own denationalization, and the other one striving with all its might to destroy this opposition.

If we consider things from this point of view—the only realistic one—the struggle of the Romanians in Transylvania, from time to time supported by free Romanians beyond the Carpathians, identifies completely with a fundamental law of nature—with the struggle for life and the instinct of self-preservation.

The great Romanian statesman, Take Ionescu, in a conversation with an English journalist in 1909, admirably articulated the aspirations for liberty and national equality of the Transylvanian Romanians.

"If I believed," said Ionescu, "that Magyarization could be successful, I should retire from politics, since in that case it would be useless for us to continue putting up resistance here in the kingdom. . . . In this case we would have no future." This sentence expressed the entire tragedy of the fate of the Transylvanian Romanians if the Magyarization program had been successful.

Do these aspirations to a national life represent a form of irredentism or Romanian imperialism? Of course not. Indeed, they were elementary aspirations, natural to any civilized man.

Ionescu in his book, *Souvenirs de Paris*, also describes a conversation he had with Banffy toward the end of the last century on the occasion of his visit to Budapest. We quote an excerpt from it here:

Ionescu: "Why shouldn't we find a modus vivendi as good neighbors? The situation of the Romanians in Hungary is intolerable. Although I do not speak officially, I don't see why, for instance, you shouldn't be able to reach an agreement like the one you patched up with the Transylvanian Saxons—at least protecting their schools, their churches, and certain electoral districts from persecution and violence.

Banffy: "Never! The two dangers are not identical. The Transylvanian Saxons amount to only 230,000, and they are 1,000 kilometers from Germany. While the Romanians. . . !"

Did the good relations between neighbors, the proposals for a modus vivendi between the Hungarian and Romanian peoples, the legitimate—and minimal—demands to protect Romanian schools and churches in Transylvania from persecution and violence—did these natural conditions constitute a manifestation against the security of Austria-Hungary, or an irredentist action, or interference in the internal affairs of the Hapsburg monarchy, or a manifestation of imperialistic tendencies? Not at all.

The Romanians in Transylvania were only claiming their just right to a free national life—and their brothers beyond the Carpathians supported their struggle within the limitations imposed by the imperatives of diplomatic relations between states. It sometimes happened that the reserve displayed by the government in Bucharest reached limits which public opinion in Romania found depressing. For example, in order to please the Hungarian government, the government of Dimitrie Sturza granted the "Crown of Romania" medal to Sandor Iezensky, of the Hungarian ministry of education, a fanatical supporter of Magyarization, whom Constantin Xeni and others described as "the man most detested in the Romanian schools in Transylvania."

Imperialist aspirations, however, found adept enthusiasts among the ever-growing number of Hungarian chauvinists.

The great journalist Eugen Rakosi, editor-in-chief of the daily *Budapesti Hyrlap*, wrote with passion about a Hungary that would comprise thirty million Hungarians within its boundaries.

A Hungary of thirty million Hungarians! Such was the Magyar chimera.

When such dreams were nurtured by a nation of approximately seven or eight million, among whom were a lot of Jews and Magyarized foreigners, how should such aspirations be qualified other than imperialistic?

This passion for an exaggerated grandeur was one of the principal factors which brought on the collapse of the Hungarian state and the disintegration of the Hapsburg monarchy—an enormous giant with feet of clay.

In the light of all the factors listed in the preceding paragraphs, the aspirations of the Transylvania Romanians appear modest in the extreme. The fulfillment of the age-old Romanian ideal—that is, the union of all Romanians—was half dream and half hope. The Transylvanians, however, nursed a much more modest and attainable ideal. They fought only to set up a legal order and to secure for themselves, within the framework of the dual monarchy, a free national life.

Today it seems almost inexplicable that the Hungarians should have refused the modest demands of the Romanians and of the other nationalities who shared Transylvania with them. At a time when the rights of nationalities were fully respected in western Europe, the attitude of the Hungarian rulers toward the subject nationalities in Hungary and toward the Transylvanian Romanians in particular was something that the average free citizen of the West could not understand.

Assuming that western Europe would never believe the accounts of their oppression of the Transylvanian Romanians, the Hungarians—with the cynicism worthy of the pejorative meaning of "propaganda"—managed to convince certain circles abroad of the absurdity of the Romanian protests. Hungary, they said, was "a country where the laws were as liberal as those of the United States and Great Britain."

Adept at propaganda, the Hungarian establishment took advantage of the good will displayed by certain intellectual circles of the west, whose information about the real state of affairs in central Europe was incomplete and sometimes completely wrong. In doing so, they used the same tools they had used before when they had managed to swing Emperor Franz Joseph completely over to their side by speaking about the danger that a possible Dacian-Romania would constitute.

Once again they had been able to avoid the question of

Magyar responsibility by talking about a vast imaginary plot, contrived by the Romanians, to overthrow the dual monarchy. The American writer Charles Upson Clark, in his work, *Greater Romania*, printed in New York in 1922, said that "the system which was specific to the Hungarians was to convince the foreign countries that the Romanians were always the guilty ones."

The Federalist Plan of Aurel Popovici

The Romanians made great efforts to pursue a policy of rapprochement with Austria-Hungary, which was at that time the only power which could provide a solid basis for state security. The best proof of the peaceful intentions nurtured by the Romanians for Austria-Hungary is the famous plan drawn up in 1906 by the Transylvanian Romanian, Aurel Popovici. This plan, incidentally, should be regarded as illustrative of a political conception specific to Transylvanian intellectuals.

In his work entitled *Die Vereinigten Staaten von Grossöesterreich* ("The United States of Great Austria"), published in Leipzig, Popovici suggested converting the Austro-Hungary dual monarchy into a federal state. He asserted that only this change could save the great monarchy from total destruction.

"The United States of Great Austria" was to comprise 15 national territories under a federal parliament, have a common army, and customs union, and German was to be the official language.

The Romanian national territory in this central European federal state was to take in all the Romanians in Transylvania proper as well as Hungary and Bukovina.

As was to be expected, this work stirred up great interest all over Europe.

Karl Renner,who was one day to become chancellor of the Austrian Republic and at a later date president of the last Austrian Parliament, wrote the following words when the plan for a great federal Austria was made public:

"The book offers enough proof that the nationalities in Hungary are not some miserable illiterate barbarians, as the Magyars would like us to believe."

This was an additional reason why the Hungarians saw fit to ban Popovici's work in the territory of Hungary.

It appears that Popovici's federalist conception had something in common with Archduke Franz Ferdinand's own plans for the future. The archduke knew about the terror imposed by the Magyars in the Romanian territories which had been under their exclusive control since the first days of the dual monarchy. Unlike his uncle, Franz Joseph, whom Hungarian intrigues had rendered completely indifferent to the sufferings of "his faithful subjects," the Romanians, the archduke favored improving the plight of the Transylvanian Romanians. In fact, he more than once expressed his indignation over the despotic Hungarian methods of governing. It is reported that one day he could no longer stifle his revulsion, and he shouted: "The Hungarians proved their lack of tact when they first came to Europe!"

According to recent books, while it may be an exaggeration to assert that the Archduke Franz Ferdinand was highly sympathetic to the Romanians, it is no exaggeration to say that the heir to the Austro-Hungarian throne had a feeling of genuine aversion for the Hungarians, a feeling which stemmed from the exaggerated ambition of the Magyar leaders. The archduke's tragic death did not grieve the Hungarians. Indeed, one had the impression that they breathed more freely after the event.

Constantin Xeni, the biographer and close personal friend of Ionescu, wrote, in a work dedicated to this great Romanian politician: "The Austro-Hungarian warmongers took advantage of the assassination in Sarajevo with macabre joy."

It is certainly true that Franz Ferdinand, in his plans to turn Austria into a federal state, was not moved so much by the desire to consolidate the position of the various nations in the multi-national monarchy as he was by the desire to consolidate the position of the Hapsburg crown. However, the interests of the Romanian people corresponded to those of the imperial crown. It was, therefore, only natural that the heir to the crown strongly favored the Romanians by taking a firm stand against the Hungarians—who were, at the same time, the enemies of a strong monarchy and of greater independence for the Romanian people. Indeed, a federalist state of Great Austria implied the end of Hungary's imperialistic dream of a state numbering "thirty million Hungarians." It also threatened the end of their centuries-old privileges, born in the usurpation of power and sustained by inhuman terror.

8. HUNGARIAN INTOLERANCE: THE PRINCIPAL REASON FOR THE COLLAPSE OF THE DUAL MONARCHY

The federal plan of 1906 failed because the Magyars had been against it. Today it is hardly venturesome to assert that, if the exaggerated ambitions of the Hungarians had not prevented the organization of the Danubian monarchy on a federal basis in 1906, European history would not have witnessed the horrors of World War I in 1914, nor would it have witnessed those of World War II, which erupted as an implacable consequence of World War I.

Those politicians who could see clearly, including publicists and newspaperman of world stature, expressed the opinion to a man that the intolerance of Hungarian policy toward the subject nationalities created a hotbed of troubled anxiety in the heart of Europe—a hotbed which was extremely destabilizing to the peace of the entire continent.

In a series of articles published in the *Pall Mall Gazette* in London in the year 1890, Lord Fitzmaurice had called the attention of the Hungarian government to the incalculable, and even fatal, consequences for the Austro-Hungarian empire that would flow from the provocative attitude of the Hungarians toward all the other nationalities in Hungary, and especially toward the Transylvanian Romanians.

Wickham Steed, in an introduction written in 1930 for G. Morianu's book *The Transylvanian Romanian Struggle for Freedom*, said that the policy of Hungarian oppression directed against the nationalities which shared Transylvania was one of the principal factors that generated World War I.

On the other hand, C. Xeni pointed out that the leaders

responsible for Magyar policy in 1914, headed by the Hungarian prime minister Count Stefan Tisza, looked upon the war as the salvation of Magyarism. It was an error which was ultimately to prove fateful both to the dual monarchy and to the Hungarian dream of limitless splendor.

Apart from the countless comments coming from abroad, there is one Hungarian comment which we must quote. The Hungarian diplomat Baron Szilassy said in his work, *Das Untergang der Donau-Monarchie* ("The Downfall of the Danubian Monarchy"), which was published after World War I in Berlin: "The cause of the monarchy's failure is to be found not only in its general policy, but also in the policy of Hungary, which rendered impossible the existence of a federal system in government. It simultaneously prevented the improvement of the system within the states of Austria-Hungary."

This Hungarian writer is one of the few who frankly admitted the past errors made by the leaders of his country. "Hungary's misfortune," he said, "began when the dual monarchy was set up in Austria-Hungary. Dualism was an anomaly which implied Hungarian and German domination over the other peoples of the monarchy—a concept which contradicts the famous theory of Hapsburg anti-Germanism expressed in *Mein Kampf.* This state of affairs could not be tolerated by the civilized world in our time." (Page 40)

Baron Szilassy continued:

Under the protection of a common army, Hungary—that is, its masters, the Hungarian magnates—put into practice the policy of the Magyarization of the non-Hungarian nationalities, believing that a policy that had proved impossible elsewhere in the world could be applied successfully in Budapest. We, the Hungarians, refused to learn anything. We did not wish to take into account that eastern Hungary was inhabited by the Romanians, who represented the majority of the people there. In 1864, Austria granted the Romanians their national independence. Three years later, Hungary violated this independence. To torture a people like this was, in the 20th century, simply intolerable. The federal system was the only system which could have avoided disaster. But still we rejected it.

Baron Szilassy was not the only politician who accepted

coram populo, the concept of the Magyars' own guilt in the destruction of Hungary, and who condemned the barbarous methods that characterized the Hungarian government during the first decade of the 20th century.

Count Stefan Bethlen himself admitted his mistakes, thus contradicting a past of chauvinistic intransigence. "If, beginning with 1867, we would have had recourse to methods compatible with the correct order of things when there was a dispute to settle, as well as to equal treatment [of the other nationalities], the essence of the nationalities problem would have been solved in 1914," he said.

Could there be more eloquent proof concerning the inhuman treatment to which the Romanians were subjected in Hungary in the 20th century, than this formal confession on the part of men who were themselves among the leaders of the oppressive system?

We understand why the contemporary Hungarian politicians and some of the Magyar historians do not possess the courage to stigmatize the actions of their past governments before world public opinion. We understand why they keep silent about this matter. Magyar vainglory is much too big to permit the necessary objectivity for this historical correction. What we cannot understand is the brazenness with which they seek to justify today the policy of forcible Magyarization that caused waves of indignation in the entire civilized world. It is naturally very difficult to ask a contemporary Hungarian writer to display the courage to condemn before world public opinion the suicidal policy of past Magyar governments.

We can understand why many Hungarian historians remain silent about the conflict between the Magyar nation and the other nationalities in Hungary. What we cannot understand is the attitude of certain Hungarian historians who apparently take pride in the forced Magyarization which for decades has been condemned by public opinion throughout the civilized world.

Professor Domanovschi and the Transylvanian Problem

In a recent book, *Le méthode historique de M. N. Iorga*, Professor Alexandru Domanovschi of the University of Budapest engaged in an argument with the famous Romanian scholar Nicolae Iorga. He first of all gives us an example of the objectivity which animates his work by calling the great Romanian historian—whose erudition inspired the respect of scholars all over the world—"a fake historian with the whims of a playwright," a "trickster," and a "perpetrator of hoaxes." Then he goes on to analyze the Magyarization practiced by his predecessors, and seeks to justify it by referring to "the ideology of human rights," which, "beginning with the French Revolution, has resulted in the disappearance of the characteristic features of all problems of local interest."

"The Hungarians," said Professor Domanovschi, "have tried to solve their political problems in the spirit of new ideas which in France, after eliminating the consequences of certain specialized developments, succeeded in creating a unified country; on the other hand, they [the non-Hungarian nationalities] had sought to have their claims and their national life acknowledged according to ancient particular features."

According to the assertions of this Hungarian historian, what we had to deal with here was the principle of unity, represented by the Hungarian nation, and the problem of maintaining the characteristic features of the various nations living in the area—a conflict which in France had terminated in the triumph of a united France over its constituent provinces. We do not know why the professor from Budapest ascribes to the French Revolution such a role in the unification of France. According to our humble knowledge of the history of France, this unification had been accomplished long before the French Revolution. But this matter is not of direct interest to our work.

What we do know for certain is that there is a total discrepancy between the unification of France and the violent struggle carried out in the name of Magyarization against the other nationalities living in Hungary. In France, the development of localized features had been directed toward the unity of the nation by a natural evolution of events. The parts of the "whole" had sacrificed on the altar of unity only the small differences which had hitherto kept them apart.

The political unity of France is an achievement which came at the end of a natural evolutionary process. But in order to achieve this positive outcome, a precondition was the existence of a sense of national unity; without this, political unity would only have been an expression which has no meaning. It appears that Domanovschi ignored this essential point on purpose.

A united France was created on the basis of people who

had a common Gallic-Roman-Frankish background. This background brought about, on the one hand, a community of remembrances and traditions and, on the other hand, a community of shared aspirations. In short, they brought about—the French nation.

What are the common elements that bind the Hungarian nation to the other nations which shared the territory of Transylvania with it? What are the traditions and aspirations, for example, that are common to both Hungarians and Romanians?

The Frenchman in the south of France had almost all things in common with the Frenchman in the north; very few things separated them. On the other hand, the Romanian in Transylvania was isolated from the Magyar in this region by almost everything. Indeed, he did not identify in any way, even where the two nations shared characteristics that tended to blend into each other.

It is true that in the regions around the Carpathians there existed a national unity similar to that found in France—a unity which compelled the recognition of the entire world for a national entity extending from the Atlantic Ocean to the Jura Mountains, and from Brittany to the Mediterranean Sea.

The Hungarians sought to prevent such a natural union of the Transylvanian peoples and to replace it with an artificial creation conjured up by their own imagination. In consequence of this, it was inevitable that this effort should wind up a lamentable failure, all the more so since it lacked the centralizing element of unity. Transylvania, after all, was a conglomerate of nations whose artificial political union did not rest on any shared ideals or recollections, but rested only on the material interests of a caste.

On this point, a valuable proof was offered in a book by a Hungarian sociologist, Josef Diner-Denes, *La Hongrie: Oligarchie, Nation, Peuple.* Diner-Denes said: "With the Hungarians, the national idea has a very special meaning. It completely excludes the popular masses, the nation being represented exclusively by the oligarchy, while the national interests are considered only the interests of a caste."

The ex-prime minister of the Hungarian republic noted that "most of the oligarchs are not of Magyar origin, and the Hungarian nobility is represented only by remnants." To this Diner-Denes added: "The nobility is composed of all kinds of nations—Huns, Avars, Slavs, Szecklers, Franks, Saxons, Wallachians, and Wallonians, as well as numerous foreign knights errant who had joined forces with the foreign kings. All these form a strange blend of races and languages. The only connecting element between them was the privileges they shared."

The Hungarian scholar Tibor Joo, after studying the structural basis of his nation, had to admit, when confronted with the evidence, that the Hungarian nation "is based neither on blood relations nor on common ethnicity." "The concept of Magyar nationality," he said, "was limited to the nation of Magyar nobility . . . The Hungarian nation is the ensemble of members of the Holy Crown, and these members are the nobility." (*La nation hongroise est l'ensemble des membres de la Sainte Couronne et ces membres sont la noblesse.*)

By the nature of things, the nations which preceded and then lived together with the Hungarians on the territory they invaded preserved their national character and were not absorbed into the politically dominant nation. Indeed, the social character of the Hungarian nation from the beginning precluded the possibility of such absorption.

According to Joo, the Hungarian state was both nonnational and supranational, with two distinct categories, "the privileged, who represented the nation, and the lower classes (*les retouriers*), that is, the bourgeoisie and the serfs, who were not members of the nation, but who lived an independent ethnic life."

But almost all of the Romanians were peasants who had been turned into serfs by the Magyar nobility. They were excluded, *ipso facto*, from the privileges enjoyed by the Hungarian nation. According to Hungarian scholars, Hungary, from the most ancient time, was inhabited by two distinct categories of people: the nobility, comprising the various ethnic groups who constituted the nation, and the people composed of the native masses who were denied Magyar nationality.

This situation was perpetuated over the centuries, serving to strengthen the national conscience of the subject nations. Once again, Magyar vainglory proved fatal to the Hungarians. When the Hungarian leaders later on declared themselves ready to accept the Romanians as Magyars, it was too late. The Romanians had by then become aware of their noble Dacian-Roman origin and were fighting, by all the means available to them, against the efforts to Magyarize them by force.

The honest explanations offered by Messrs. Denes and Joo completely destroyed the feeble structure erected by Domanovschi. When considered in conjunction with these categorical explanations, the struggle of the Hungarian nobles against the subject nationalities acquired a completely different aspect from that which the Budapest professors sought to impose.

Far from resembling an ideological struggle between an almost accomplished unity and its constituent parts, the struggle took on a completely materialist aspect. The problem at issue, which has to do with Magyarization by force, was basically a problem of domination.

The Hungarians belonged to the peoples with "a weak or moderate demographic force. On Transylvania's territory, they met a Romanian population which constituted a great demographic force." (Dr. Anton Reithinger). The only logical and rational solution for the problem was to arrange a cooperative program designed to improve the welfare of both nations which shared the area. But the Hungarians refused such a cooperative arrangement; they clearly meant to incorporate the quite impressive numbers of Romanians into their own nation, which had been very much weakened numerically.

If the low numbers of Hungarians had been offset by the strength of their race, it goes without saying that the correlation of forces between the Hungarians and the minorities would not have been so unfavorable to the Hungarians. But the Hungarian nation, as the absorbing element, was composed of a heterogeneous mass, while the minorities which it thought to absorb by force had not in recent centuries suffered from any racial weakening. For this reason, the policy of forced Magyarization was contrary to the laws of nature. The leaders of Magyar chauvinism were fully aware that the racial forces were favorable to the Romanians in Transylvania, but, in line with their habit of taking wishes for realities, they hoped to bring about a radical change in the situation, even though it meant a violation of conscience.

In 1869, the Austrian Colonel Jankovschy recommended the union of the Saxons with the Magyars in order to overcome "the brute force of the Romanians." In 1905, Andrei Balabas, an obdurate supporter of Magyarization, spoke to the Hungarians about a Transylvania where the Romanians would one day come to power. "It is only a question of time," he wrote, in describing the growing strength of the Romanian masses in

Transylvania. In 1913, ex-Prime Minister Coloman Szell was even more explicit, asserting in Cluj: "The Hungarians have lost Transylvania."

Instead of weakening the resistance of the Romanians, persecution strengthened it. Indeed, Romanian solidarity was forged under the injustice of oppression.

After all his fruitless attempts to justify the policy of forced Magyarization, Professor Domanovschi admitted that his predecessors would have been better off if, in the interest of self-preservation, they had followed a policy of "respecting the national life of all the peoples living in Hungary."

"We have to confess," the professor said, "that we would have been much better served by reaching an agreement with the nationalities, recognizing in each case their ancient special privileges."

The Apponyi Law

Domanovschi, of course, had in mind the berserk campaign of denationalization which began with the onset of the 20th century and reached its climax in 1907 with the famous Apponyi law. According to the intention of the author, this law was to do away with what had until then been the most powerful weapon of the Romanians in Transylvania—the school.

The Romanians, a peasant people, had succeeded in preserving their national culture intact through the primary instrumentality of their native language. The elementary schools represented the backbone of Romanian national life, on which depended the future of Romanian people in Transylvania.

The higher schools could be Magyarized, but the elementary schools provided the basis of Romanian cultural life. So long as these schools remained Romanian, there was no danger that the nation would lose its national identity.

Count Albert Apponyi, who was minister of education in 1907, had no use for the existing laws which stipulated the right of other nationalities to use their native language in the schools. Through a series of measures, which provoked the indignation of the civilized world, Apponyi ruled that it was compulsory to use the Magyar language in Romanian elementary schools. It was difficult to know which was more despicable—the plan to denationalize the Romanian people in Transylvania or the perfidy of the effort to conceal the real character of the laws which provided for the Magyarization of the Romanians.

Romanian is a Romance language, completely unrelated to the Hungarian language, which belongs to the smallest group of Indo-European languages, the so-called Finno-Ugrian group, which comprises only four languages: Magyar, Finnish, Estonian, and Lapp.

There is no characteristic common to both languages which might serve as a support and make the study of the other nation's language easier. The two languages are completely different. But in contrast to the Magyar language, which is rough and harsh sounding—the consequence of the large number of consonants of which its words are composed—the Romanian language has the brilliance of crystal, each vowel giving it the perfect grace and luminosity of the Mediterranean.

I have talked to dozens of Romanian peasants who had become refugees from Transylvania after the Vienna *Diktat* of 1940. Natives of those areas where Magyarism had managed, over the centuries, to make some headway, these Romanians nevertheless had not been able to learn to pronounce correctly a single Hungarian sentence, despite the fact that they were in continual contact with the Hungarians. This inability was due primarily to the harsh character of the Hungarian language. Under these circumstances, to oblige a Romanian child to learn Hungarian, or to oblige a teacher to teach the Hungarian language so well that, at graduation, after four elementary grades, the child could express himself "intelligibly, both in oral and written form" (Article 19 of the Apponyi law), simply meant to turn the Romanian school into a Hungarian one. In order to observe the law, the teachers had to teach Hungarian at all times in class, and other subjects which were supposed to be taught in Romanian were completely neglected.

Article 12 of the same law stipulated that the government had the right to close down any Romanian school on the pretext that such action was demanded by "superior state interests." The decision of the minister of education was final. Thus, the very existence of the Romanian schools depended on the arbitrary interpretation of the measures taken by the Hungarian government.

What was even more reprehensible was that Romanian teachers in Romanian schools, in addition to teaching pupils the Hungarian language, had to accustom them to the idea that they "belonged to the Hungarian nation."

Article 17 of the Apponyi law said, textually: "Teachers

must strengthen the pupils' affection for the Hungarian motherland [*sic!*] and the feeling that they belong to the Hungarian
nation."

Denationalization, therefore, was to be carried out, first,
by gradually replacing the native language of the area and,
second, by insinuating into the child's mind the impression
that he was somehow affiliated with Magyarism.

It was a program which tried to pervert the most inner
psyche of children—something that had never happened before
in the history of civilized peoples. Because there was a scarcity
of those who had been born Magyar, the Hungarians apparently wanted to fill out their ranks with artificial Magyars.

The confessional schools, for religious reasons which are
easy to understand, were to a certain extent favored in comparison with the other Romanian schools, public or private.

But Apponyi found a way to subdue these schools, too,
through a Magyarization program which escaped the attention
of public opinion abroad. For instance, the law stipulated that
minimum salaries be paid to teachers in the Romanian confessional schools. This imposed great sacrifices. Not being able to
maintain minimum salaries because of lack of funds, many
schools had to appeal to the Magyar state. In giving teachers
the minimum salary, the state, however, also gained complete
power over the schools. In one county only (Hunedoara), 180
schools belonging to the Orthodox church had to close their
doors after the infamous Apponyi law came into effect. It is not
difficult, therefore, to imagine the strong, anti-Hungarian feeling which prevailed in European public opinion as the result
of the Apponyi law.

Count Leo Tolstoy Condemns the Magyar Methods

The world figure who found the most biting words in criticism of Magyarization as conceived by Count Apponyi was the
famous Russian novelist, Count Leo Tolstoy. In a letter addressed to the Hungarian magazine, *A Hir* of Budapest, the
apostle from Yasnaya Polyana said: "What is even more sad-
dening is the fact that Count Apponyi had a reputation abroad
for being a pacifist, while in Hungary he is not prepared to
acknowledge that non-Magyars possess the quality of being
people. Any man of sound mind should tear the mask from the
face of this demented person, to reveal to the whole world that
he is not a benefactor but a bird of prey."

Magyar Voices Oppose the Policy of Forced Magyarization

Even inside Hungary there were voices which were ready to condemn the assault on Romanian national life committed by the Magyar government in enforcing the Apponyi law.

Ludivoc de Mocsany, one of the most enlightened Hungarian politicians at the beginning of the 20th century, spoke prophetically for a long time from the tribune of the Parliament about the need for applying the most liberal ideas in the relations between the Hungarian people and the other nationalities. In an article on December 25, 1907, published in the important daily, *Egyeteres*, he laid bare for Magyar public opinion the truth about the nationalities problem. The chauvinists attempted to stifle this truth with grandiloquent but vain words. In the same article, Mocsany denounced the danger which the inhuman and cruel attitude of the Hungarian government represented for the future of Hungary. Mocsany said:

> Excessive fear makes us commit actions which are essentially imprudent. I refer to the general tendency to support Magyarization. I know very well that here and there, in the four corners of our country, there is frenzied applause whenever that great chauvinist, Desider Banffy, repeats unremittingly that our motherland will never be happy until the last person belonging to the Romanian or Slovak races is turned into a genuine Magyar. And why is it that in our Parliament one could declaim, without fear of punishment, that the Magyar language has to be made the exclusive instrument of public education? What is the rationale of the law which stipulates that half of the classes in all of the elementary schools belonging to the other nationalities should be dedicated to the study of the Magyar language?

"It is in vain," Mocsany emphasized, "that we seek to deny all of these things because this unwholesome wish exists within us and represents one of the principal elements at the root of our nationalities policy."

Mocsany concluded his article with these words:

> Let us not strive after impossible things. We are not dealing with the remnants of peoples, like the Flemish or the

Basques. We are confronted with national blocs which are fully aware of their status and what progress in this status means. Their centrifugal movement cannot be stopped by force. Indeed, we will not be able to stop centrifugal tendencies among the nationalities unless we manage to secure for them, within our present boundaries, the possibilities of satisfying their cultural aspirations.

Unfortunately, people who possessed the breadth of principle displayed by Mocsany were very few in the kingdom of Hungary.

Far from thinking to satisfy the cultural aspirations of the Romanian people, the Hungarian ruling class, in measure after measure, sought to stifle such aspirations. Hungarian public opinion, as a whole, hyperstimulated by articles in the popular press and, indeed, by an entire vehement literature on the subject, enthusiastically embraced the Apponyi law calling for the denationalization of other peoples, because they perceived such measures to be a determining step in the direction of achieving a united, homogeneous Hungary.

In legislating against the Romanian schools, the Hungarians were aware of the fact that they were striking a deadly blow to the Romanian people. Indeed, during the brief interval from the suppression of Kossuth's revolution until the era of the dual monarchy, the Romanian people demonstrated handsomely that they knew how to use the little liberty the Austrian monarch had granted them for the purpose of restraining the impetus of the Hungarian revolutionaries, which threatened the Crown.

In those regions where there were limits on the ability of the Hungarian administration to govern tyrannically, either because of the preponderance of the Saxon element in public offices or because of the proximity of the Romanian kingdom, the Romanian people embarked, in an almost frenzied manner, on the study of their native tongue—a privilege which had been denied to them until that time.

"So strong was the trend directed toward the bright light of education," says Professor Silviu Dragomir, "that there is no similar example in the history of any other people."

At Sibiu, 50 percent of the total number of students were Romanians, and at Lugoj, in Banat, Romanian pupils constituted 70 percent of the student body.

Why the Romanian Peasant Was Illiterate

The nature of the facts constituted reason for Hungarian concern. The Romanians had been a people of illiterates so long as an education in their native language was denied to them. (Until the beginning of the 19th century, the Transylvanian Romanians had almost no schools where the Romanian language was taught.) But once they were free to study in the language of their forefathers, the Transylvanian peasants surpassed all the other nationalities which lived in the area in their desire to learn and thus emancipate themselves from the yoke of their centuries-old bondage.

That is why the nobility always wished to keep the Romanian peasant in darkness and why the Magyar leaders, when the Romanian people—against their will—had begun to see the light, did their best to distort this light through the Magyarizing laws of Count Apponyi. This is openly admitted by the Hungarian historiographer, Acsady. In *Kozgazdasagi Lexicon* (Vol. II, p. 223), "The Transylvanian nobility," wrote Acsady, "has always shivered from the fear inspired by the Romanian serfs. This nobility was very irritated when, after the union with the Catholics, Romanian schools were built. The nobility feared that the Romanians would refuse to bear their yoke once they began to get an education and had more educated leaders. That is why they did not accept the existence of schools for the poor. [Here is the real measure of the much-touted Hungarian democracy!] But the old economic system in this way became a totally anti-cultural factor. In order to save the imaginary interests of 200 families of big landowners, an entire family was compelled to live in eternal ignorance, darkness, and material and spiritual misery."

In tandem with Apponyi's measures in the field of education, other fervent Hungarian politicians who supported the policy of Magyarization urged that the Magyarizing offensive be carried over into the fields of social and economic life.

The Hungarian Colonization of Transylvania

Count Bethlen, one of the most obdurate defenders of the policy of forced assimilation, warned against the danger of a "Romanian ocean between the Tisa River, the Danube, and the Carpathians." Influenced by considerations inspired by the old colonizing law of Daranyi, he recommended breaking up the compact bloc of Romanians in Transylvania through a massive program of Hungarian colonization.

"The Hungarian government," says Charles Upson Clark in *Greater Romania,* "spent millions of crowns for the purpose of colonizing Transylvania with Hungarians, and after the war it embarked on stepped-up efforts to implement this plan."

Bethlen's plan of 1912 also recommended a whole series of measures designed in the first place to undermine Romanian rural property, which was at the base of Romanian life in the countryside; and, in the second place, to hinder the free economic development of millions of Romanian citizens.

In order to reach the first goal, which was the most important, Bethlen simply demanded that the Romanians be dispossessed of their rural goods—that is, their only goods. As for paralyzing Romanian economic life in Transylvania, the man who was to become the next prime minister of Hungary sought the elimination of the Romanian credit structure and the sabotage of the Romanian banks.

If Bethlen's plan had ever been put into operation, the old feudal traditions would have come to life again in the 20th century, and the Romanians would again have become, thanks to the Hungarians, slaves on their own land, as they had been for centuries.

But fortunately for the Transylvanian Romanians, the Austro-Hungarian monarchy collapsed in time, and this Machiavellian plan for the Magyarization of the onetime province of Dacia came to an end before it could show any significant effects.

The implementation of this plan had been embarked on, in preliminary form, before World War I. Count I. Mailath had drawn up an agrarian plan based on the principle of transferring rural properties from Romanian ownership to Hungarian ownership—while, simultaneously, the members of OMGE (the Hungarian Agrarian Society) declared at the top of their lungs that Transylvania's land must belong to the Hungarians since "he who owns the land also owns the country."

In the plan to transform Romanian Transylvania into Hungarian Transylvania, the Hungarian politicians worked in two stages. First of all, there was the Magyarization of the human element; and, secondly, there was the Magyarization of the land itself. But this effort was at once both too audacious and too inhuman to enjoy a significant chance of success, coming as it did at a time when national liberty had become accepted as the basic principle in the life of the state.

Their effort was doomed to failure. But the Hungarian leaders did not give up on their effort to achieve Magyarization by violence even in the final moments of their political domination of Transylvania.

Professor Silviu Dragomir, who, in his role of Romanian minister of nationalities, proved himself to be a man whose sense of justice and equity would do honor to any politician in the West, condemned the nationalities policy of the Magyars as "criminal." In the light of the actions by the Hungarian government which came to power before World War I erupted, this term does not appear to us to be exaggerated. Indeed, when we survey the long line of decrees on the Transylvanian Romanians which Count Tisza's government issued after Austria-Hungary had entered the war, the term seems to us to be too mild.

Count Tisza's Government

Tisza, who, by his energy and intellect dominated the entire political life of Hungary during the second decade of the 20th century, was known as an implacable enemy of Romanian national aspirations.

First of all, Tisza, for all practical purposes, wiped out the Romanian presence in Parliament. This he did with the help of a law which reduced the number of electoral wards where the Romanians were in the majority from 42 to 17. Thus, 3,500,000 Romanians were represented by only 17 deputies, while 200,000 Transylvanian Saxons had 14 deputies in Parliament. When this was done, Tisza was cynical enough to declare from the rostrum of the House: "We have succeeded in getting rid of these gentlemen, with only a few distressing exceptions!"

For Tisza, "these gentlemen" were the outstanding Romanian patriots whose reelection had been prevented by the new electoral law, and especially by the arbitrary means which characterized the election. Tisza in his speech in Parliament on July 11, 1910, described them as "foam fortresses" and a *fata morgana* ["an illusion"]. What is clear is that he preferred them out of Parliament rather than occupying seats in it. The "distressing exceptions" were the handful of deputies who had managed to overcome all the difficulties and obstacles which the Hungarian electoral system had placed in their way, so that they could come to Budapest and there voice the claims of the millions of oppressed Romanians.

And even this small number of Romanian deputies was too many for Tisza!

One can easily imagine how Tisza felt on the day when Austria-Hungary was at war with the Allies, while Romania, rejecting proposals that came from Vienna and Berlin, sided diplomatically with the Allies. It is easier to imagine his attitude toward the Transylvanian Romanians when free Romania declared war on Hungary.

In 1914 the government headed by Tisza issued no less than thirty-three decrees designed to "increase the material means necessary to carry out the Magyarization policy"—to quote Ion Clopotel, the historian of events in Transylvania from 1914 until its union with Romania.

The freedom of the Romanian press was eliminated. Vasile Goldis's newspaper, *The Romanian*, was suppressed. Romanian public meetings were prohibited. The Hungarian state assumed control over the administration of the Romanian banks. The autonomy of the Romanian church was violated, and its national gatherings and congresses were permitted to convene in session only in the presence of government inspectors. The Romanian population in Transylvania was removed from the jurisdiction of the courts of law and placed under the jurisdiction of the military courts—an exceptional procedure. The law dealing with traitors to the motherland, which was originally decreed in 1915 (Law XVIII), intensified even more the atmosphere of terror in which the Transylvanian Romanians had been living since World War I broke out. Mere information lodged against someone was enough to have a Romanian's possessions sequestered, while he himself was interned or subjected to other perils.

The prisons in Brasov, Fagaras, Cluj, and Seghedin were packed with these "traitors" whose only sin was that of being born Romanian on the Romanian land of Transylvania.

Archpriests, priests, old men, women, and children filled the camps that had been set up at Sopron, near the Austrian border, at Vepred, and at other points. The people were arrested for the most part in their own homes and in the most abusive manner. The detention regime under which they were obliged to live must have been very severe if one can be guided by the number of deaths in the camps and prisons, and if one recalls the harsh treatment meted out to Transylvanian Romanians in Hungarian prisons, even in time of peace.

Decree no. 4,000, put out in 1917 in the name of the presidency of the Hungarian council of ministers, put the crown on the former government's efforts at denationalization. It was designed to put into practice the program of Count Bethlen. According to this decree, Romanians could no longer buy any plot of land in the country without the prior permission of the ministry of agriculture in Budapest; in other words, the Romanians were prohibited from buying any land in the country because permission was flatly refused whenever they asked for it. In fact, this was precisely why the need for a permit had been instituted.

In the same year, Count Apponyi, who had again become minister of education and culture, set up a so-called "cultural zone" in southeastern Transylvania for the sole purpose of securing the complete Magyarization of the Romanian schools in the counties of Nasaud, Trei Scaune, Brasov, Fagaras, Hunedoara, and others—that is, precisely in those regions where the Romanian schools had offered resistance against previous Magyarizing actions. The immediate consequence of Apponyi's new law was the suppression of 507 Romanian elementary schools in the above-mentioned counties.

All of these legislative measures were accompanied by what the American publicist Charles Upson Clark called the "petty persecution" of the police, exercised in all fields of activity. This persecution is compared by the same author with the persecution exercised by the Austrians in Riva and the Germans in Schleswig. This oppression included dozens of insults and injustices which the country and town policemen committed against the Romanians, who did not have any means to defend themselves.

Persecution

These small persecutions, which took place day in and day out, acted like a daily poison. They were to assume an exceptionally serious character when Romania declared war on the Central Powers.

It is estimated that some 500,000 Transylvanian Romanians were arrested and sent to fight on various battlefields for a cause which was not theirs. It is easy to imagine which Hungarian soldiers had the honor of fighting in the front lines if one keeps in mind Hungarian hostility toward the Romanians.

"After depriving Transylvania of all of its youth," said N. Polizu-Micsunesti in his book dedicated to Nicolae Filipescu, "atrocities were committed against the old people. Even the wounded had to serve as wagoners. Priests and old women were thrown into dungeons."

At Sibiu, according to the Transylvanian poet, Octavian Goga, women and priests were placed in chains and then taken out into the streets at a time when people were emerging from the theaters, where Magyars and Transylvanian Saxons spat in their faces. [N. Polizu-Micsunesti: "N. Filipescu."]

"There was no field of public activity," wrote Ion Clopotel, in his book, *The 1918 Revolution and Transylvania's Union with Romania*, "where liberties were not suspended, and no one knew what the next day might bring."

The Romanians on the other side of the Carpathians were not indifferent to the fate of their brothers over the mountains. During the period of neutrality, a strong nationalist political current had become evident in the kingdom of Romania, which asked for Romania to enter the war on the side of the Allies as a matter of urgency in order to liberate the Transylvanian Romanians from the yoke of Magyar domination.

9. TRANSYLVANIA AND WORLD WAR I

The National Action Movement

The Romanian masses were electrified by the National Action movement which had gathered around a number of prominent Romanians, conspicuous among whom were the two famous Romanian statesmen, Take Ionescu (the "European," as Clemenceau called him) and Nicolae Filipescu, about whom Robert de Flers wrote that "not only does he love this country but he is crazy (*il est fou*) about it." In addition, there was Octavian Goga, Vasile Lucaci, a martyr of the Transylvanian cause, and many other political leaders.

The enthusiasm which greeted General Pau when he passed through Romania provided significant evidence of the sentiments which animated the Romanians of the kingdom at that time, the more so because the arrival of a German field marshal in Bucharest had been met with noteworthy coldness by Romanian public opinion.

In order to understand the mindset which was characteristic of the city of Bucharest during the second year of Romania's neutrality, it is sufficient to quote from the final words of a speech made by Filipescu on behalf of National Action on February 15, 1915.

Addressing the country's sovereign, King Ferdinand, Filipescu said: "You are God's missionary, sent here to fulfill the dream of the nation. Your Majesty, the glory we all wish you is to be crowned at Alba-Julia—for which we are prepared to die on the Plain of Turda."

One should not forget that, at the time this speech was made, Romania was bound to the Central Powers by treaty and that the country's government had a strict policy of neutrality.

If the enthusiastic solidarity of the Romanian people on the other side of the Carpathians with their brothers in Hungary can be characterized as a purely sentimental one, the rapprochement with the Allies, which was forcefully demanded by Romanian political leaders, was also given strength by imperious practical considerations.

If Austria-Hungary were to emerge victorious when the war was over, the fate of the Transylvanian Romanians as a nation was forever sealed—all the more so because the victorious Hungarians would have represented one of the greatest dangers to the independence of Romania itself.

In a famous speech in the Chamber of Deputies on December 16-17, 1915, the great Romanian statesman Take Ionescu, raised the matter of a possible Austro-Hungary victory in the war. Addressing the deputies, he said: "Can you imagine that Hungary would tolerate that we go on living independently here?"

The Romanians had no other choice. In order to preserve the Romanian national character and spirit in Transylvania, and in order to assure the independence and territorial integrity of the kingdom, they were constrained to follow the only policy which complied both with national ideas and the vital interests of the Romanian people—a policy which Ionescu called "the policy of national instinct."

"In the heart of all Romanians, from the village teacher to the politician," said Ionescu, "there is written: 'Transylvanian national unity!' . . . Each people has the right to live its own life, to live it with all other people who share its national identity, because only in that way can it have a civilization of its own which can then become part of world civilization."

There were two ideals in conflict. The first was that of a united and heterogeneous Hungary. The second was that of a united Romania embracing the onetime province of Dacia—the fulfillment of a natural aspiration to make whole again an entity which had been divided over the centuries. The clash between these two ideals was becoming visible on both sides of the Carpathians. By the policy of violence, the Hungarians had created an abyss between these two conceptions. Things had gone so far that, in the words of Ionescu, "No concession was any longer possible, one party's life excluding the life of the other."

Count Tisza had dealt with this same situation in one of

his better known speeches in the Hungarian Parliament on July 11, 1910. On that occasion he said:

Our non-Magyar fellow citizens should, in the first place, take into account the fact that they belong to a national state—a state which is not a conglomerate of a peoples of different races, but a state which was created and brought to its present status by only one nation. This nation imprinted upon it the ineffaceable stamp of its own individuality. I have always been a partisan of brotherly understanding with our nationalities [*sic!*], and I shall remain one. It is my greatest joy to offer them everything which can serve the national character and the national unity of the Magyar state. But I am not going to do more than that. This is the rock that will break the head of anyone who tries to shatter it!

At the time he made this speech, Tisza was not an unimportant deputy whose statements had value only as a personal opinion. He was, on the contrary, the leader of a major party, the Party of National Labor, which, with 257 deputies, had a large majority in parliament.

His viewpoint was that of virtually all Hungarians. Hungary was regarded as a united, homogeneous state, in the life of which the problem of the nationalities was only incidental. The conclusion was as false as the premise on which it was based. It was, indeed, an aberration from reality to assert that Hungary was a homogeneous state in the face of the fact that the millions of non-Magyars who lived in it conferred on the Hungarian state a most impressive heterogeneous and polynational aspect.

But Tisza in the passage we have quoted, gave perhaps the best characterization, in reverse, of his state when he said that it was *not* a "conglomerate of peoples of different races." In reality, the subject peoples of the Hungarian kingdom enjoyed all rights on one condition only: That they give up their nationality and be swallowed up by Magyarism.

"Let them join our ranks!" Tisza exclaimed one day, addressing himself to the Romanians in Transylvania from the tribune of the Parliament. "In this way we shall be able to have a big and strong Hungary."

Mutatis mutandis, virtually the same words could be heard

from the other side of the Carpathians—but this time the condition was not posed that the subject people give up its national life. On the contrary, they were told that what was waiting for them was the fulfillment of their hopes and ideals, which had been handed down from one generation to the next of Transylvanian Romanians. In a language that they didn't even understand, they were asked by Budapest to bind themselves to a concept of glory to which they remained absolutely indifferent. From Romania, on the other hand, they were able to hear "the call of the heart," urging them, in the language of their Dacian-Roman ancestors, to achieve their natural unity—an organic unity which brought together the sons of the same nation.

Thus, Hungarian intransigence hastened the evolution of history in Transylvania.

Erzberger and Iuliu Maniu

In his memoirs, *Souvenirs de Guerre* (Paris, 1921), Erzberger, the head of the Catholic center in the German Parliament and a former minister of the Reich, described the mission on which he had been sent by Germany for the purpose of preventing Italy and Romania from declaring war on his country and siding with the Allies. He spoke about the stubbornness with which the Hungarian leaders, during the first year of the war, refused to satisfy legitimate Romanian demands. The Hungarian viewpoint, he said, was unchanged over the centuries: "No concessions for the Romanians!"

"These were not territorial concessions," said Erzberger, "but had to do only with the legitimate aspirations of the Romanians in Hungary. Baron Burian, who was considered Tisza's spokesman in Vienna, flatly rejected any suggestion of conciliation vis-à-vis the Romanians." The Hungarian prime minister, whom Erzberger had visited prior to writing this, would not even admit that the Romanian demands were legitimate. "He asserted," said Erzberger, "that there was no power which pursued such a tolerant policy towards its nationalities as Hungary did." In short, everything was fine and everything was going to be better in the most happy Hungary of the last Hapsburg.

Voltaire's hero, Candide, could not have put it better.

Iuliu Maniu, who had been a member of the Romanian

delegation received by Erzberger in Vienna and whose mission it had been to inform the German envoy of the demands of the Transylvanian Romanians, described in the following words the progress of the talks between Erzberger and the Transylvanian representatives:

> In 1915, the Central Powers were in a difficult situation. Emperor Wilhelm tried to win the Romanians in Transylvania over to the side of the Central Powers. With this end in view, he sent Erzberger to Vienna in charge of a mission to negotiate an agreement with the Romanian delegates. In Lichtenstein Palace in Vienna, a delegation consisting of Aurel Popovici, Goldis, and myself contacted Erzberger. We, the delegates, explained to Erzberger that the Romanians in Transylvania possessed no rights, and that it was only natural that Romania would not fight side by side with those who were disposed to kill its sons. Erzberger replied that the Romanians would be given the rights they were claiming. I answered that I did not believe this because promises had been made many times before, but the Romanian people had never been given anything.

The outcome of the negotiations, as had been expected and as Maniu had foreseen, was completely negative.

Erzberger related that "Stefan Tisza refused to enter any negotiations with Romania concerning the granting of new rights to the Romanians in Hungary."

The boundless ambition of the Hungarians and the total blindness of the Hungarian political leaders "made impossible a friendly solution of the conflict between the dominating and the dominated nations." Thanks to Hungarian intransigence, only one solution was left that might settle the problem—an appeal to arms.

The Romanian War (Ion Bratianu)

It was the fate of Ion Bratianu, as head of state of the Romanian government, to make the decision on Romanian entrance into the war on the side of the Allies for the purpose of achieving the national ideal of Transylvanian freedom.

In the light of the documentation available today, Bratianu's actions during the period of Romania's neutrality can be better understood than it was by contemporaries who were in possession of all the details.

Bratianu pursued the realization of the Romanian national ideal with great statesmanship and in very difficult circumstances. On the one hand, Romanian public opinion favored the immediate entrance of Romania on the side of the Allies. On the other hand, there was the insistent pressure of Germany and Austria-Hungary which sought to have Romania opt for their side and which at times took the form of direct threats of invasion. Finally, there were the pressures of the Allies designed to force the hand of Bratianu even before they had agreed to the Romanian demands for Transylvania, Banat, and Bukovina. In this complex situation, Bratianu guided the course of Romanian politics with unique ability.

"The diplomatic history of the European war," wrote C. Kiritescu, a Romanian professor, "no matter what the viewpoint of the historians judging the events, unanimously acknowledges the basic truth that Romania was represented in the negotiations by a statesman who was a great patriot, a man of great intellectual power and extraordinary diplomatic ability." (*The History of the War for the Realization of Romania.*)

When the Allies registered their agreement on Romanian claims, Romania immediately entered the war against Austria-Hungary. In fact, on August 13, 1916, Sturmer, Sazonov's successor at the Russian ministry for external affairs, accepted Romania's conditions dealing with the cession of the Romanian territories by the Austro-Hungarian empire. Four days later, on August 17, Romania signed a treaty of alliance with the Allies. In return for a guarantee on the part of the Allies that there would be a definitive solution to the Transylvanian problem, Romania obligated itself to enter the war against the Central Powers by August 28, 1916, at the very latest.

Today, when, thanks to the documents in our possession, we can better understand the history of this recent past, we can appreciate the precise foresight which Romanian statesmen displayed in dealing with the fate of the Transylvanian Romanians, allowing for the possibility of an Austrian victory.

The Secret Plans of the Magyars

In his book about Transylvania, Romulus Seisanu lays bare one of the famous plans, drawn up by the Hungarians at a time when they still hoped to emerge from the war victorious, with regard to the problem of nationalities in general and of the Romanians in particular. On the one hand, Tisza paraded a conciliatory attitude toward the Romanians and negotiated a reconciliation with the Romanian national party, which had been revived in Transylvania. The secret goal of the Hungarians was to weaken the position of the leaders of this party if the Romanians in Transylvania sided with the Central Powers. On the other hand, the Hungarians had made secret plans, in agreement with Archduke Joseph, with a view to seeking a slice of Romanian territory on the eastern side of the Carpathians.

"In the same way that a military security zone had been set up in the eastern regions of the German empire during the Middle Ages," said Seisanu, "a zone later known under the name of Oest-Mark and which later on was the nucleus of Austria—in this same way, Tisza, with Archduke Joseph's consent, aspired to stab the Romanian spirit in the heart by setting up the military strategic zone—under the guise of a Magyar Oest-Mark—which was to dominate both sizes of the Carpathians."

According to the plans of the two Austro-Hungarian statesmen, the dividing line cut deeply into both Moldavia and Wallachia. The territories which were to be Magyar included the whole eastern part of the Carpathians, the valleys of the Lotru, the Olt, the Dambovita, the Buzau, the Teleajen and the Bistrita Rivers, and, last but not least, the oil fields, the most important asset of the Romanian soil on this side of the Carpathians.

In order to accomplish the complete Magyarization of the region, Archduke Joseph's plans provided for the Hungarian colonization of the entire security region on both sides of the Carpathians. This was designed to prevent forever a Romanian revival in Transylvania by interposing a string of Magyar posts between the two Romanian blocs on either side of the Carpathians.

Even more revealing of the mentality of the Magyar leaders is the fact that the image of a Romanian spirit, submerged forever within the hulk of Magyarism, persisted even after the Hungarians had begun to lose hope in the final success of the Central Powers.

In the peace proposals addressed to the Allies by Austria-

Hungary, through the agency of Prince Sixte de Bourbon, the question of the eastern borders of the empire was passed over in silence because it was the intention of the Hungarians to give themselves free scope in the east, so that they could settle as they pleased the question of the border between Hungary and Romania.

But World War I had not been fought for four years and millions of people had not shed their blood on the battlefields so that they could have a new Hungarian despotism established in Europe, or so that the anachronistic form of government previously maintained by the Hungarians in central Europe could be resurrected.

It was predestined that, according to the inexorable evolution of mankind's destiny, the conglomerate represented by the dual monarchy would collapse like a sandcastle at the first violent commotion.

The attitude of the Hungarian leaders when the failure of their policy had begun to take shape is deserving of mention. Not even in those final moments before the disaster struck did their understanding permit them to give up any of their elitist political conceptions.

Count Tisza's words addressed to the Croats and Serbs a few weeks before the fall of the monarchy could serve as a preface to an anthology on intolerance: "We may lose," said Tisza, on the occasion of a visit to Bosnia and Herzegovina at the end of September 1918. "But before losing we shall still find the necessary force to destroy you." [Kr. Novak, *Der Sturtz der Mittelmächte*—"The Collapse of the Central Powers."]

This was the same Tisza who four years previously had declared in the Hungarian Parliament, "we have against us the hostility of the nationalities because our kind of patriotism manifests itself in such baneful ways and is unworthy of the gallant character of the Magyar people." It is worth noting, too, that the words he addressed to the Bosnians were uttered at a time when President [Woodrow] Wilson's voice, favoring the self-determination of the peoples of the Hapsburg monarchy, had already been raised.

10. THE END OF WORLD WAR I BRINGS FREEDOM

"The national aspiration of peoples," President Wilson had declared in the American Congress on February 11, 1918, "must be respected: In the future, peoples must be governed only according to their own free will. Self-determination is not an empty phrase. It is a principle, an imperative which statesmen can no longer ignore, for if they do so, it will turn against them."

The president of the United States was announcing to the peoples who had been oppressed for centuries the news that a new world order had come into existence. The Hungarian prime minister, it is noteworthy, had threatened the same peoples with destruction because they had dared to take up Wilson's words as their creed.

But events, moving with the speed of lightning, left the Hungarian political leaders far behind. At the eleventh hour, they were unable to carry out their odious plan to destroy the nationalities—a goal they had not been able to achieve in a thousand years despite the use of the most violent methods.

The end of the dual monarchy—this state monstrosity which had endured for so long in the heart of Europe—was hastened by a complex of circumstances. There was Marshal Franchet d'Esperey's offensive in the south of the Balkans; there was the breaking of the front at Drobropolje; there was the rapid advance of the Allies toward Sofia and Constantinople; there was the surrender of Bulgaria and Turkey; there was the reentry of Romania into the war at the end of October 1918*; and, finally, there were the movements for national liberation of the non-Magyar peoples in the dual monarchy.

---

*When Romania declared war on the Central Powers in August 1917, it did so on the expectation that this action would be supported by Russian troops. However, the Bolshevik revolution intervened, the Russian troops did not arrive, and much of Romania was occupied by the Central Powers. Romania re-entered the war in October 1918.

In a written statement to Napoleon after the battle of Austerlitz, in which he had advised the emperor to maintain Austria as a state, the great Talleyrand described in a few cogent words the grave instability of the Austro-Hungarian empire—which was nevertheless to continue its existence for another century.

"The Austrian monarchy," said the brilliant French diplomat, "is a mixture of states which are weakly united and which are divided from each other by language, custom, religion, and political and civil regime. In fact, they do not have anything in common but their head of state. It goes without saying that such a power is weak."

. . . And, of course, doomed to destruction!

In the Crown Council which took place in Vienna on October 15, 1918, Emperor Carol, the last Hapsburg, made a serious effort to prevent the downfall of the monarchy by attempting to turn it into a federal state, in which independence was granted to all nationalities. This was a belated acknowledgement of the justice of the principle which had been formulated by the Romanian Aurel Popovici, in 1906.

The Crown Council took place only two weeks before the revolution broke out in Hungary. The attitude of the participants in the Council defies comprehension. Although the ground was disappearing from under their feet, the blind passion which governed their nationalities policy prevented them from understanding the real state of affairs.

Hungary's Prime Minister, Wekele, who had succeeded Tisza in April 1918, but who acted under the political direction of the ex-prime minister, strongly opposed any change in the regime of the dual monarchy. Indeed, he went to the extent of threatening Austria with starvation if the Emperor included Hungary in the proposed federation.

A year before this, Tisza had taken the same attitude on the question of Romanian independence within a federal Austrian state. To one of Count Czernen's envoys who had suggested the idea, he declared that "anyone trying to deprive Hungary of as much as one square meter of its territory will be shot."

The Hungarian threat had a major effect on the decisions the emperor was to take the day after the Crown Council met in Vienna. Indeed, in the message he addressed to "his peoples" on October 16, 1918, he granted them the right to organize themselves according to the principle of national autonomy—with the exception of the Romanians and other nations coming under the "Holy Crown of Hungary." These nations, according to the announced intention of the emperor, were to go on bearing the yoke of Magyar domination forever.

While the Hapsburg empire tottered on the brink of collapse, and while the wind of liberty was demolishing all artificial obstacles which absolutist rule had created between sons of the same nation, the Hungarians stubbornly clung to the maintenance of an antiquated political system which was bound to disappear forever in darkness. Indeed, this was one of the most surprising historical examples of improvidence and lack of political skill, combined with obstinacy in embracing a hopelessly lost cause.

While the emperor's message proclaimed the untouchability of the territories belonging to the Holy Crown, Hungary's unity had ceased being a reality and was no more than an apparent formality. The peoples who had until that point been subdued by violence were on the march to liberty, and nothing could stop them any longer.

The Hungarian Revolution

Surrounded by hostile faces, the Romanian deputy, Alexandru Vaida Voievod, took the floor in the Hungarian Chamber on October 18, 1918, and declared on behalf of the Romanian nation in Hungary that he "did not acknowledge the right of the Magyar parliament to represent it at the peace conference." He demanded that "in line with the natural right of any nation to dispose of its own destiny, the Romanian nation should be entitled to decide on its form of government and on its status among the free nations."

Amidst a terrible uproar in the Chamber, Voievod, who was later to become a Romanian prime minister, finished his historic declaration with these words: "After much suffering and after struggles that have gone on for centuries, the Romanian nation in the Austro-Hungarian monarchy expects and demands the acknowledgement of its undeniable and inalienable right to a national life."

At the end of October 1918, the revolution broke out in Hungary. On October 31, Count Tisza was assassinated. On November 1, Emperor Carol abdicated. A new government, headed by Count Mihail Karoly, was set up.

Oscar Iaszi, who was the minister of nationalities in the radical government of Karoly, defined the state of affairs in Hungary at the time of the revolution as "chaotic." In *Revolution and Counterrevolution in Hungary*, Iaszi further said that "even under the new regime, the old mistakes of the past were still committed."

"The old regime," said Iaszi, "owed its strength primarily to three political leaders, Windischgratz, Vazsonyi, and Sztereny."

The concessions these leaders offered the Romanians were minimal. Even during the revolution, the Hungarians failed to understand the great demands of the time. They tried to secure their own freedom as a result of the revolution of 1918—but they offered only a glimmer of liberty to the other nationalities. In this skillful political maneuver, Karoly, who favored the entente, tried to win the sympathy of the Allies so that he would not be obliged to make larger sacrifices afterwards. It was a repetition of the experience with the "liberal" revolutionaries of 1848.

December 1, 1918

The Romanians in Transylvania, who had never forgotten the betrayal of the Romanian cause by Kossuth's revolutionaries in 1848, did not wait any longer to be offered their liberty by the new Hungarian republic which had been set up on November 16, 1918. On December 1, in a huge meeting and plebiscite held at Alba-Julia, under the leadership of the old Transylvanian patriot, Gheorghe Pop de Basesti, they declared enthusiastically: "What we want is the union with Romania of the Romanians on this side of the mountains and the other territories in which they live."

The Hungarian newspapers of the time estimated the number of Transylvanian Romanian representatives attending this meeting at approximately 100,000.

The union of Transylvania with Romania was not, as the Magyar propagandists wanted those abroad to believe, the consequence of treaties that "Hungary had been forced to sign" or of "outside influences." [See Horvath, *Weltkrieg, Friedensdiktat und Nachkriegsregelung*. ("The Dictated Peace and the Postwar Settlement.")] It was the result of a slow process of evolution. Transylvania had achieved its destiny.

For the Romanians on both sides of the Carpathians, the 1st of December 1918 was like a light flickering near the horizon at the end of a long journey. From somewhere in the future, it indicated the way to them. On the day they reached this light, their ideal was fulfilled, and the union with Romania was accomplished.

The patience with which the Romanians had been awaiting the coming of this day was characteristic of the nature of the Romanian people, tempered by historical experience. Perhaps it is also a consequence of the quiet confidence of the Romanian people that their centuries-old dreams would come true. The Transylvanians *knew* that the day of union with Romania, the day of liberty, would eventually arrive. They knew that the promise of this liberty lay in a natural law which moved inexorably toward fulfillment, and that this law could not forever be obstructed by obstacles erected to serve the baser interests of other peoples.

The Beginning of a New Era

Transylvania was joined to Romania. It was not done by the will of others, but by the will of its own people. It was in vain that the professors in Budapest took issue with this development by falsifying in the most flagrant way the real evolution of events.

The action of the Allied powers was limited to ascertaining and ratifying the desire of a province which had been Romanian for centuries to be united with the Romanians on the other side of the Carpathians.

"The union of the Romanian people," said the Romanian academician Ion Lupas, himself a Transylvanian, "is not the work of a single person, or of a province, or of a generation. It is the product rather of an intense struggle over the centuries by the best sons of the Romanian people."

Professor Horvath and his colleagues at the University of Budapest, in all their works intended for distribution abroad, spoke of "bilateral agreements which had been vitiated by the lack of free consent on the part of one of the parties involved." They also spoke of "arbitrary decisions" and of many other petty things, worthy of a trivial trial in a small country courthouse over the possession of a square foot of land.

The process which came to an end on December 1, 1918,

as a result of the firm and explicit decision of the Transylvanian Romanians to be united with the kingdom of Romania, was centuries in the making. This process was not brought to an end by a verdict coldly pronounced by an indifferent court, but by a national revolution.

Fortunately for Transylvania, the Romanian revolution of December 1, 1918, took place without any bloodshed. The explosive desire for liberty on the part of the oppressed peoples was so great, indeed, that no one could have stifled it even with bloodshed. On October 28, revolution erupted in Prague and Krakow. On October 29, the flag of liberty was hoisted in Zagreb and Lubin. On October 30, revolt broke out in Austria. On October 31, there began the disintegration of the Hungarian conglomerate. As clear-sighted minds had foreseen for decades, a mighty shakeup in central Europe was enough to expose the fictitious unity of the Austro-Hungarian empire, which disintegrated into its component parts. This was the authentic political reality.

"Like any evil," said Loucarevici in his book, *Jugoslawiens Enstähung* ("The Birth of Yugoslavia") [Vienna, 1928], "the world war also had its good aspects: The last remnants of a medieval feudal absolutism were abolished."

The historic action at Alba-Julia brought to an end a sad chapter in the history of the Romanian people in Transylvania. At the same time it marked the beginning of a new era—an era that was not without difficult moments at the beginning, nor devoid of great suffering in more recent times. After a thousand years of bondage, intolerance, and oppression, the Romanian people had finally achieved the element needed to complete their normal evolution—liberty.

"The Romanian people," said Nicolae Iorga, "is a people which has been born free and lived free, and liberty is the quintessential and imperative condition for its existence."

The Alba-Julia Proclamation

The proclamation of December 1, 1918, represented the manner of living the Romanians had selected for themselves at the moment when they stepped over the threshold of national history. Its essential points are deserving of mention since they not only constitute a political program but also because of what they say about the attitude of yesterday's slaves, now masters in their land, toward their centuries-old oppressors.

The Romanians did not think of revenge, but in a gesture of high moral standing, reached out a conciliatory hand to the Hungarians with whom they were destined to live together on Transylvania's land.

The national assembly in Alba-Julia decided:

1. There shall be complete national liberty for all the peoples living in the area. Each people has the right to be educated, governed, and judged in its own language by its own representatives. Each people will be granted the right to be represented in the legal structure of the government of the country, in proportion to its numbers.

2. There shall be complete freedom for all religions existing in the state.

3. A truly democratic regime shall be introduced in all fields of public life.

The right to vote shall be universal, direct, equal, and secret.

4. Freedom of the press and of association shall be guaranteed, as shall the right to convene meetings and to distribute propaganda representing all human creeds.

What a contrast between the liberal attitude of the Romanian revolutionaries of 1918 and the narrowness of conception which characterized the Hungarian revolution of 1848!

No branch of social life was omitted from the guarantees in this declaration whose charter was to govern the future life of the peoples of Transylvania.

Since the overwhelming majority of the people were peasants, Transylvania urgently needed a land reform program designed "to promote both a social leveling and an increase of production."

"Every peasant," said the proclamation of December 1, "should have as much land as he and his family can work."

In a country where great landlords owned immense land areas, sometimes of 420,000 hectares, the agrarian expropriation announced by the Romanians had an even more pronounced revolutionary impact than did the national revolution which led to Transylvania's union with Romania.

Born in bondage, but nurtured by the most sanguine ideals of liberty and brotherhood, the inaugural declaration which opened the period of free Romanian history in Transylvania, terminated with this commitment to a better future: "The general assembly expresses its wish that the peace conference accomplish the cooperation of all the free nations, in such a way that liberty and justice are guaranteed for all nations, big or small, and that war ceases to be a means for the settlement of international disputes."

Unfortunately, these hopes for an international order in which war was to be forever abolished were scattered to the winds, only two decades after they were articulated by the Transylvanian Romanians meeting at Alba-Julia. But we must not forget that, during those two decades, as a member of the European family of nations, Romania did nothing to disturb the peace. Indeed, its politicians, headed by Ion I. C. Bratianu, Take Ionescu, Iuliu Maniu, Nicolae Titulescu, G. G. Mironescu, Grigore Gafencu, and all the others who succeeded them in the direction of Romanian foreign policy, endeavored over the years to cooperate in the effort to strengthen peace in Europe.

In particular, Romania's attitude toward the other nationalities who resided in Transylvania played an essential role in the maintenance of peace in the Danubian region. This was so because the Romanians always kept alive in their minds the memory of the lamentable end of the vast Austro-Hungarian empire, which was a natural consequence of the total lack of understanding of the nationalities issue displayed by the Hungarian leaders.

Sol lucet omnibus

An eminently tolerant people, as are all peoples of Latin origin, the Romanians wanted to make friends, by kindness and equal treatment, with the Magyars living within Romania's borders.

In May 1924, Iuliu Maniu declared: "We must guarantee the civil and political rights of those who belong to a racial, language, or religious minority."

Himself a Transylvanian who had condemned the intolerant methods of previous Magyar governments, Maniu did everything possible to win the support of the Hungarian minority, with the help of the liberal laws which governed them.

In the same year, Vaida-Voievod, in a speech at the Social Institute in Bucharest, supported the policy of liberal treatment of the Hungarians. On that occasion he said:

The Hungarians made a suicidal mistake. We can draw instructive conclusions from the Magyars' fall. The weakening of the minorities does not automatically result in a strengthening of the Romanian element. To consume the energy of the state in an endless internal struggle between a fourth or a fifth part of the population and the rest of its citizens, while it might not jeopardize the state's political-geographic borders, would mean to shock the sentiments and the secure feeling about their rights, which is in the hearts of our citizens, and this would lead to internal unrest.

Finally, in order to present a complete picture of the preponderant conception at the time that the laws governing minorities were legislated, we quote the following declaration by the minister for internal affairs Octavian Goga in 1927: "We are trying to satisfy everyone, not by committing acts of violence against our fellow citizens, but by making use of the feeling for justice which must be the foundation of our political principles."

These principles did not derive from any momentary interest—this is confirmed by the manner in which they were put into practice—but were the expression of the Romanian approach toward the treatment of foreign peoples whom history had brought to the territory of Romania. After the passage of half a century, the two contrasting mentalities were characterized by different active attitudes.

When Count Tisza had been attacked before the war in the Hungarian Parliament by the ultrachauvinistic deputies for what seemed to them his moderate policy toward the Romanians, the Hungarian prime minister—who in his negotiations with the Romanians in 1913 had preserved intact his orthodox approach to total Magyarization—backed down. Thus, in the history of Magyarism, he could not be accused of abdicating from Magyarism's higher cause, which for the entire governing class of the Hungarian nation was identified with the policy of ostentatious and intransigent domination.

When in 1868 an ultranationalist deputy in the Romanian Parliament argued in favor of the intolerant treatment of Romanian minorities, Bratianu, who later was to play so important a role in Romanian history, immediately assailed this proposal, using the weight of his very great influence.

Addressing himself to the handful of Romanian ultrana-
tionalists, Bratianu said: "If some of you can get some of your
electors drunk with such words, you are going to have to do it
on your own account, and you are going to have to pay a heavy
price for it. You convey false ideas to your electors—and false
ideas can never serve the good interests of any society."

Thus, the attitude of tolerance and understanding which
characterized Romanian treatment of the minority nationalities was an enduring phenomenon. This attitude is an attribute
of the truly strong. After ten centuries of living in darkness,
the Transylvanian Romanians proved to the world that, in
their return to a national life, they were as strong as their
Dacian-Roman ancestors.

The political approach which they chose at the moment
they regained their strength constituted a repudiation of that
darkness which had been their implacable fate for a thousand
years.

Sol lucet omnibus ("The sun shines upon all").

Under this insignia, the life of the various nationalities in
Transylvania continued, but now it was under Romanian rule.

11. HUNGARY AFTER THE TRIANON TREATY

> *"On ne doit pas oublier que la trace des frontières de la Hongrie a fait l'objet de la part de tous les Alliés d'un examen minutieux, que chacun de ses éléments a été discuté, qu'il existe entre eux une étroite solidarité."*
> (One should not forget that the delineation of the frontiers of Hungary was the subject of very careful examination by all of the Allies, that every one of its elements was discussed, and that there exists between them [the Allies] a close solidarity of viewpoint.)
>
> *M. Guernier*
> Reporter of the law sanctioning the Trianon treaty

Hungary after Trianon:
A Unitary, Homogeneous State

In Granger's *World Geography* published in 1922, the Hungarian population in 1910 is given as 20,886,000 inhabitants, according to Hungarian statistics. Of this number, the Hungarians constituted a little more than 9,000,000 and the non-Magyars more than 11,000,000. The latter category included 3,000,000 Romanians, 2,000,000 Germans, 2,000,000 Slovaks, 1,800,000 Croats, 1,100,000 Serbs, 472,000 Ruthenians, a few hundred thousand Jews, and 470,000 other nationalities. According to traditional practice, the Jews were included in the Hungarian total.

Again, according to Hungarian statistics, Hungary's population on January 1, 1930, consisted of only 8,686,519 inhabitants, of whom 8,100,812 were Hungarian, and 685,000 belonged to the non-Magyar nationalities.

A comparison between these two Hungarian population statistics shows that, while the figure for the non-Magyar population had decreased enormously, from 11,000,000 to 685,000, the figures for the Hungarian population proper had dropped by only a little more than 1,000,000. This comparison also reveals a fundamental change between the ethnic structure of the two Hungarian states—the Hungarian state of before World War I and the Hungary which came into existence after the national revolutions which led to the disintegration of the Hapsburg empire in 1918.

In prewar Hungary, the Hungarians were submerged in an enormous mass of ethnic minorities which constituted the mixture of nations that came under the Holy Crown of Hungary. In the postwar period, the Hungarians secured for themselves a state of a unitarian, homogeneous character, thus realizing the dream of the Magyar nationalists of the first decades of our century.

"From an ethnic and linguistic viewpoint," said Alajos Kovacs in his study of the population of Hungary, "the Hungarian state after the Trianon treaty is more unitary than greater Hungary before the world war. The inhabitants who used Hungarian as their mother tongue constituted 92.1 percent of the total population." Kovacs noted that 74.2 percent of those who did not count Hungarian as their mother tongue could nevertheless speak Hungarian. Accordingly, within the geographic limits of the Hungary established by the Treaty of Trianon, the percentage of those who spoke Hungarian rose to the overwhelming figure of 98 percent.

A comparative diagram of the two Hungarian statistics—that for the prewar period and that for the postwar period—constitutes, even on summary examination, conclusive proof of the scrupulous manner in which Hungary's borders had been delineated at Trianon.

In a state which presented such a large variety of nationalities as Hungary—which in many places formed inlets and islands of Hungarians within the surrounding mass of nationalities, as well as inlets and islands of nationalities within the surrounding Hungarian mass—it was, of course, impossible to achieve a perfect delineation of frontiers.

While perfection may not have been achieved, it was nevertheless possible, on the basis of the enormous informational material submitted by the interested parties, to achieve at least a satisfactory delineation. It is true that in the regions ceded by the dual monarchy one might find Hungarian islands here and there—the result of an age-old infiltration. But it is no less true that Hungary, despite the fact that it was much smaller after the Trianon treaty, also contained minority enclaves, which included, according to Hungarian statistics, 700,000 non-Magyars—Germans, Slovaks, Serbs, Croats, and Romanians.

Although the Hungarians had succeeded at last in achieving, within the framework of the new Magyar state, the homogeneous unity which they had sought after, they still found little comfort in the thought that the Great Hungary of thirty million Magyars was a dead dream.

For twenty years the Hungarians kept on complaining, to the four corners of the world, about the "great injustice" that had been done to them by what they called the "dictated peace" (*Friedensdiktat*), on the basis of which their country had lost 71 percent of its territory and 63 percent of its population. In fact, the Trianon Treaty only represented the ratification of the will of millions of non-Magyars.

It is quite true that the figures presented by the Hungarian geographers and historians are impressive, but they do not tell us what relationship existed between the size of the losses suffered by post-World War I Hungary and the justice of minority claims.

What was taken away from the Hungarians was only equal to what they had conquered over the centuries by arbitrary methods and by violence. In short, the Hungarians themselves are the only ones to blame for the size of the sacrifice they had to accept in 1920.

How Much Territory do the Hungarians Need?

The Hungarians wished to seize more territory than they were able to control with the limited means at their disposal—far too much in comparison with what fate had in store for them.

If we look at a Hungarian map showing the migrations of the Magyars over the centuries, we are constrained to wonder at the small space which sustained their ancestors in the region of the Ural Mountains before their invasion of Europe. After this invasion, they occupied the region between the Don and Dnieper rivers (Revieda) and, later on, the region situated south of Bessarabia and Moldavia (Atelkuz). They had occupied these regions only temporarily during the 6th, 8th, and 9th centuries A.D. Any one of these regions represented at the most one-tenth of the area which later maps gave to St. Stephen's Hungary. But they corresponded precisely to the territory the Magyar nation occupied on ethnographic maps drawn in the 19th and 20th centuries, especially that of the Hungarian cartographer Sandor Farkas, published in the *Magyar Geographic Atlas* of 1902.

This disparity between their numbers and the size of their territory could have been settled by the Hungarians in one of two ways—either by limiting themselves to the Alfold, or the low plain, which provided perhaps the most adequate conditions for the development of the national culture of the Magyar people, or else by pursuing a desperate policy of unlimited expansion, which would necessarily violate all the laws of natural evolution. Unfortunately, for themselves and for the native peoples who lived in the territories adjoining the areas where Arpad's tribes had settled down, the ancestors of today's Magyars chose the latter solution.

As a result of this choice, the Hungarians became lost in a historically negativist approach. Their efforts to achieve progress for their own people were tied to a parallel effort to impede the development of the native peoples—peaceful peoples, almost exclusively cultivators and shepherds, whom they found in Transylvania and the other regions surrounding the Alfold.

The ceaseless conflict between the dominant nation and the peoples dominated by it reached its climax with the national revolution of 1918, which resulted in the collapse of those states which had constituted the domain of the Holy Crown of Hungary.

The Hungarian state created after the war certainly had enough territory to secure for the Magyar nation a happy material and spiritual development. In this way the Hungarian state could have become an important factor in the maintenance of peace—if it had cooperated peacefully with the nations surrounding it. In fact, such cooperation was the goal of the peace treaties which had put an end to the bloodiest war mankind had ever known. George Clemenceau, addressing the German delegation to the peace conference on June 16, 1919, defined the role which the treaties were designed to play in the new order brought into existence by the Versailles Treaty. "The peace treaty," said the great French statesman, "establishes the basis for the peaceful and equitable cooperation of the peoples of Europe."

Revisionism at Any Cost

Agreements between nations, like all things human, cannot have an eternal character. Realizing this, those who drew up the Versailles Treaty had foreseen the probability that the text of the treaty under international law would have to undergo adjustment because of the imperious necessities which might later arise.

"The agreement," said Clemenceau, "can be modified from time to time in order to cope with new situations and conditions that might make their appearance."

It was only natural, therefore, that any revision of the treaty should, in the final analysis, be subordinated to the appearance of new situations. It was a very minor exception to the basic immutability of the treaty, which could not be extended to apply to its express provisions.

The new Hungarian leaders, however, endeavored to make a general rule of this exception. Without waiting for the development of a new situation which might have justified it, they began to make trouble by asking for a revision of the essential text of the treaty, in this way assailing the basic principles which constituted the European order after World War I. This was the first blow against a treaty which had brought peace to the continent; it was the first action to disturb the peace in postwar Europe.

"The mutilation of Hungary" was presented as one of the gravest injustices resulting from the treaty. The problem of revising the treaty, therefore, was no longer justified on the ground that certain provisions had become void due to new developments; the Hungarians were now arguing about the justice or the injustice of some of the basic terms that had been agreed to in 1919-20.

The Plan of Revisionist Action

The revisionist propaganda campaign mounted by the Magyars was very well planned. The Hungarians admittedly managed to impress some circles abroad through their persistent and skillful propaganda. (Had they not managed at a given moment to win sympathy even within the British Foreign Office, so that the famous case of the counterfeit French banknotes was no longer considered a serious offense but was described as a "nationalist activity?") As evidence there was the widely read article in the *London Times* of February 4, 1925, entitled "The Case of Hungary," in which Hungary was presented as an unfortunate country, surrounded by hostile and suspicious nations. The entire plan of this propaganda campaign—whose sophisticated arguments entrapped in its web hundreds of outstanding personalities who were completely ignorant of the real facts of the problem—can be reduced to two essential points:

1. When the new frontiers had been decided at Trianon, Hungary had been robbed of large territories which, by the nature of things, properly belonged to Hungary—in perpetuity.

2. Within the successor states that now governed in the areas that had been stripped from Hungary, the plight of the Hungarian minority was disastrous—so that in addition to being the victim of "unilateral" action, the Hungarian people also qualified as "unfortunate."

The premises on which the Hungarian spokesmen based their case were totally false. Magyar propaganda presented the Hungarian state which existed before the war as a model of ideal justice. True, a Hungary reduced in size to its postwar frontiers, when compared to the "ideal" Hungary that existed previously, appeared to have been "mutilated" by the postwar settlement. But the real facts were completely different. The Hungary which existed before the war was the product of the most flagrant injustices. To right this situation, the peoples had taken justice into their own hands, and the action they had taken had later been ratified by the peace agreements and treaties.

Premise no. 2 was as false as no. 1. The Hungarians claimed that prewar Hungary had been a real Eden for the subject nationalities, and that, conversely, the fate of the Hungarians who now lived as an ethnic minority in the successor states (Romania, Czechoslovakia, and Yugoslavia) was a real hell. Once again, reality was turned upside down—and this on purpose. The treatment of the Romanians in prewar Hungary had been described as "barbarous" by the most famous writers of the 19th and 20th centuries. As for the human treatment of the minority Hungarians in post-World War I Romania, we shall limit ourselves to quoting in the following pages the words of a number of the "persecuted" minority Hungarians themselves.

The Trianon "Injustice"

First of all, let us analyze the most important Hungarian accusation—an accusation which resulted in so many debates after the war and which, unfortunately, led anew to a violation of the integrity of the Romanian state and the Romanian people. This accusation has to do with the "injustice" the Hungarian people had suffered at Trianon through the allotment to Romania of territories which were ethnically Hungarian.

Needless to say, there are still many Hungarians who take the stand that the whole of Transylvania should have been allotted to Hungary since it had been under their domination for a thousand years. This is as though, in the history of peoples, there was a time limit which governs territorial acquisition, so that an injustice which is a thousand years old could be turned automatically, by the lapse of time, into a just order.

This was the viewpoint of the Hungarian chauvinists. It did not find an echo within the ranks of even the most passionate supporters of the Magyar case abroad. Indeed, this approach was considered unworkable and exaggerated even by famous Magyar personalities, such as the Hungarian ex-minister of justice, Dr. Emil Nagy. Nagy declared, "The Hungarians must give up the concept of the integrity of their prewar territories and should resign themselves to the loss of certain territories which were populated by compact masses of foreign nationalities."

What was left was the more modest viewpoint of those who, as late as 1940, had raised the question of a "correction" of the Romanian-Hungarian frontier established in 1920. These people were unquestionably surprised to find that even their most daring hopes were surpassed in the summer of 1940 when Transylvania was taken away from Romania, annexed to Hungary, and abused in the most senseless way. The nightmare of the Transylvanian-Romanians had started anew.

The Hungarians had always talked about the fact that a vast territory which was ethnically Hungarian had been allotted to Romania. This theory was also inexact. At Trianon, Romania was given a territory which was smaller than the one it was entitled to, according to the ethnic principles elaborated by President Wilson.

The true ethnic-linguistic frontiers between Romania and Hungary had been traced by the treaty concluded in 1916 between the Romanians and the Allied powers.

The frontiers which were decided on at Trianon were situated east of the true ethnic Romanian frontier, leaving important Romanian enclaves within Hungarian territory. At the peace conference in Paris, Ion I. C. Bratianu, the head of Romania's delegation, firmly defended Romania's rights, demanding the recognition of the frontiers that had been agreed to by the Allies in 1916, after long and detailed negotiations. The Romanian delegation to the peace conference did not content itself with simply demanding the observance of the treaty signed by the Allies in 1916 as their sacred right—they supported their territorial claims on every point with well-documented studies and carefully written statements, accompanied by carefully drawn and historically accurate ethnographic maps.

Further than this, in the interests of peace, the free development of peoples and Europe's economic progress, Ion Bratianu no longer lay claim to the territories populated by Romanians south of the Danube and those in the Tisza region. [Speech of February 1, 1919.]

But the peace conference denied Romania the borders that had been established by the treaty of alliance in 1916 by moving the dividing line between Romania and Hungary considerably to the east—in fact, this dividing line closely followed the line on the map which had been drawn at an earlier date at the suggestion of the great Hungarian patriot, Kossuth. In this way, certain regions in which the Romanians constituted an ethnic majority were excluded from the territory awarded to Romania.

All the ethnographic and linguistic maps which were drawn up toward the end of the 18th century and over the course of the 19th and 20th centuries—by geographers, ethnographers, and linguists, including Hungarians, Germans, Austrians, Frenchmen, Englishmen, and Italians—all the monographs and lexicons, all the studies that dealt with the ethnic dividing line between Hungarian and Romanian concentrations in the contested area, more than proved that the proper ethnic frontier of Romania on the western side substantially exceeded the political frontier established by the Trianon Treaty in 1920.

Thus, in the *Geographical Compendium of Hungary* published in 1779 by Mathias Bell, the author, in describing the distribution of the nationalities on the western border of Transylvania, wrote that the Romanians could be found as far as Bereg, Ugocsa, Bekes, and Bihor counties. The first three of these counties remained outside the borders granted to Romania by the Trianon treaty, while the last-named county was divided between Romania and Hungary.

The *Geographical Lexicon of Hungary*, written by I. M. Korabinszky in 1786, which was published in Presburg (Bratislava), mentions several regions on the western side of Transylvania, heavily populated by Romanians, which were also allotted to Hungary by the Trianon Treaty. Among others, there were the villages of Nyir-Adony, Nagy-Kallo, and Bir situated in the county of Szabolcs, Poceni and Peterd situated in the Hungarian part of Bihor County, and Suged in Borsod County.

On the other hand, in his great book, *Magyarorszagnak Leirasa* ("Writing about Hungary"), published in Buda in 1796, A. Valyi counted a whole series of hamlets, villages, small towns, and big towns where the Romanian population was in the majority. All of these remained on Hungarian territory after 1920.

In 1829, J. V. Csaplovits published in Pesta two volumes entitled, *Gemälde von Ungarn* ("Portraits of Hungary"), at the end of which one finds a colored ethnographic map of Hungary and the provinces dependent on it, except Transylvania proper. (*Ethnographische Karte des Königreichs Ungarn, nach Lipszcky*: "Ethnographic Map of the Hungarian Kingdom, according to Lipszcky)." This map is valuable for the contribution it makes to establishing proper ethnic frontiers between the Romanians and the Hungarians. This frontier, once again, exceeds the borderline established by the Trianon treaty. The ethnic frontier intrudes into the territory of post-World War I Hungary in the county of Szabolcs, in which seven communities are listed as purely Romanian. In that part of Bihor County which was

assigned to Hungary after 1920, there are another eight large
Romanian villages. In the northern part of Arad county, the
Romanian ethnic frontier depicted by Csaplovits in 1829 shows
a substantial intrusion into territory assigned to Hungary in
1920, with Romanian villages extending as far as Gyula.

In 1857, Karl F. Czornig published in Vienna, as an annex
to his monograph, *Ethnographie der Osterreichischen Monarchie* ("Ethnography of the Austrian Monarchy"), a map in
which the ethnic Romanian-Hungarian frontier coincided at
almost all points with the Romanian-Hungarian border after
1920. However, in the county of Bihor, it exceeded the political
borders established in 1920 and, following the Crisul Negru
River, reached the villages of Szaka and Dordos which were
allotted to Hungary at Trianon.

In a map published in 1860 by Dr. A. Ficker, as an annex
to his study *The Inhabitants of the Austrian Monarchy*, Romanian presence was also recorded (it is true it constituted
only a small percentage of the total population) in Szabolcs,
Ugocsa, and Bereg counties. These counties, too, remained outside the Romanian frontiers established in 1920. The fact is
that by 1860 Magyarization had already had visible effects.
The Romanian presence beyond the dividing line to be established at Trianon was diminishing little by little.

In 1869, H. Kiepert published in Berlin an ethnographic
map of the region drawn according to the data of the 1869
census in Austria (*Völker und Sprachenkarte von Österreich
und Unterdonauländer*—"Ethnic and Linguistic Map of Austria and the Danubian Lands"). The Romanian-Hungarian ethnic frontier on this map also exceeded the political borders
established at Trianon in 1920. On this map, Romanian concentrations reached as far into post-Trianon Hungary as the
villages of Vekerd and Zsaka. The town of Gyula constituted
the most advanced point of Romanian penetration into the territory assigned to Hungary in 1920.

This map was most displeasing to the Hungarians, who
had launched a vigorous campaign aimed at the denationalization of the Romanian element in Transylvania. The presence
of so many Romanians on what was claimed to be Hungarian
territory was not at all encouraging to the partisans of the
"unitary Hungarian Magyar state." Accordingly, they immediately banned the publication and distribution of Kiepert's
map in the territory of Transylvania—as if this measure could

somehow bring to an end the continuing increase in Romanian national consciousness. Many other works, even less dangerous for the Hungarian state order than Kiepert's map, were also banned.

At the time, the work of denationalization was registering important ostensible progress. Hungarian statistics assimilated to the Hungarian people all those of Romanian origin who had converted to a Magyar religion or who could speak Hungarian.

The Hungarian ethnographic maps of the period reflected the statistics which had been compiled according to these guidelines and adopted as part of the nefarious work of denationalization.

Nevertheless, in this battle between the Romanians of western Transylvania and the deceitful methods of denationalization, the Romanians emerged victorious. That this is so, is demonstrated by the author, Peter Balogh, in his book dealing with Hungary's nationalities at the beginning of the 20th century, *A nepfajok magyarorszagon* ("Popular Legends of Hungary") [Budapest, 1902]. Although it makes good use of the statistics provided by the census of 1900, it establishes the ethnic Romanian-Hungarian boundary along a line which, here and there, exceeds the Romanian frontier established at Trianon in 1920. Balogh is highly instructive on the hypothetical "linguistic frontier" separating the Romanians and the Hungarians. According to Balogh's studies, the Romanian-Hungarian frontiers which were established in 1920 were well inside the linguistic frontier which he had charted.

More recent Hungarian maps solved the problem of the Romanians in western Transylvania in a more radical manner and according to the old Hungarian method. They simply did away with the compact masses of Romanians which existed in that area, depicting entire regions—the mountainous ones in particular—as being not inhabited at all. This was one of the countless methods employed by the Hungarians to mislead people abroad. The Romanian population in Transylvania was in fact more or less evenly spread over the entire territory of the province. In Transylvania there is absolutely no *terra deserta*.

Stephen Manciulea, an expert on problems relating to Transylvania's western border, wrote in his work *La frontière ouest de la Roumanie* ("The Western Border of Romania"): "Recent studies have established beyond any doubt that in

Romania there is no uninhabited mountain zone; human life is busily active in our Carpathian mountains, from the first moment of spring until late in autumn. The Romanian people are deeply bound to their mountains—an attachment which is reflected in the old Romanian saying: 'The woods and the Romanian are brothers.' "

A mere look at the maps of Transylvania which are the work of foreigners is sufficient to make one realize the meaning of the "empty areas" that appear in the Hungarian maps.

It can be stated as an absolute fact that all the maps made at the end of the 19th century, as well as those which were products of the 20th century, demonstrate that the Romanian ethnic frontier exceeds the Romanian-Hungarian border established at Trianon in 1920. We shall limit ourselves to mentioning only the best-known maps—the map published in 1889 by the Austrian Geographical Institute (*Völkerkarte von Europe*—"Ethnic Map of Europe"); the map published in 1888 by Gustav Grober, professor of Romance philology at the University of Strasbourg (*Ausbreitung der rumänischen Sprachen in Europa*—"The Distribution of the Romanian Language in Europe"); the maps published by Novikov in 1866, by James Caterly in 1908, and by Paul Langhans in 1915 (*Der rumänische Volksboden und die Staatliche Entwicklung des Römanentums*—"The Romanian Body Politic and the Governmental Development of the Romanians," by Élisée Reclus), and the maps published by the Agostini Institute in Navara by Karl Haushoffer, and others. On all of these maps, the towns of Sighetul Marmatiei, Oradea Mare, Arad, and Timisoara are located within the regions marked as Romanian ethnic territory, and the towns themselves were surrounded by compact masses of Romanian peasants.

So, if an injustice was committed in 1920, it is the Romanians and not the Hungarians who are entitled to complain, since significant islands of Romanians were left within Hungarian territory, outside the political frontiers which separated them from Romania.

But, in order not to disturb the peace of Europe, the Romanians accepted things as they were after the Trianon treaty, devoting all their energies to the positive goal of enhancing the national prosperity.

The least that can be said is that, with the possible exception of a number of Romanian ethnic intrusions into Hungary, the borders which were delineated at Trianon, if not perfect, corresponded, to the best of human ability, to a demarcation line between the Romanian and Hungarian nations.

As a matter of fact, such a frontier was one of the goals, among others, of the war which the Romanians fought on the Allied side from 1916 to 1918. When asked in 1916 by President Wilson to identify their goals, the Western Allies, in a Minute dated January 10 of that year, replied that one of their goals was "the liberation from foreign domination of the Italians, Croats, Romanians, Czechs, and Serbs."

When the war was over, Lord Northcliffe, brother of the famous revisionist leader, Lord Rothermere, declared in a speech made on November 4, 1918:

> We must secure for the peoples in Austria-Hungary a place among the free nations of the world and offer them the right to unite with their brothers beyond the present boundaries of Austria-Hungary. This implies the birth of the independent states of Czechoslovakia and Yugoslavia, the reducing of Hungary to the ethnographic limits of the Magyar race, as well as the union of all the Romanians with the present Romanian kingdom.

When the frontiers dividing the states of post-World War I Europe were drawn up, the peace conference took into consideration in the first place Europe's ethnic configuration. The accent was placed on achieving the most ideal distribution of ethnic areas to the respective national states.

"I am going to guide myself in the work of building up peace, as much as is humanly possible," said Lloyd George in a memorandum to the conference on March 23, 1919, "so that the different races belong to their own motherlands. This human criterion has priority over strategic, economic, or commercial considerations, which present problems that may be settled by other means."

It was this spirit which prevailed when the treaties were concluded. Sir Robert Donald was the author of a book published in London in 1928, *The Tragedy of Trianon* (whose title is at the same time an indication of attitude!). Even Sir Robert had this to say about the proceedings of the conference:

> The Peace Conference did not decide Hungary's fate with-

out its full knowledge of the case: the Hungarian delegation in Paris came to the Conference with three thick
volumes of 600 pages each, containing an admirable collection of maps, diagrams, tables, all of them supported
by oral evidence . . .

In the light of this, how can anyone persist in spreading
the groundless revisionist propaganda that the Peace Conference acted in ignorance of what the Hungarians had to say in
defense of their case?

The Hungarian politician, Tibor Eckhardt, who had no
friendly feeling for the Romanian nation, made a concession
to the historical truth in dealing with the question of Hungarian ethnic space.

"Let us imagine," he said in *Magyororszag Tortenete* (Budapest, 1933), "that the Hungarians—the conquerors—populated
the entire country. Their number was too small to achieve this,
perhaps because of the defeats they had suffered in their former
motherland. The territory occupied by them fitted approximately into the territory established by the Trianon treaty, to
which Great Hungary was reduced after a thousand years."

But why go so far as that into the past when the present
can offer the most radical answer to the problem? In fact, available statistics throw much light on the problem, which the
Hungarians wish to present in its most complicated form but
which is really extremely simple. On the western border of the
Romanian kingdom, as this border was established by the Trianon treaty in 1920, there are four counties which are immediate neighbors of Hungary: Satu-Mare, Salaj, Bihor, and Arad.
In 1930, the total population of these four counties in the Romanian-Hungarian border area was approximately 1,600,000,
of whom 943,692 were Romanians; 417,183 were Hungarians;
80,030 were Germans; 68,377 were Jews; and so on. In short,
the Hungarians represented only 26 percent of the population
in these counties on the Romanian-Hungarian border.

We have available to us *The Dictionary of Transylvania,
Banat, and the Other Annexed Regions*, published at Cluj in
1921, that is, only a short time after the Trianon treaty had
been concluded. At that time, the ethnic aspect of the region
on the western border still suffered from the dominant effects
of the long period of Magyarization on the part of the Hungarian state administration and from the massive Hungarian

colonization campaign in the towns of this frontier area of Transylvania.

Indeed, in this area, the campaign of Magyarization had been implemented with much greater force than in any other region in Transylvania, because it was here in the counties of Satu-Mare, Bihor, Salaj, and Arad that the limits of the ethnic Romanian element could be found and where this element made contact with the Magyar masses.

The large towns in the area—Arad, Oradea Mare, Careii Mari, Satu-Mare—were looked upon by the Hungarians as the starting point of an offensive for the denationalization of the Transylvanian Romanians, which might later create the possibility of penetrating the state of the long-established Romanian kingdom.

After many years of actively trying to bring about the denationalization of the native population, one would have expected to find in these regions a dominant Hungarian ethnic structure. Nevertheless, so deeply was the Romanian ethnic spirit rooted in this area—even in the regions which came into contact with the plain, which had for many hundreds of years been preeminently Magyar—that the Hungarians were not able to exercise a decisive influence over the ethnic structure of the western border area, taken as a whole. Indeed, the Romanian population in western Transylvania is more heavily concentrated than in the central and eastern parts, where the compact colonization practices of the Szecklers had created a foreign island within the cradle of Roman Dacia. On the western border, the Romanians represented 60.4 percent of the total number of inhabitants, compared to only 57.6 percent in the central and eastern regions which had been colonized with Hungarians and Szecklers.

Characteristic of this region—a fact that is worthy of mention because it reveals the basic weakness of denationalization by violent methods—was the contrast between the ethnic aspect of the towns and that of the nearby villages. Most of the villages were Romanian, while the towns had an unmistakably foreign aspect, although not always a Magyar one. What more visible proof could there be of the persistence of the Romanian spirit in Transylvania than this essentially Romanian aspect of the territory which lay at the western border of the province, the western limit of the ancient Roman *Dacia Felix*?

In 1921, only a short while after the age-old Hungarian

domination had come to an end, we found this situation in the areas where the Hungarian and Romanian nations had made contact—and it should be recalled that this was the area where the dominant Hungarians had the greatest possibilities to influence the dominated Romanians.

In the county of Bihor, small rural districts were revealed to be preponderantly Romanian. Alesd, with 50,265 inhabitants and 50 communes, had 40,110 Romanians and only 5,155 Hungarians; Beliu with 18,733 inhabitants and 33 communes, had 17,696 Romanians and only 792 Hungarians; Ceica with 31,497 inhabitants—after a thousand years of Hungarian domination—had 30,078 Romanians to 963 Hungarians. Finally, there was a small rural district of Vascau with 28,148 inhabitants, of whom 27,276 were Romanian and only 491 Hungarians—in short, the Romanians represented almost 98 percent of the total population.

In the county of Satu-Mare, the small rural district of Somcuta-Mare which consisted of 41 communes, counted 24,885 Romanians and 1,179 Hungarians out of a total population of 28,393.

In the county of Maramures in the small rural district of Iza, which was composed of 13 communes, the Romanians found, when the district had been integrated into Romania, that there were 22,379 Romanians and only 74 Hungarians. [Dragomir Esti.]

In Arad which is situated near the border, out of a total of 397,969 inhabitants, 245,113 were Romanian and 98,208 Magyar. In the nearby villages, the percentage of Romanians, as compared with Hungarians, was overwhelming. For example, in the 36 communes of the small rural district of Radna, there were 27,155 Romanians and only 1,825 Hungarians. In Sebis, which had 49 communes, there were 30,390 Romanians and only 2,141 Hungarians.

From all this we have to conclude that, in the villages which were clustered near the Hungarian frontier, the Hungarians, despite a thousand years of domination and attempted denationalization, had not been able to attain a population accounting for 10 percent of the total number of inhabitants.

If all these supporters of the theory that "Hungary had been wronged at Trianon" had taken a good look at these figures—which, beneath their cold and impassive aspect, concealed an overwhelming reality—neither Lord Rothermere, nor the former French minister Anatole de Monzie, nor the French deputy Charles Tisseyre, nor Sir Robert Donald, nor Franco Vellani Dionisi, would have accused Romania of incorporating Hungarian peasants in the western part of Transylvania into its ethnic structure.

What right did the Hungarians have to claim that Oradea Mare was theirs, when the county of Bihor had hundreds of villages surrounding the Magyarized town which were Romanian to their innermost core?

Under what rationale were they able to ask that the towns in the western border area be returned to Hungary, when all the hamlets and villages in the area—that is, the *land* of western Transylvania—were Romanian?

How were they able to claim that towns which were lost in a Romanian sea were "Hungarian"? At the most, one might have said that these towns were "Magyarized," but this is not the kind of reason on the basis of which one lays claim to territory.

What was most detrimental to the peace of Europe was the lack of seriousness with which some foreign personalities declared themselves partisans of the Magyar cause. Their desire may have been to make justice triumph. Their actions had the opposite effect. The best that can be said about them is that they were not responsible for the data they were defending.

De Monzie, for example, with characteristic vigor, asked this pathetic question in 1922: "According to what aberration did these people, who bragged to the four winds about the rights of races and nationalities, rob the Magyars of their towns, where the inhabitants, with minor exception, were of Magyar origin, mind, and culture? Why, yes, why?"

And Charles Tisseyre, in his book *Une erreur diplomatique, La Hongrie mutilée* ("A Diplomatic Error: Mutilated Hungary"), which was published in Paris immediately after the close of World War I, said that the Szecklers were "pure Hungarians" and that the Hungarians were "victims of their own liberalism." Exclaimed Tisseyre: "The birthplace of the famous king of Hungary, Matei Corvin, the son of the great Hungarian captain, Ioan Huniade, which can still be seen today, lies on Romanian territory. Isn't that a cruel irony?"

Other critics, more or less interested, more or less in good faith, more or less pathetic in their innocence of the facts, distorted historical realities and even the palpable evidence of the present.

If de Monzie had visited the mountains and the plains of Maramures, Bihor, Salaj, and Arad, at the very frontier of Magyarism, he would have found in the language spoken by hundreds of thousands of Romanian peasants and in the melodious accents of their tongue, all the beauty of the language of his own ancestors—which has been perpetuated until the present day both by the neo-Latins in the western part of Europe and those on the eastern frontier of the Latin-speaking world.

If de Monzie had studied the history of this preeminently Romanian province, he would have realized that, if many towns appeared Magyar, this was due to the artificial measures of the Hungarian state. And, if he had thoroughly investigated the ethnic structure of these towns, he could have satisfied himself that many of the ostensibly "pure" Hungarians were, in fact, Romanians, who had come to the towns from the nearby Romanian villages and had been Magyarized over the years by inducements and pressures applied by the "liberal" Hungarian administration.

Of course, neither de Monzie nor his less prominent disciples were aware that Oradea-Mare, which, according to Hungarian propaganda was "preeminently Magyar," had a united Romanian diocese in 1776, and that this diocese was set up by the Empress Maria Theresa and acknowledged by the *Bula Indefessum* of Pope Pius VI on June 10, 1777. Or perhaps the supporters of the Magyar cause who dwell on the banks of the Seine were under the impression that a Romanian Catholic diocese had, 150 years previously, been set up for the benefit of the inhabitants of Hungarian origin, who obviously must have had Hungarian feelings and a Hungarian culture.

As to the "cruel irony of fate" which had determined that after World War I Romania was to shelter in the town of Cluj the birthplace of the Hungarian king, Matei Corvin, the son of the "Hungarian" Captain Ioan Huniade, Tisseyre would have been much less impressed and his feeling of revulsion would have been much more modest if he had been aware of the true facts. If, for example, he had read a history of Hungary, even a history written by such a Hungarian as Professor Domanovschy of the University of Budapest, he would have found that the famous captain Ioan Huniade, of whom the Magyar nation is so proud, as well as his son, King Matei Corvin, had been Transylvanian Romanians!

The great sin of all those who attacked the authors of the peace treaty so fiercely was that they wanted to write history anew, ignoring the real history of Transylvania which for a thousand years had been written with many tears and with even more blood.

More than once, in supporting the desiderata of Hungarian chauvinist propaganda, the protectors of the Magyar cause found themselves in disagreement—even in conflict—with the Hungarian political leaders and the most outstanding representatives of Magyar science, as well as Hungarian publications prior to World War I. They did not know the real state of affairs, but they put a lot of passion into discussing it.

Documents on the Romanians in Pannonia and in the Western Part of Transylvania

In ancient times, not only did the Romanians constitute the overwhelming majority in the western part of Transylvania, but they were also to be found in large numbers, even in the Pannonian plain, far from Transylvania's border.

In 1777, Ricardus said that when the Hungarians invaded Pannonia it was already known by the name of the "Plain of the Romans."

In his work, *The Romanians Between the Ninth to the Fourteenth Centuries*, which was published in 1932, the famous Romanian historian N. Bragan quotes a whole series of historical sources as saying that, for a long time after the Hungarian invasion, Romanian shepherds were still present in Pannonia—that is, in Hungary proper. Among the more important sources he cites are Thomas de Spalato who, writing about the year 1250, spoke of Pannonia as "the Roman pasturelands." He also cited a Catholic monk who wrote about the Romanian presence in Pannonia in the year 1308. Specifically, he spoke about the "the Wallachian and Romanian shepherds" (*Blachi ac pastores Romanorum*).

The firm proof left by the Hungarian chroniclers, Thuroczi and Simonis de Geza, is also worth mentioning. These chroniclers assert that, when the Huns invaded Pannonia, they found only Romanian shepherds. These were clearly the ancestors of today's Romanians. Finally, these Hungarian proofs are confirmed by the anonymous chronicler who positively affirmed the existence of the Wallachians and the Romanian shepherds in the western regions of Transylvania and Pannonia.

The existence of the Romanians in the western part of Transylvania since the oldest times is today a scientifically proved fact. The distinguished Hungarian historian Marki, in a work published at Oradea-Mare in 1887, wrote these words: "As to the Crisul Negru valley, I must admit that our Hungarians found the Romanians already there." The Romanian presence in the county of Bihor in the 11th century is confirmed by the Hungarian writer E. Gyarfas, in his work entitled *A roman grog katolikusok autonomiaja*—("The Autonomy of the Romanian Greek Catholic Church"), which was published in Budapest in 1905. The Romanian *knezats* in the Arad region are mentioned in the 13th century by the chronicler Rogerius in his work *Carmen Miserabile*. Silviu Dragomir quotes documents from the time of King Carol Robert (1318), which speak about the Romanian villages around the old monastery near Ineu. Stefan Manciulea, in the above-mentioned work on *The Western Border of Romania*, supports his theory about the Romanian presence in this area in the 14th and 15th centuries by mentioning documents attesting to this presence, which are dated 1364, 1415, and 1544. He also speaks of evidence dated 1475 dealing with the residence of a Romanian *voivode* at Nicolesti, a village which no longer exists.

In Bihor County, the Romanians are mentioned in documents dating back to the 11th century, including King Geza's action in bestowing certain properties to the Benedictine monks at Gran. A document from the year 1202 mentions the presence in Bihor County of Romanians bearing the names Micus (small), Tata, Qurud (cruel), Karachin (Christmas). The register of the bishopric in Oradea contains a whole series of Romanian names from the areas of Bihor and Oradea. In a work published in Budapest in 1892, V. Bunytay showed that documents going back as far as 1294 already spoke about the Romanian population living in the Crisul Negru valley. During the same period, the Romanians are mentioned as residents of the villages in the valley of the Crisul Repede River.

Marki wrote that the Romanians were present in Arad County in the first years of the 14th century, while the historian, Czanky, said that, in the region of western Transylvania, the Romanians constituted the majority of the population in the counties of Bihor, Arad and Zarand, in the 14th and 15th centuries.

A complete listing of the documents which speak of the

Romanian presence in the border area of western Transylvania during the 13th, 14th, and 15th centuries would go on without end.

In more recent times, the Hungarians themselves admitted that, of all the nationalities that inhabited the western counties of Transylvania, the Romanians constituted the preponderant majority. Thus, in 1912, Count Bethlen, writing about the distribution of the various nationalities in the region which was later to become the Romanian border area, frankly admitted the overwhelming superiority in numbers of the Romanian element in western Transylvania.

"The Romanians in Hungary," said the one-time prime minister, "are more numerous than the Magyars and the other peoples, in the following regions: in the whole of historic Transylvania, in three districts of Maremures, in all the districts of Salaj, and in the great majority of those in Satu-Mare, Bihor, and Arad."

The Romanians are more numerous than the Hungarians in Salaj, Satu-Mare, Bihorr, and Arad! If Messrs. de Monzie and Tisseyre in France, and Sir Robert Donald and Lord Rothermere in England had read this passage by Count Bethlen, perhaps they would have given up pleading the cause of "mutilated" Hungary—especially since the regions the one-time prime minister listed as being dominated by the Romanian presence were all situated in the shadow of the borders assigned to Romania by the Trianon treaty.

Speaking of the situation in the other regions of Transylvania, Count Bethlen reached the following conclusion (a conclusion which he did not mention in his pro-Hungarian lectures in eastern Europe): "The Romanian masses in Transylvania, in comparison with the other nationalities, represent an ocean, a sea, an avalanche." Before he said this, Count Bethlen, in commenting upon the distribution of the several nationalities in the countryside of the eleven western districts of Transylvania, confirmed that the Romanians ranked first among the nationalities which inhabited the area, with 75.1 percent of the population as compared with 15 percent for the Hungarians.

When Hungarians were animated by purely scientific motivation, the data they presented was completely different from that spread around by Hungarian propaganda abroad, the purpose of which was to distort those statistics which militated against Hungarian expansionism and to otherwise misinterpret annoying realities.

For instance, in *The Geography of Arad County*, a textbook created for use in the Hungarian elementary schools, the Hungarian authors, Ianos Gyorffy and Ildebert Kiss, wrote in 1905, "the inhabitants of Arad County total 386,100, and they live on a territory 6,643 kilometers in size. The majority of the population is of Romanian origin. Then there are Germans, Magyars, and others."

In *The Ethnographic Statistics of Hungary*, published in 1906, the author, Kenez Bella, stated that "the Romanians constitute the absolute majority in twelve counties, to wit: Salaj, Alba, Caras-Severin, . . ." [The quotation went on to list the other Transylvanian counties in which the Romanians were in the majority.]

What all this adds up to is that, according to Magyar sources, the Romanians in western Transylvania, after a thousand years of Hungarian rule, still constituted an absolute majority compared with the other nationalities that resided in the area.

In 1912, the Hungarian academician Gyula Varga, in drawing an ethnographic dividing line between the Romanians and the Hungarians in the territory, again showed that Romanian ethnic territory extended beyond the border which was established by the Trianon treaty in the counties of Crisul Repede and Careii Mici.

When confronted with such explicit findings on the massive preponderance of the Romanian element in the Romanian-Hungarian border areas, what value can be attached to the assertions of Magyar propaganda, except that it consists of empty words totally lacking in substance?

If Lord Buckmaster, whom Sir Robert Donald mentioned in *The Tragedy of Trianon*, had been more familiar with the real state of affairs in Transylvania, he would not have ventured to say in the House of Lords' speech on November 17, 1927, that "peace had come to Hungary in the shape of a falcon, tearing its body to pieces." And none of the English politicians or of the prominent newspapermen, on the banks of the Tiber as well as the banks of the Thames, would have taken so warmly to a cause which could be sustained only by ignoring the most elementary historical truths concerning the Romanian province of Transylvania.

The Union Has a "Live" Basis

The Romanians were right in believing that fundamental truths which had manifested themselves with the force of an axiom after being suppressed for a thousand years by the most rigid intolerance, no longer needed to be proved.

The correctness of the Romanian cause was beyond the reach of any opportunistic argument and not subject to dispute. Indeed, it resulted from the nature of things. The triumph of this cause was the natural consequence of that law of nature which demands that the walls existing between brothers belonging to the same nation—walls erected by forces which were hostile to the unity of this nation—should be burnt to the ground.

For this reason, Magyar propaganda abroad had very little effect in Romania. The Romanians were convinced that no argument could cause any trouble to the new order that had been established at Trianon in 1920.

We should emphasize the fact that this order was based more on the steadfast will of the millions of Transylvanian Romanians to live their lives freely in a Romanian Transylvania than it was on the dry text of treaties.

In the appeal to the peoples of the world which the Romanian National Committee in Arad sent out between November 7 and 20, 1918, the leaders of the Transylvanian Romanians, Stefan Ciceo Pop and Gheorghe Crisan, asked for the help of the civilized world in achieving the just ideals of the Romanian people. These ideals corresponded completely to the expressed goals of the Allies. But the Romanian leaders made it clear that it was their firm decision to preserve the freedoms they had won after so many sacrifices, even if the western powers refused to give them the help they were seeking.

The Romanians, said the authors of the appeal, would sooner die than live in bondage again.

In their propaganda, the Hungarian politicians kept completely silent about this "live" basis of the union which had been accomplished in 1918. They attacked only the treaty which had sanctioned the union in 1920.

In this way, the Hungarians showed the weakness of the cause they were defending. They avoided all mention of the real reason for the Hungarian collapse: the desire for liberty and independence by the non-Magyar nationalities which had resided in the former Hapsburg monarchy.

Since Magyar propaganda could not set forth any major reason to support their contention, the Hungarians contented themselves with posing as martyrs. They made a tragedy out

of a situation which was indeed distressing to those who championed the chimera of a pure Magyar Hungary thirty million
strong. But this situation was the logical consequence of an
implacable historic evolution.

Magyar Propaganda Takes the Offensive

The Hungarian leaders launched an intense revisionist
attack in the western countries. In essence, their complaint
was that the territory of Hungary had been drastically reduced.
The ethnographic, linguistic, and historical reasons which justified the Trianon treaty, as well as the sovereign right of the
subject peoples to self-determination, were never mentioned in
the furious propaganda attacks directed against Romania,
Czechoslovakia, and Yugoslavia by the Magyar irredentist
forces.

Making use of various means, ranging from minor propagandist actions to the most brazen attempts to court the
sympathy of political parties and important newspapers in the
western world, the Hungarians sought to present the new order
which had been established in the Carpathian-Danubian region as intrinsically unjust and, therefore, inevitably subject
to revision.

Nem! Nem! Soha! ("No! No! Never!") was the cry carried
to the four corners of the world by the Magyar propagandists—a
cry which was the equivalent to a declaration of war against
a peace which the Hungarians refused to accept.

"Hungary," said Sir Robert Donald, "had become a country
of patriotic slogans," intended to keep alive "the spirit of Magyarism" inside the borders of Hungary, while attempting to
appeal to the hearts of those abroad rather than impressing
them with documentary evidence.

Revisionist, irredentist, and chauvinistic slogans filled the
entire country. One could meet them everywhere—in railroad
stations, in trains, buses and trams, on their maps, postcards
and envelopes, and on many other small articles in everyday
use.

The symbol of irredentist Magyarism appeared on their
flags, was carved on rings and seals and on building facades,
was engraved on brooches, tiepins, and cufflinks, and was fitted
into old songs or introduced in new ones. Hundreds of times a
day Hungarians could hear and read the slogan: "Let us

remember and not forget Trianon!" The Hungarian irredentist motto, "I believe there is only one God; I believe in Hungary's revival," was repeated like a monomania.

The vindictive spirit, in short, was kept alive by the constant propaganda, day in and day out, for twenty years. As anyone can imagine, such an atmosphere was not in the least conducive to the establishment of friendly relations with the states surrounding Hungary.

12. HUNGARIAN REVISIONIST PROPAGANDA ABROAD

Hungarian propaganda abroad sought to impress foreign public opinion with the dramatic contrast in magnitude between the two Hungarian states—prewar Hungary and the Hungarian state which had been produced by the peace treaty. At the same time, they said not a word about the real causes of the territorial losses suffered by the excessively large Hungarian state which had existed before the war.

In Great Britain, the Hungarian propagandists distributed thousands of maps showing a comparably "mutilated" Britain and bearing the following caption: "Would the English accept this peace? It would be identical to the one forced on Hungary!" Similar maps were distributed in unlimited numbers in France, Italy, Spain, and other countries, showing the territories of these countries "mutilated," as the territory of prewar Hungary had been by the Trianon treaty.

Another map which was circulated depicted a post-Trianon Hungary inside a prewar polyglot Hungary, over the following caption: "Justice is the only guarantee of peace and prosperity. But is this justice?" Nowhere was it indicated that the postwar Hungary had simply been reduced to its ethnic frontiers.

A similar map, engraved on an aluminum plate, was distributed in Hungary. It bore the Magyar words: *Moradht ez igy? Nem! Nem! Soha!* ("Can this go on forever? No! No! Never!").

The Hungarians Distort the Truth

All Magyar propaganda was based exclusively on the contrasts between the respective territories of prewar Hungary and postwar Hungary. No ethnic or linguistic argument was advanced as a unifying theme for the avalanche of pamphlets and revisionist claims. Indeed, when one of the excessively fervent propagandists happened to mention the ethnic problem, he was obliged to distort the truth in order to show the Hungarian cause in a favorable light.

Thus, Sir Robert Donald, in writing his well-known work on Transylvania and the Trianon treaty *The Tragedy of Trianon,* was greatly influenced by Magyar propaganda in Great Britain. As frequently happened, the "facts" presented were quoted without first being checked by the author. Inevitably, one found errors so flagrant that they could easily be refuted by those who were in the least informed about the real state of affairs in Transylvania. In the paragraphs that follow, we deal with some of the most flagrant errors of which Sir Robert was guilty.

1. *Among other things Sir Robert said, "The sacred principles of self determination were ignored in the Trianon Treaty, and irredentism was perpetuated."*

One must ask, in talking about the sacred principles of self determination, what was the huge national assembly at Alba-Julia if it was not a plebiscite which demonstrated the enthusiastic desire of the Transylvanian Romanians to be united with their motherland?

This great assembly had been convened, as a matter of fact, in support of the principles set forth by President Wilson.

"History calls upon us to take action," said the document summoning the assembly, which was addressed to the three million Transylvanian Romanians by the Great National Council. "The irresistible advance of human civilization has brought the great Romanian nation to the light after it had known the darkness of age-old bondage. In the name of eternal justice and of the principle of the independence of nations—a principle which has been consecrated by the evolution of history—the Romanian nation in Transylvanian-Hungary wishes to be the master of its own destiny from now on."

A short while after the Romanian plebiscite, the Transylvanian Germans, in a huge meeting in Medias on January 8, 1919, voted heavily in favor of "their union with the kingdom of Romania, on the basis of the people's right to self-determination."

This is what the British politicians who supported the Hungarian cause would have learned if they had sought, not to read in detail the history of the Romanian province of Transylvania—this was unnecessary—but to read only the basic documents having to do with the popular decisions of the nationalities in the former kingdom of Hungary.

2. *At one point Sir Robert said that the Hungarians represented 70 percent or more of the total population in the region which had been allotted to Romania, Czechoslovakia, and Yugoslavia after World War I.*

The question under discussion is that of Transylvania, which had been united to Romania after the revolution of 1918. In 1930, there were in this region 3,026,998 Romanians, as compared to 882,000 authentic Hungarians and the 500,000 Szecklers who had colonized the eastern part of Transylvania. Thus, the Romanian population in Transylvania outnumbered the authentic Hungarian population by the proportion of four to one.

To assert under these circumstances that the Hungarian element was dominant in comparison with the Romanian element, obviously means that a fictional history of the province was written, in which full scope was given to the imagination.

Statistics are inflexible in their rigidity. It is, of course, the historian's job to interpret them. But to misinterpret them for propagandistic reasons exceeds the mission of any historian. This is completely characteristic, however, of what the Hungarians have always tried to do through their propaganda: to present a distorted image of the truth in order to conceal the real facts from foreign public opinion—for the simple reason that these facts were not in their favor. In this way, Hungarian propaganda has succeeded more than once in misleading the governments of the western nations.

But distorting figures is a method which is too weak to stand up even under the most hasty examination. That is why the Hungarians used this method more in order to create an atmosphere than to convince people. One must admit, however, that, for many honest-minded people, the figures put out by the Magyar propagandists represented the most objective statistics. Sir Robert, who was one of these people, clearly did not mean to mislead anyone when he asserted that the Hungarians constituted the majority in those regions which had been allotted after the fall of the Hapsburg empire to the various successor states.

3. *"There are thousands of inhabitants in Hungary,"* Sir

Robert said in 1928, "whose language is not Magyar but who are good, patriotic Hungarians."

The conclusions which the author obviously wished to reach for is that the linguistic criterion, which had been considered together with the ethnic criterion when the great powers had ratified Transylvania's union with Romania, is not infallible; thus, the inhabitants of Romanian origin who spoke Romanian did not consider themselves less Hungarian than the authentic Hungarians whose mother tongue was Magyar.

In all the books that were published before World War II, this was the most glaring aberration from the truth.

The Romanian language and Transylvanian Romanianism are so closely connected that they constitute an indestructible whole. The Romanian who suffered under the centuries-old Magyar oppression and who managed to preserve his language intact, despite repeated Magyarization programs, was aware of his Dacian-Roman origin, and he thought and felt like a Romanian.

In Transylvania, the Romanian language was like a granite rock against which wave after wave of Magyarization broke.

It is true that there were many good Romanians who were forced by circumstances to speak Hungarian. But the fact that they used Hungarian in their social relations did not prevent them from manifesting their Romanian spirit when political circumstances were more favorable. In doing so, they immediately and almost invariably started speaking again in the tongue of their ancestors and gave up using the language they had borrowed.

But what the history of Transylvania had never known was a Romanian who spoke Romanian—but considered himself Hungarian!

"National unity is compatible with a variety of spoken languages," continued Sir Robert.

Nothing could be truer where variety of language has been added to a unity of traditions and aspirations, as is the case in Switzerland—an example which Sir Robert himself mentions.

In the case of Hungary, nothing could be more false. There, the variety of spoken languages constituted the most visible aspect of a wider diversity which separated the various nationalities inhabiting Transylvania.

None of the foreign writers who made use of the enormous quantity of propaganda materials circulated by the Hungarians throughout western Europe had ever tried to discover what was accurate and what was inaccurate in allegations which, by the nature of things, were bound to use exaggerated arguments or even to distort the truth. They contented themselves with accepting the materials placed at their disposal by the Hungarians. Inevitably, they reached conclusions which were totally at odds with reality.

For Sir Robert, the Trianon treaty represented "the product of a warlike spirit"—while, as has been demonstrated in previous chapters, the Trianon treaty did not create rights but only "ascertained the fact that it was Transylvania's will to unite with Romania." This will had been expressed in the most categorical manner in a spontaneous plebiscite involving the great majority of the Transylvanian population. For the same British author, "the new borders were not the result of national principles; they had been established arbitrarily." He also said that the decision of the great powers was influenced by the fact that the Romanians were already in possession of the territory, and possession, according to an English phrase, "is nine-tenths of the law."

We have had a good deal to say about the western border areas of Transylvania. We believe the reader of this treatise has already been able to arrive at the opinion that it was not the new dividing line between Romania and Hungary that was arbitrary, but the assertion which supported such nonsensical declarations.

For the indefatigible defender of the Magyar cause in Great Britain, the way in which the dividing line between Romania and Hungary had been established was also defective because Romania had been allotted regions which were more dependent on Hungary economically and had only insignificant ties with the rest of Transylvania. Sir Robert does not trouble to present any concrete examples of such areas, contenting himself with repeating the claims of the Hungarian delegation to the peace conference in Paris. If this passionate Magyarophile in London had taken the time to study, even in the most general way, the geographic and economic facts about western Transylvania, he could not have agreed with the claims pressed by the Hungarian delegation to the peace conference, which were fatally subjective for the simple reason that they were presented by an interested party. Among other things, he would have found out, first of all, that the towns of Satu-Mare, Oradea, Arad, and even Timisoara were situated in an area which, from a geographic standpoint, belonged to Transylvania and not to Hungary.

Economically speaking, the towns of Satu-Mare, Careii Mari, Oradea Mare, Arad and Timisoara, which were situated at the western frontier of Transylvania, were closely connected with Transylvania and heavily dependent on it—despite the fact that Sir Robert, following in the steps of Lord Rothermere, would have liked this region to be acknowledged as belonging to Hungary.

Indeed, the lines of communication from these towns are connected to the Hungarian plain by only twelve roads, while there are thirty-four roads to the eastern parts of Transylvania. As Laurian Somesan remarked in his study of the western frontier of Romania, these roads were built "before the period of Romanian domination and by a state which was preeminently centralized." According to the Hungarian writer Hanus Istvan, in 1886 "these industrial centers situated in the western part of Transylvania were supplied with raw materials (coal, wood, metal ores, and other materials), which came from the central and eastern parts of Transylvania."

But to the foreign authors who had fallen under the influence of the Magyar propaganda, all these facts were totally unknown. This accounts for their favorable attitude to a cause which no honest man aware of the real state of affairs could support.

Magyar Opportunism

One must concede that the Magyar propagandists made tremendous efforts in the western countries to win the sympathies of the upper classes. In terms of magnitude, this effort can only be compared to the effort the Hungarians had made over the centuries to denationalize the subject nationalities who lived alongside them.

The autocratic Hungary of yesterday—the Hungary of the counts and nobles—against which the protests of the civilized world had been directed for decades, had become overnight a country where various nationalities lived in the same territory under paradisiacal conditions. Hungary was "the great victim of World War I," and for all the partisans of the Magyar cause, the Hungarians were "the wronged ones."

Charles Tisseyre, who was the author of a distinctly propagandist tract to which we have already referred (*Une erreur
diplomatique: la Hongrie mutilée*), declared that the Hungarians, although endowed with all other human qualities, lacked
only that of "diplomatic skill." It is difficult for us to agree with
him. If the Hungarian propagandists succeeded in gaining the
sympathy of important circles in countries like Great Britain,
Germany, France and Italy, they did so by shrewd and una-
bashed emotional outpourings, tailored individually for each
country. This they could not have done if they had not possessed
a particularly "skillful and cunning (*avisé et retors*) spirit," as
Tisseyre put it.

The Magyars Are Pro-English

Like many British politicians and prominent Fleet Street
journalists, Sir Robert Donald was convinced that "all Hungarian statesmen deeply admired Great Britain and British
institutions." As a matter of fact, in 1849 their predecessors
had been persuaded by Kossuth's envoys that all Magyar intellectuals came spiritually under the direct influence of the
British. Indeed, if one could believe the Hungarian propagandists in London, every Magyar intellectual kept beside his
bed either John Milton's "Paradise Lost" or Lord Byron's
"Childe Harold."

The Magyars Are Pro-French

While this was the image they propagated on the banks
of the Thames, on the banks of the Seine Hungarian propagandists managed to persuade important French political, jour-
nalistic, and intellectual circles in general, that there was no
country in the world more friendly to France than Hungary.
So dramatically had some of the French publicists been influenced by Hungarian propaganda that they even declared, as
was the case with Tisseyre, that Budapest—the citadel of Ger-
manized Magyarism—was spiritually far closer to the French
than Bucharest, which was widely known as the "little Paris
of middle Europe," and which was a city whose Latinity pul-
sated in every aspect of its being. Tisseyre assumed the unre-
warding task of demonstrating to the average Frenchman that
the Romanians, who had come to regard France as the second

motherland, were less attached to France than were the Hungarians, who in fact, to a much larger extent than any other European nation, were very close to the German culture, under whose influence they had lived for centuries.

In order to achieve such dramatic results, while denying even the most elementary truth, the Hungarians must have disposed of a very special diplomatic ability. Not only were the Hungarian propagandists able to win the sympathy of important circles in France and England, but beyond this they endeavored to keep in hand all of the best cards.

While the Hungarian propagandists in Paris and London paid exaggerated compliments to the French and British, and while special envoys to the United States of America traveled all over that country with the myth that Admiral Horthy and his clique in Budapest were pro-American, other propagandists on the banks of the Seine and the Tiber spoke a completely different language.

The Magyars Are Pro-German

It was in Berlin that the first celebration of German-Hungarian friendship took place. According to Karacsony's Gepidae theory, the Hungarians are of German origin, and proofs going back many centuries were invoked for the purpose of proving the close ties that exist between Hungarian spirituality and German culture.

This age-old friendship was the subject of an exuberant literature. Permanent bonds between Budapest and Berlin were based on cultural ties, but while elevated voices concerned with cultural matters were being heard, other voices let it be understood that the same closeness characterized political relations, when necessary. And this was really what happened a short time later. In order to show their strong desire to make friends with the countries of the Iron Pact, the Hungarians set up branches of a *Collegium Hungaricum* in Berlin, Vienna, and Rome, while Hungarian propaganda in Germany and Italy moved rapidly to bring its output into tune with the revisionist policies which were being pushed ever more vigorously by Adolf Hitler and Benito Mussolini.

In Berlin in 1930, Eugen Horvath published his violent book, entitled *So starb der Friede* ("This is How Peace Died").

In Vienna in 1932, Josef Kuncz published his completely

revisionist book entitled *Die Revision der Friedensvertrage eine volkerrechtliche Untersuchung* ("The Revision of the Peace Treaties: An Examination from the Standpoint of International Law").

At the same time, Wolfgang Peters published his pro-Hungarian book *Ein Volk hasst* ("A People's Hatred"). In the words of his title, Kuncz synthesized the feeling of the Hungarian magnates towards their neighbors, who, in fact, desired nothing more than to have peaceful relations with Hungary.

Last but not least, in 1940, the publishing house of the Royal University of Budapest published a voluminous study *Ungarn: Das Antlitz einer Nation* ("Hungary: The Aspect of a Nation"). This book was designed to demonstrate to the Germans the strength of the Germanic influence over a thousand years of Hungarian history.

In this study, in the volume entitled *Hungary and the German Culture*, Bela Szent-Ivanyi showed that the bonds between Hungary and the German culture dated back to the time of Stephen the Holy—that is, around 1,000 A.D.—and that political relations between the two countries were already friendly under the first Arpad monarch. The study also argued that, after the World War of 1914-18, the ties between the two countries had become closer and closer. Szent-Ivanyi concluded at the end of this study that "among the western cultural influences which had had the most important impact on Hungary, there had been a persistent German one."

In the same volume, Bela Pukanszky wrote in his study *German Writings on Hungary*, that no description could fit Hungary better than the one conveyed by the word *Deutschungarn* (German Hungary). Indeed, Pukanszky described his phrase as "a luminous and meaningful formula."

During World War II, no European country made greater efforts than Hungary to prove its strong philo-Germanic sentiments. In 1942, under the presidency of Andreas von Rasnadi Nagy and the real leadership of State Councillor Alexandru von Kidebu Varga, the Hungarian-German Society (Ungarische-Deutsche Gesellschaft) in Budapest carried on an intense activity with a view to bringing about a Hungarian-German rapprochement. Outstanding Magyar personalities delivered numerous lectures in Germany. Among these personalities were: Professor Bela Pukanszky, ministerial advisor Geza von Palert, Professor Vitez Theo Suranyi Unger, Professor Julius von Farkas, Professor Josef Deer, and the writers Lorenz Szabo and Ladislau Hoffman, as well as many others. Most of these talks were not limited to dissertations on the cultural relations between the two countries, but were manifestations of an effort to find convincing reasons for strengthened political, economic, and ideological relations between Hungary and Germany. The events of the years 1940-44 proved to the world how close these relations had become during the present war. The crimes, the plundering, and the savage horrors committed by the Germans during the war, far from producing indignation in Hungary, found their most enthusiastic supporters there.

The Hungarians had finally discovered their true companions: the Nazis in Berlin. Thanks to them they were able with relatively little difficulty to pillage all of their neighbors—the Yugoslavs, the Romanians, and the Czechs. Together, the Nazis and the Hungarians spread terror in invaded Transylvania.

Needless to say, all of their philo-Germanic effusions did not prevent the Hungarians, when it was demanded that part of western Hungary be annexed to Austria, from launching an intense propaganda in France in which they spoke about the danger which a strong Germany represented for France. The fact is that their numerous pro-German manifestations did not prevent them from plucking at the strings of their polyphonic instrument, in what one might describe as "nationally tailored propaganda."

The Magyars Are Pro-American

A series of special emissaries was sent to the United States in an effort to win over American public opinion to "the righteousness of the Magyar cause."

English language magazines were published for the express purpose of persuading the American people that "close relations had always existed" between the great North American republic and the Magyar kingdom (without a king!) in central Europe.

The Hungarian Quarterly, which was published expressly for Anglo-Saxon readers on the other side of the Atlantic, defined its mission in these words: "A quarterly meant to strengthen cultural relations between Hungary and the Anglo-Saxon world."

The Magyar government set up in New York a huge library

containing all the English language works that dealt with Hungary, and they opened a Magyar propaganda office bearing the guise of a "Reference Library," where they gave lectures about Hungary and figuratively threw stones at all the peoples surrounding Hungary. It should be conceded that at this reference library one could get almost any information about the Magyar people—but this information was, of course, presented only in the form of Magyar propaganda.

The Hungarians published an entire literature specially tailored for the American people, in which, under the most inoffensive aspects, the poison of their daily propaganda was concealed. The manner in which this literature covered the Hungarian annexation of Transylvania pursuant to the Vienna agreement between the Axis powers in highly instructive. In order to inform their English language readers about the attitude of the Transylvanian population when the Hungarian troops entered the territory, *The Hungarian Quarterly*, in its autumn issue of 1941, published a short story entitled "The New Frontier." In this story, its author, Count Wass, described the joy the Transylvanian-Romanians felt when they learned how Transylvania had been overrun. Count Wass pretended that, in a conversation with an ordinary Romanian peasant named Iosub, Iosub had said to him "to us peasants it matters little who rules the land."

I have seen many of these peasants from the regions occupied by the Hungarians immediately after their escape from Romania. I have seen them coming by the thousands, leaving behind them their modest possessions, and the plots of land which their ancestors had worked by the sweat of their brow—and on which, for two decades, they had toiled themselves, happily, knowing that the crops would be theirs. I have seen them arriving with grief in their eyes and walking timidly. Fear of the unknown had made them shy, but they were, at the same time, strong. To leave the villages of their fathers and forefathers and to start life again in a world which was unknown to them, required strength and heroic decision.

Whoever thinks a little about this heroic decision made by people who were deeply rooted in the soil of Transylvania, going back a thousand years, will easily understand the real feeling of the Romanian peasants for the Hungarian invaders when, in August 1940, their country was again carved up pursuant to the Vienna agreement.

We do not know what the Romanian peasant actually told Count Wass—that is, if that peasant really existed and was not a product of patriotic fervor and propaganda fiction. But we do know that hundreds of thousands of Romanian peasants, of whom many thousands were old, preferred the uncertainty of embarking on a new life in another world to living in their native villages under the domination of foreigners, whose previous period of domination had left them with bad memories.

The Hungarians had not only distorted history; they had falsified their real sentiments toward the Allied nations. Thus, after extolling fascism and Benito Mussolini for more than two decades and Führer Adolf Hitler for a decade—these praises were among the most effusive addressed to the Führer—the Hungarians started praising President Roosevelt.

In Stephen Coal's article, "American Presidents through Hungarian Eyes," which was published in 1941, one can read the following characterization of the United States President: "Franklin Delano Roosevelt, the political genius of today, the great political thinker who has a well-established reputation on the distant banks of the Danube."

The Hungarians were indeed unwise! They should have prevented items which were written for the Americans from falling into the hands of the Europeans—and vice versa. For instance, we think the Americans would hardly tread on air after reading the following characterization of the American woman written by a Hungarian immigrant, Alexander Lukacs, in the last century. Lukacs had come to the United States believing it to be "the promised land." But he was unhappy about the state of affairs he found there. This is how he expressed his dissatisfaction in a letter sent to a fellow countryman in Hungary on November 19, 1850.

"I have never seen," says this forerunner of Tibor Eckhardt and Oscar Jaszi, "lazier, dirtier, more primitive and untidy creatures than the American woman. They have no notion of the sublime, are completely vain and devoid of love for their children. They are all alike, from the richest to the poorest."

This is how one Hungarian spoke to another Hungarian about the American people. But in addressing themselves to the American people, they speak of the boundless love which the Hungarians have for President Roosevelt and other American leaders.

The Magyars Are Pro-Japanese

Is there any strategem the Hungarians did not try in their efforts to achieve their goal? Not so long ago they discovered ties which gave them an affinity to the Japanese. This newly discovered affinity is no less interesting than the other affinities they profess. The pro-Japanese sentiments of the Hungarians date back to the time when, at the beginning of the war between Japan and the United States, the Japanese appeared to have a chance of success. Thinking that the United States would be defeated, Hungary found it convenient to start showing admiration for the country of the geishas and samurai.

Characteristic of the pro-Japanese effusion is an article in the Hungarian newspaper, *Nemzeti Elet*, of December 12, 1942. We shall quote it at length:

> In this great war which involves the entire world, not only the European and Anglo-Saxon peoples are fighting for their race and their economy [*sic*!], but also the Turanian peoples, who represent one-third of the entire population of the world. Under Japan's leadership they are embarking on their fight for liberty. The struggle of the Turanian peoples is not a secondary one; it has become a decisive factor in determining the future image of the world. This struggle, whose pulse can hardly be felt today, will lead to the achievement of the Turanian conception. It is only a question of time before a world empire emerges [here it comes! M.L.]—an Eastern Asiatic-Japanese-Manchurian-Chinese-Mongolian empire in which all the Turanian states, marching side by side, will be able to turn to good account their worldwide political and economic will.

In this quotation, the Hungarians appear to have become the supporters of the Mongols and to look upon Mongolia as a world power.

Those in the western countries who might think that the above-quoted lines represent the warped conception of a nobody in the field of journalism are in error. The mania for grandeur is characteristic of the entire people and not of certain select individuals.

Thus, Baron Atzel Ede wrote the following in the newspaper *Szekely Nep*, of December 20, 1941: "If we were to reward the Hungarians according to their talents, then we should be the first in the world."

Thus far we have quoted a newspaperman and a representative of the Hungarian nobility. Now it is the turn of a distinguished professor. In a lecture on the cultural superiority of the Turanians, Professor Chelnoky said: "When the Hungarians came to the country they are living in today, they had a culture which was quite superior to that of the European peoples they conquered and subdued. We have given a lot of our material values and especially our spiritual values, to the peoples living here." [Values they had brought with them from Asia! M.L.]

Professor Chelnoky went on speaking about the Hungarian contribution to European culture. He said: "We were the first to have a constitution. We also decreed liberty of religion." [See the sections dealing with the law on tolerated religions. M.L.]

Perhaps we are perverse, but we have always believed that the liberal institutions of Europe had their foundations in the British Magna Charta of the 13th century. Certainly we knew as a fact that there was not another country in the world where religious intolerance had a more honored place than in the homeland of Arpad.

If there is anyone who has any doubts that the Magyars suffered from megalomania, let him read the following lines from the Hungarian newspaper *Szekely Nep* of August 2, 1942, which appeared over the signature of Ember Odom: "To whom should the German troops be thankful for their rapid successes? Surprise attacks and the swift movement of troops represent the decisive elements in warfare. Is there anyone who still doubts that we are the ones who proved these axioms in Europe?" Indeed, there are many who doubt this assertion—but not the Magyar megalomaniacs.

But the Hungarians did not content themselves with civilizing Europe. In their English publications, they sought to prove that they have played a decisive role in the spiritual progress of the United States. An examination of the numerous articles on this theme written by Hungarians for American readers, leaves one with the feeling that of all the European peoples who populate the territory of the United States, the Hungarians stand out as those who have always enjoyed the greatest sympathy in White House circles. One is also left with the impression that they gave the greatest support to the northern states in the abolition of slavery (haven't the Hungarians always been the champions of liberty?), and that the 580,000 Hungarians living in the United States have always, in all fields of activity, ranked first among European ethnic groups living in the New World. (In books intended for German distribution, the figure of 580,000 Hungarians is given, but books written for British distribution speak of over one million Hungarian Americans.)

We should not be surprised if one day we were told that American literature, art, and science were totally attributable to the Hungarian people and the Mongolian race. With Hungarians, everything is possible. As an English author put the matter, "everything with them [the Magyars] runs to extremes."

In Europe there were already passionate philo-Hungarians who were ready to declare with Tisseyre that "Hungarian culture is spreading its beneficence over the peoples living around Hungary," and that the "little civilization existing around Hungary exists only because of Hungary."

Never fear, America's turn will come one day!

13. HUNGARIANS AND ROMANIANS

The Romanian Modesty

What a difference between Magyar opportunism and the modest attitude of Romanian Americans, who, in times of peace, have silently but palpably contributed to the industrialization of the United States through their hard work in the factories and mills of Detroit, Cleveland, and Chicago, and who, during World War I, enthusiastically and spontaneously joined in the battles fought by the American army against the liberty-stifling policy of the Austro-Hungarian monarchy. Recently the United States named one of its large warships after a Romanian immigrant who had become a general in the American army during the American Civil War. The Romanians had received the news with much joy. If the general had been Hungarian, there is no doubt that the arrogant clique in Budapest would have claimed for the "great Magyar people" the honor of bearing the burden of the entire American Civil War. What an occasion this would have presented for the Magyars at "the Reference Library" in New York to extol the heroism of the Magyar nation, which had been described by the Hungarian writer, I. Mikecs, as "the leader of the small European peoples." [*Romania*, Budapest, 1940.]

Anyone who is familiar with the character of the Romanian peasant would not be able to hide the deep admiration and respect he felt for the sincere modesty of the Romanian immigrant population in the United States, which stood in such visible contrast with the arrogance characteristic of Arpad's descendants.

For centuries the Romanians have carried out their historic mission at the frontier between the two worlds, the west and the east. In those areas where they had been placed by providence, they had always served as a protecting shield against repeated barbarian invasions.

Mircea *Cel Batrin,* "the most courageous and skillful among the Christian princes," as contemporary Turkish chroniclers called him, defending western Europe against the fury of the Turkish invaders, courageously stopped the heathen torrent in the battles fought at Rovine (October 10, 1394) and Nicopole (1396). According to contemporary Serbian chronicles, Baiazid, the Turkish leader, was put to flight by "the brave Christian prince," Mircea *Cel Batrin.*

Ioan Huniade, the famous Transylvanian Romanian crusader; Stephen the Great, who was described by the historian, Nicolae Iorga, as a "captain of the crusades" and by the Pope himself as "Christ's athlete;" Michael the Brave, the hero of Calugareni; Vlad Tepes, the victor of Tirgoviste—these have all been Romanian heroes and representatives of the eastern Latin spirit. They were men who turned Romanian Transylvania and the Romanian principalities into a shield against the Turkish danger.

While the Turkish troops, on the offensive to the West, were passing through Budapest, the great Romanian prince, Michael the Brave, forced the invaders to turn their attention to the Romanian army by smiting them with all his force, in this way frustrating the Turkish attack against the West. And Vlad Tepes, the Prince of Wallachia, boldly asserted that "the Romanians should fight the Turks at any price, for if they lose, disaster would strike not only the Romanian people but the whole of Christendom."

The Fruit of Romanian Propaganda

The characteristic modesty of the Romanian people prevented them from bragging to the four corners of the world about the merits of which they had given evidence over the centuries, and which they saw only as their natural contribution to the maintenance and progress of European culture. Magyar propaganda took advantage of this characteristic Romanian modesty. Skillfully making use of all circumstances, the Magyars managed to create, even in Rome, an atmosphere sympathetic to the achievement of Hungarian political ideals. This, despite the fact that Transylvanian Romanians referred to Rome as "Mother Rome," as an expression of the ties which bound them to the everlasting Latin spirit symbolized by the eternal city.

The lack of any aptitude for noisy propaganda of the type at which the Hungarians excel had the effect that Romanian national ideals found less sympathy in Italy's capital—a Latin, but Mussolinian Italy—than did the political goals of Hungary. This, despite a thousand years of history which closely bound the Romanian and Italian peoples and which were marked by bitter enmity between the descendants of ancient Rome and the tribes which had invaded northern Italy, "pillaging and killing 20,000 people in a single day." [According to *The Fulda Annals*, this event took place approximately 894 A.D.]

Hungary's foreign policy after the Versailles peace conference was really carried on under the banner of friendship for fascist Italy and, later on, under that of friendship for the Third Reich. The interest which post-Versailles Hungary succeeded in stirring up in Italy is the most visible proof of the fruitful results which can be achieved by a persevering and unscrupulous propaganda, directed against the most elementary principles of equity and justice.

Rome and the Romanians

For the Romanians in Transylvania, Rome has always represented the most illustrative proof of the common origin of all Romanians—the essence of the national ideal of unity.

"For the Romanians in Transylvania," wrote the Transylvanian writer Gabriel Tepelea, "their contact with Rome has been a continuing source of spiritual and national revival. The knowledge of their noble origin helped them to keep their heads erect during their centuries of oppressive bondage. Both for our peasants and our intellectuals, 'Mother Rome,' or 'Eternal Rome,' were words that they pronounced piously, as if in prayer."

It was in Rome that Transylvanian Romanians Gheorghe Sincai and Inocentiu Micu-Klein first experienced the revelation of Romanian unity. It was also in Rome that they were exposed to the evidence of Romania's centuries-old past, and that they had the sublime vision of the rebirth of the Roman province of Dacia—which was finally realized in 1918. It was also in Rome that Sincai found the inspiration for the Romanian chronicle, which the Hungarians apparently thought so dangerous for their continued rule of Transylvania that they banned its publication. [Decision of the Transylvanian government of March 23, 1814.] It is there, in the crypt of a small church near Trajan's Column, that lie the mortal remains of the patriot Bishop Micu-Klein, who, in 1735, had the courage to challenge the Hungarian nobility with these words, sublime in their strength and simplicity: "From a hereditary standpoint, we have been the masters of Transylvania since the days of the Emperor Trajan."

Nevertheless, it is from Rome—where Romanian leaders had, for the first time, conceived a vision of national unity and where they had, over the centuries, found sustenance for the ideal of union—that the proposal for the mutilation of Romanian national integrity came in 1940.

All of this was the outcome of a wicked propaganda conducted in fascist Italy, which had a *Collegium Hungaricum* in the Falconieri Palace ("Academia d'Unghere," as the Italians called it), with dozens of Hungarian professors—one might say propagandists—at the Universities of Rome, Genoa, Milan, Naples, Pavia, Pisa, Turin, and Trieste, and the hundreds of Magyar lecturers swarming through all the towns of Mussolini's Italy, as though they were at home, while the Romanians were, in general, conspicuous by their absence from the Eternal City.

Because those who are absent are always guilty, the Hungarian propaganda in Rome bore fruit on August 30, 1940.

The Champions of Civilization

> "Oh God, protect Thou us against the Hungarians!"
> (Richard Wagner—Lohengrin, Act I, Scene 1)

Medieval historical sources supply much data concerning the Hungarian invaders who, after pillaging western Europe, settled down on the Pannonian plains in central Europe after their western offensive had been stopped by the armies of the German Emperor, Otho the Great.

Popa-Lisseanu was correct when he observed that the data available about the Hungarian invaders is more ample in these chronicles than the data about previous invaders, precisely because of their penchant for pillaging.

In the year 889 A.D., the chronicler Regino wrote these words about the Magyar race, *Gens Hungarorum ferocissima et omni belua crudelior . . . Vivunt non hominum sed beluarum more* ("The Hungarian people are a more ferocious and cruel race than any wild beast [in the chronicle the superlative 'ferocissima' is used]. They do not live like human beings but like wild beasts.")

After this the chronicler tells us that the Hungarians "eat raw meat and drink blood, and the hearts of their prisoners they eat as medicine." Then he adds: *Nulla miseratione flectuntur nullis pietatis visceribus commoventur* ("They do not know what pity means and they have no sentiment of piety.").

The Fulda Annals, in their turn, speak about the Finno-Ugrian race which invaded the west from the direction of the Urals, and describe the ancestors of today's Hungarians in the same dark colors: "A predatory, cruel race, lacking any human feeling."

This is how the Magyar people appear in the arena of European history. The ancestors of today's Hungarians spread only terror and misery in the lands they passed through. As an illustration of how they were regarded by other people, let us quote what a Hungarian scholar—who cannot be accused of being anti-Hungarian—had to say on this point.

"The Hungarian conquerors," said prelate Endre Sebestyen, writing in the *Hungarian Quarterly*, "immediately after their rule had been established in their new country, instead of settling down peacefully, embarked on a series of pillaging raids in the neighboring countries, which made their name both feared and hated all over western Europe." The peoples in the countries which were "visited" by the pillaging Hungarians added another line to their Sunday prayers—*De sagittis Hungarorum libera nos Domine* ("God protect us from the arrows of the Hungarians").

Sebestyen, who was an English language lecturer at Debrecen University, ended his historical notes with the words, "The peoples thought the Hungarians were a calamity visited upon them by God."

When a people appears on the European continent under such circumstances, we think it is at the very least a trifle risky to speak today about its "civilizing" mission in central Europe.

Count de Fiquelmont, one-time president of the Austrian council of ministers, wrote that it should not be forgotten that the Hungarian people had been the last Europeans to enter

Europe from Asia, and that they did so without annals, which might have provided a clue to their historical antecedents, and without any remembrance of their history and motherland. Such a people is the least entitled to speak about the superior or inferior civilization of a people who descend directly from the Emperor Trajan's Romans.

Of course, it is not our intention to pronounce a judgment on matters of current history in the light of these far-off events. That Regino's chronicle refers to the Hungarians who lived over a thousand years ago is a fact that cannot be challenged. These events would have been buried a long time ago, and the characterizations critical of the Hungarians which appear in medieval chronicles would have been forgotten, if the Hungarians themselves had not again given them currency in more recent historical times.

In 1939, that is, 1,050 years after the Magyar tribes had settled on the Pannonian plain, a Hungarian writer, Ducso Csaba, wrote this characterization in Budapest: "The Hungarian nation is the most glorious achievement of the dominant Mongolian race, which has known only victories. In our veins there flows the blood of Attila, Arpad, and Genghis Khan."

Csaba, the author of this characterization of the Hungarian nation, appeared set in his determination to convince us that blood is thicker than water and that today's Hungarians have inherited all the primitive qualities [*sic*!] of the Finno-Ugrian race. In his violently nationalistic work, *Nincs Kegyelem* ("No Mercy"), which was published in Budapest in 1939, he wipes the slate clean of the thousand years of civilization and culture from the era of the Hungarian invasion, singing a paen of praise to the primitive and barbarian qualities of his ancestors.

The message of Csaba's work, there is no pity and no mercy, reminds one of the famous *nulla miseratione* ("No Pity") in Regino's chronicles. In the chapter entitled "Levent's Mission," Csaba demonstrated that the goal of the Hungarian youth organization known as the Levents was the extermination of the Romanians in Hungary at any price—by assassination, by poison, by fire, or other means. We quote verbatim from "Levent's Mission." The Magyar Levent, Torday, is speaking to his sweetheart, Pirosca:

I will not wait until the time for revenge comes. I won't.

I'm going to kill any Wallachian I meet. I'll kill every one of them. I shall be ruthless. I'll set the Wallachian villages on fire at night. I'll put the entire population to the sword. I'll poison all the springs, and I'll kill even the children in their cradles. I'll destroy this miserable thieving race in the bud. I'll have mercy on no one—neither the children in their cradles nor the mother giving birth to a baby. . . . I'll kill every Wallachian—and then there will be only one nationality left in Transylvania, the Magyar nationality, my nation, my blood. I'll make the future Closcas and Crisans impotent. I'll be merciless!

After reading this pathological confession of faith of the young Levent, Torday—Csaba is, after all, a 20th century writer—I confess to being profoundly perplexed. Indeed, it is dumbfounding that the Magyar government, which patronized the Levent movement as a legally instituted organization for the paramilitary training of Hungarian youth, should encourage or even condone language inciting to assassination and bestialities and to the most odious cruelties.

The total extermination of the Romanians in Transylvania so that it could finally become Magyar! Why not the extermination of all the other nations on the continent so that the whole of Europe could become Magyar? It would give the Magyars more *Lebensraum*, and the Hungarians would at last find the earthly paradise they coveted.

The death of mothers carrying small babies, the killing of babies in their cradles? What other certificate of superior culture is needed than the record of fanatical manifestations of hypernationalism?

Civilization and culture are intended to stifle man's primitive instincts, his primeval impulses and the sometimes bloody examples of his ancient forefathers who lived at a time when the mind of the barbarian was in darkness. Ducso Csaba wished to do away with the invisible links wrought by the progress of civilization in relations between men. He wanted a license to kill, to pillage, to exterminate even children, to destroy everything in his way—and all of this in the name of the triumph of the superior civilization characterized by Attila the Hun, Genghis Khan, and Arpad. Under the spiritual patronage of this dark triumvirate, the Hungarian extremists intended to create a new mode of life in central Europe. In effect, they were saying, "Let us return to the barbarian era, so that Hungary may rule Romanian Transylvania again."

Yet, Hungary's "civilizing mission" was praised by many people. Thus, the Italian writer Franco Vellano Dionisi, spoke of "fertile, civilized Hungary"; the Hungarian writer L. Mikecs saw his country as the "leader of the neighboring peoples"; while Count Apponyi claimed that Hungary was the "civilizing missionary at the frontier of western Europe."

The future of Europe would appear dark indeed if we were to look upon the Hungarian nation as the missionary of central European civilization. The neighboring Romanians are, however, modest peasants. Romania is a country which has only recently joined the great family of cultured European states. Fate has been cruel to this younger branch of European Latinity. Indeed, the Romanian people had to defend themselves for centuries in order to be able to exist as a nation.

This state of uncertainty, which was the product of a long struggle, resulted in many drawbacks and suffering and troubles. Such a state of uncertainty hardly favors the flourishing of culture and progress. *Inter arma silent musae!* ("When weapons clash, the muses are silent.")

One should not forget that, unlike the Hungarians, the Romanians never made war on other peoples with the intention of conquering, pillaging, and destroying. There are many wars in Romanian history, but all of them were defensive wars, intended to protect their ancestral land and their national spirit.

Since the Romanians won their freedom, they have made surprising progress in all areas of activity. However, it would be childish to draw a parallel between the spiritual values which the two nations—the Romanians and the Hungarians—have contributed to world culture.

Cultural contributions do not lend themselves to qualitative analysis. It would also be ridiculous to follow in the path of modern Hungarian anthologies, which lumped together as "Magyar" literary productions the works written by various writers, not only Hungarian, but also members of the nationalities which lived on the territories ruled by the Hungarian crown.

In their efforts to look magnificent at any cost, the Hungarians boast about spiritual values which really belong to other peoples and which have nothing in common with the descendants of St. Stephen. Professor Gyula Pal, for example, in his book *The Lives and Works of the Magyar Writers*, which has just come out in Budapest, speaks of the most outstanding figures of Romanian national cultural life in Transylvania as "Magyar writers." It is quite true that Transylvania lived under Hungarian domination. But this does not give the Magyars the right to count as Hungarian writers men who wrote in Romanian, considered themselves Romanian, fought for the Romanian cause, and were the most fervent enemies of Magyar denationalization.

It is, for example, an elementary lack of common sense, if not a provocation, to present as a Magyar a man such as Gheorghe Baritiu, one of the most enlightened Transylvanian Romanian patriots, often considered the founder of Transylvanian journalism, a martyr of the Romanian cause in Transylvania. It is equally provocative to list as a "Magyar writer" people like Inocentiu Micu-Klein, an author who wrote, *Elements linguae daco-romanae sive valachicae* ("Elements of the Daco-Romanian or Wallachian Language"), or Samuel Klein, one of the first fighters against Magyar domination, or Simeon Barnutiu, Ion Agarbiceanu, Teodor Capidan, Emanoil Bucuta, and Gheorghe Bodgan Duica, who represent the most important Romanian authors in Transylvania.

Pal has managed, through the forced Magyarization of all the non-Hungarian writers who ever lived under the Austro-Hungarian monarchy, to list 14,117 so-called Magyar writers for only the first three letters of the alphabet. Zenovie Paclisanu, a competent specialist in problems of the former Austro-Hungarian monarchy, has estimated that the total number of writers Pal will manage to collect, when the remaining volumes containing the rest of the letters up to Z are completed, might be approximately 100,000.

We should not be at all surprised if, making use of the same method, Pal were to list among the Magyar writers the great Romanian poet Octavian Goga, the singer of Transylvania's sufferings, who wrote that in Transylvania "there are songs and flowers, and many, many tears are shed." It would also be natural for such an anthology to present as Magyar writers men like Andrei Muresanu, the author of the famous poem, *Response*, the first stanza of which constitutes the best proof of his "pro-Magyar" sentiments:

Awake, Romanian, from thy death's slumber

In which the tyrants have kept you!

But this method is not new, and it can no longer surprise those who are familiar with the ways of the Magyars. Don't the Hungarians derive glory from the beautiful *Rondo all'ongresse* ("Hungarian Rondo"), which Haydn immortalized in one of his trios—a composition which is as Hungarian as the works of Ion Agarbiceanu, a Romanian prose writer who was selected as national laureate for 1927, or as the works of Octavian Goga, the poet of Romanian Transylvania's mountain roads?

Nobody can deny the beauty and originality of the Hungarian folk music which inspired Brahms, Liszt, Schubert and Sarasate, and nobody can dispute the charm of Alexander Petöfy's poems or the philosophical poems of Emerich Marach, the author of the famous *Tragedy of Man*.

It is unfair to include in the patrimony of Magyar culture productions which unchallengeably belong to the culture of other peoples who inhabited the same areas of central Europe. The Hungarians have made a lot of fuss when musical productions of the Hungarian folk genius made their way to the west under the caption of "gypsy music." And they were especially indignant when Maestro Sarasate called his famous violin composition, which was really inspired by the sentimental Hungarian song by Elemer Szentirmay, "Gypsy Airs" (*Zigeunerweisen*).

Then, one may ask, why don't they refrain from committing the same sin by ascribing to the Magyar culture productions which are pregnant with the most characteristic Romanian spirit?

The explanation is to be found in the traditional Hungarian method of creating confusion, a method intended to make things so intricate that it requires great effort to bring truth to light.

If one takes into consideration those 100,000 Magyar writers—a figure which represents 1.2 percent of the entire Hungarian population of the Magyar kingdom of 1920—the Hungarians would have justice on their side in posing not only as the spiritual leaders of the "barbarian" people surrounding them, but also of the entire world!

Indeed, the western neighbors of the Romanians have had little hesitation, whenever the occasion arose, to refer to the

Romanians as a nation of illiterate and backward shepherds, or as barbarians who clustered around a highly civilized Hungary, the country of 100,000 men of letters. The answer given by the Romanians to such Hungarian graciousness was sober and eloquent. It is written for all time and for all men to see in the permanent presence of many Romanian representatives in the annals of European culture.

The glory of the historian Nicolae Iorga has transcended his country's frontier, as has that of the great neurologist Gheorghe Marinescu.

In the history of European diplomacy, the names of the Romanians, Take Ionescu and Nicolae Titulescu, are inscribed in golden letters.

In the sphere of music, the name of George Enescu—violinist, conductor, and composer—will belong forever, together with that of Stan Golestan, to the group of great musicians of the 20th century.

DeMax, Marioara Ventura, Younel, have all been gifted representatives of Romanian art in Paris; Raoul Aslan and Grozavescu have taken the fame of Romanian art to Vienna; Maria Cebotari to LaScala in Milan. Artists such as Countess de Noailles, Elena Vacarescu, Martha Bibescu, Panait Istrati, and Matei Russo have Europeanized the name of Romania, while Mihail Eminescu's poetry is on the verge of taking hold of a well-deserved place among the most illustrious creations of the genre, including the poetry of Leopardi, Musset, and Shelley. Finally, Petru Neagoie's glory has taken the good name of the Romanian people across the ocean to the United States of America.

As one can see, a large group of Romanian thinkers, poets, artists, and writers have brought their country a different kind of fame from that which the Hungarians were disposed to attribute to them. But the Hungarians have meditated deeply on the famous words: *Calomniez, calomniez, il en resters toujours quelque chose!* ("Calumniate, calumniate—something will always stick!"). Indeed, they have used these words as their dogma.

They have made use of every opportunity that presented itself to disparage the Romanians and to portray them to world public opinion as inferior to the Magyars in every respect.

The Romanians in Budapest

The most convincing example of the traditional Hungarian penchant for distorting the truth at any cost and for slandering everything Romanian was a product of the Romanian occupation in the summer of 1919.

Today, the facts about what really happened are recognized, undistorted by political passion. They are recorded in history by impartial scholars.

The military occupation of Hungary had been approved by leading military figures and politicians in the West. Indeed, the occupation had been suggested by General Pelle, the chief of the French military delegation in Prague, even before the Romanian troops had crossed the Tisa River. In his letter of July 6, 1919, addressed to the Allied Supreme Council, General Pelle wrote: "The Hungarians are determined to win back their former boundaries. The only means to deter them is to occupy Hungary by military intervention, as in the case of Germany."

The Romanian occupation of Hungary caused the Hungarians to embark on an energetic and vicious propaganda campaign against the Romanian army, a campaign in which they outrageously distorted the truth. There was no conceivable charge that the Romanians were not accused of in order to make the civilized world stop sympathizing with them and start worrying, instead, about "unhappy" Hungary.

First, they were accused of starving the Hungarian capital and of taking by force everything on which they could lay their hands, in other words, they were accused of devastating the entire country.

On this occasion, Hungarian propaganda resorted to a barrage of heavy artillery. Once more we are compelled to admit that their vicious propaganda, based on imaginary facts which were difficult to check at a distance of thousands of miles, succeeded in surrounding the Hungarian people with an aura of martyrdom. The echo of this propaganda can be heard to this day.

We shall continue to be faithful to the principles that have thus far guided us. To settle the matter to which we have just referred, we shall not quote the Romanian evidence presented by General Mardarescu, the commander of the Romanian occupation army in Budapest, but we shall have recourse instead to a source whose objectivity cannot be challenged, an American newspaperman who was in the Hungarian capital during the Romanian occupation.

Fortunately for the triumph of truth, the American journalist Charles Upson Clark, Ph.D., was able to bear witness on the spot to what the Romanian occupation of Hungary was really like. In his work *Greater Romania*, which was published in New York in 1922, Clark described in detail the life of the Hungarian capital under the occupation. "Since I happened to see Budapest under the Romanian occupation in October 1919," he said, "I shall be able to describe what I saw there myself without the assistance of any official translator or guide who could prevent me from finding out the truth."

Clark admitted that before he left for Budapest, important members of the American Commission at the peace conference in Paris had painted in most somber colors the situation he would discover in Budapest. A leading American diplomat had even told him—obviously from hearsay—that the Romanians had left untouched only the cobblestones in the streets of Budapest.

"I have to confess," said Clark, "that to my great surprise not only had the Romanians not ruined the life of the Hungarian capital but had even normalized it. The Romanians should be praised for their constructive point of view in everything they did in Budapest."

Clark declared that the goods captured from the Hungarian army were put at the disposal of the civilian authority, and that four trainloads of food, coming from four different directions, had been stopped and the food used for the capital's population. "The markets," said Clark, "were full of peasants and their customers. There was plenty of poultry. In addition to food, the markets were also full of goods. In fact, life was cheaper than it was in Bucharest where the shops did not offer so large a display of products."

All the theaters were open. On the evening of October 28, 1919, the American journalist could choose between Shakespeare's *Othello*, Mozart's *The Magic Flute*, Schiller's *The Robbers*, and other plays or musical comedies—to say nothing about the cimenas. For a town living "under the humiliating occupation of a Balkan army," Budapest was doing very well, indeed. Clark also related that under the Romanian occupation art exhibitions had opened their doors, and even the horse races had been resumed.

The Romanians did not in any way impede the exercise of civil rights by the Hungarian people. Indeed, during the Romanian occupation, there was one public manifestation which brought together 150,000 people. This fact confirms General

Mardarescu's statement that "the Romanian troops of occupation did not interfere in any way in the internal life of the Hungarian state."

The Magyar "Civilization" and the "Savageness" of the Romanians

Today it is an historically accepted fact that the German-Austrian-Hungarian occupation troops during World War I devastated occupied Romania.

If one were to draw a parallel between the two occupations—the Romanian occupation of Hungary and the German-Austrian-Hungarian occupation of Romania—the Romanians could not have been addressed with the injurious epithets that the Magyar propaganda hurled at them for some two decades.

The question arises: How did the lies about the ruin of Budapest achieve currency, and how is it that these lies can still be heard today?

The answer is quite simple. The Hungarians have always sought—and are still seeking—to publicize the notion that the Romanians are a people with barbarian instincts, and for this reason are incapable of being a major element among peoples of superior race—such as the Finno-Ugrian Magyar people, for example.

Hungarian "civilization" has been set against the "savageness" of the Romanian people.

And what are the means used by the Hungarians to paint themselves as champions of civilization in the eyes of world public opinion?

When they cannot find enough heroic deeds in their own history to round out "the magnificent story of the most glorious central European nation," the Hungarians have not shrunk from concocting heroic deeds or from turning the great disasters of their history into pages of eternal glory. Thus, the Magyar histories which have been written for the use of non-Magyars have generally been historical transfigurations, where fiction replaces reality and a legend, full of subjectivism and expressly created for the reader, is presented as an objective historical account.

Thus, for consumption by Spanish public opinion, the Hungarians invented an original Hungarian history, in which the battles of Mohi (1241 A.D.) and Mohaci (1526 A.D.), both of which constituted genuine national disasters, were described as victories unique in the history of Europe, with incalculable consequences for western civilization. It is sufficient to open Henrik Marczali's history of the period where one reads that "in 1241 A.D. Batu [the leader of the Mongolians] was forced to withdraw, not by Hungarian pressure, but by the death of Oktai Khan in the Far East and Batu's desire to take his place." [Henrik Marczali, *The History of the Arpad Dynasty.*] Count Paul Teleki's study, *Ungarn, Vergangenheit und Gegenwart* ("Hungary, Past and Present"), also tells us that the withdrawal of the Tartar forces did not come about thanks to the heroism of the Magyar troops, but as the result of an accident in the form of "the death of Oktai Khan." Any Hungarian history book intended for Hungarian readers makes one realize the proportions of the Hungarian disaster at Mohaci. In Fraknoi Vilmo's book *The Era of the Huniades and the Jagellons*, he wrote that in only one hour and a half the Magyar army had been destroyed and "the corpses, of about 24,000 (out of 28,000 Magyar soldiers), covered the battlefield."

When an outstanding historian like Balint Homan writes that the ravaging expeditions of the first Magyars were just "sportive undertakings" (*sportartige Unternehmungen*), what can one expect from so-called historians who write for political propaganda purposes?

If the "ravaging expeditions," which according to the *Fulda Annals* involved the killing of as many as 20,000 people in one day, could be regarded as a sportive indulgence, one is constrained to ask what limits would have been observed if the "representatives of civilization in central Europe" had decided to be really cruel. The answer to this question is provided by Ducso Csaba and his Levent organization. In order to achieve a final settlement of the Transylvanian problem, they proposed the extermination of the three million Transylvanian Romanians. This, of course, would have involved killings on a much larger scale than the 20,000 who were killed in a single day by the early Magyar invaders—but then one has to defer to the laws of progress and the modern emphasis on speed.

But if they can rewrite history so easily, why don't the Hungarians invent a Hungarian King Louis XIV or a Queen Victoria to further their cause? Then they could really speak—as they in fact speak today in the Spanish magazine *Destino*—in the name of a Hungary without which "the European continent would become the most forgotten corner on earth."

The cause of truth could not be better served than by quoting, at the end of this chapter, two distinguished opinions regarding the "backward Romanian people," who live at the frontiers of eastern Europe.

"I don't think there is among our allies," said Louis Barthou, the French politician and man of letters, "another country which is closer to us through so many affinities, through its origin, its tradition, and its culture. There is no other allied country where the French language is spoken as it is in Romania—with such ease, grace, and force."

The great French historian Jules Michelet, addressing himself to the western peoples, defended the Romanians in these terms against the incessant Magyar propaganda campaign:

Peoples of the West, who have for a long time cultivated peace, remote from the danger of barbarism—you should be forever grateful to the nations living at Europe's eastern frontier, because they have protected you from the Tartar invasions and the Turkish Army. You should not forget what you owe in particular to unhappy Romania.

Barthou and Michelet! Let us be allowed to prefer their words, written for eternity, to those of Tisseyre, Franco Vellani-Dionisi or Robert Donald. Let us prefer what is eternal over that which is transient. Let us prefer objectivity to the passionate and convoluted distortions of the pseudo-historians.

Barthou and Michelet, your names will be eternally remembered by the Romanian people, while the names of those who have slandered the Romanian people will surely sink into oblivion!

14. NATIONAL MINORITIES POLICY UNDER THE HUNGARIANS AND THE ROMANIANS

> *Magyarorszag vagy lesz magyar vagy nem lesz.*
> ("Either Hungary will become Magyar or it will disappear.")
>
> Hungarian slogan

> "Today, the fate of the minorities cannot be compared to that of the peoples in prewar Europe."
>
> *Aristide Briand*

When the Hungarians, taking advantage of the weaknesses of the Hapsburg crown, had become sufficiently strong under the dual monarchy, their policy toward the other people who shared the territory with them was carried forward under the slogan of "Magyarization at any price." As a policy statement, this referred to all the non-Magyar peoples, with the chimerical goal of achieving a unitary Hungarian state.

When this ultranationalistic policy was put into effect in 1867, Hungary had a population of 13,579,000 inhabitants, of whom only 5,665,000 were Magyar, as compared with 7,959,000 non-Magyar.

Therefore, within the Hungary of that time, the Hungarians constituted a distinct minority, while the majority consisted of non-Magyar peoples. These latter lived together not because of the nature of things or because this was their will, but because of an absurd destiny against which these nationalities had always fought until their final liberation. Between the dominant Magyar element and those they oppressed, there had always been an abyss, which was the result not only of differences of race, tradition, ideals, and religion but also of centuries of oppression on the part of the Magyar leaders.

The Hungarians did not refrain from any measure, no matter how grave, in their efforts to bring about the denationalization of the subject nationalities. All the efforts of the Hungarian state, all the endeavors of the Budapest leaders, from the most moderate ones to the most chauvinistic ones, were directed towards one central goal—the Magyarization of the millions of non-Magyars.

With his customary cynicism, Geza Kostelszky put the matter in unmistakable terms: "We can either Magyarize them or disappear ourselves; *tertium non datur* ('there is no middle course')."

The effects of this immense negative undertaking can be seen in the sad but flexible reality of population statistics. In 1869, the Magyars constituted 44.4 percent of the entire population, while non-Magyar elements combined constituted 55.6 percent. In 1880, the Hungarians rose to 46.6 percent of the total population, while the non-Magyars dropped to 53.4 percent. In 1890, the proportion was 48.5 percent Magyars and 51.5 percent non-Magyars. in 1900, Hungarian statistics showed that the proportion had changed to 51.4 percent Magyar as compared with 48.6 percent non-Magyar. Finally, in the year 1910, the Magyars had become unmistakably the most numerous nationality, with 54.5 percent of the population against 45.5 percent of the non-Magyar elements. This is set forth in the table that follows:

	1869	1880	1890	1900	1910
Magyar	44.4%	46.6%	48.5%	51.4%	54.5%
Non-Magyar	55.6%	53.4%	51.5%	48.6%	45.5%

The first line shows the increase in the Hungarian percentage of the total population as a result of the policy of denationalization, while the second line shows the decrease in the population percentage of the non-Magyar peoples, who were the victims of the policy of progressive denationalization.

If it had not been for the outbreak of World War I and the collapse of the Austro-Hungarian monarchy, Kostelszky's dream might indeed have come true one day, because Europe was obviously unable to put a stop to the most monstrous denationalization program in history. Indeed, during the first decade of the 20th century, the Magyar population, as compared with the entire population of Hungary, recorded an increase of 3.1 percent, while the non-Magyars decreased by 3.1 percent during the same time period.

In 1880, the Hungarians numbered only 5,404,070, as compared with 7,345,553 non-Magyars. Taking into consideration the natural increase due to births, there should have been 10 million non-Magyars by 1910 and at the most 8 million Magyars. But the denationalization program was in full swing so that by 1910 the Hungarian state had 9,944,620 Hungarians, or so-called Hungarians, and only 8,319,966 non-Magyars.

One may ask what happened to the Romanians, Germans, Slovaks, Croats, and Serbs, who historically had had such a high birth rate? Did they lose themselves so quickly in the mass of what had been until recently the Magyar minority? Did the Romanians—from the standpoint of their birth rate, one of the most vigorous peoples in Europe—actually diminish in number? And what about the highly prolific Germans?

Perhaps they were assimilated of their own free will, especially during the first decade of the 20th century which was so auspicious for the Magyar denationalization program. Perhaps they spontaneously and enthusiastically declared themselves to be Hungarians, after declining for centuries the honor of being counted among Arpad's descendants. Such an assumption is simply unbelievable. And on closer examination, one discovers how really preposterous it is.

For example, in the region of the western part of Transylvania inhabited by Swabian colonists, there is the commune of Petresti in the former Satu-Mare district. Hungarian statistics in 1890 recorded the existence of 134 Hungarians as compared with 1,076 Germans. In 1900, that is, ten years later, the statistics show increases of 3 Hungarians and 146 Germans—which was normal given the comparative birth rates of the two peoples. But over the next decade, the official statistics record a very strange phenomenon. From the 137 Magyars existing in 1900, the number suddenly rose to 1,453—an increase of 1,000 percent—while the Germans, who counted 1,202 in the statistics of 1900, disappeared as if by magic, without leaving any trace.

In order to arrive at this miraculous result, two highly unlikely conditions should have existed. First, there could have been a calamity which, mercilessly and miraculously, killed off the Germans—but only the Germans—in the commune of Petresti. And, second, there would have had to be a phenomenon, of the same order, which converted the dead Germans into living Hungarians. At that point, Hungary would have ceased to be "the country of 100,000 writers," and it would have become the country of all miracles—in an age when nobody any longer believed in miracles. The explanation, however, is much simpler and closer to earth.

In the statistics for the commune of Petresti, recorded according to the criterion of language, we find that in 1900 there were 1,202 inhabitants recorded in the German language column. These were "Magyars" who could speak German—of course, with a pronounced Swabian accent. In 1910, however, these statistics for Petresti record no German-speaking population. The case of Petresti is not an isolated one. Indeed, Zenovie Paclisanu mentions dozens of similar cases in his book *Deutsche und Magyaren* ("Germans and Hungarians").

For a civilized person, such phenomena, which occurred all the time and on such a large scale in all areas of activity, are simply inconceivable. Nevertheless, they were the natural results of a policy about which the Magyar leaders made no bones (within the boundaries of Hungary), and even encouraged with all their might. When the goal of Hungarian policy was the extermination of the subject nationalities, and when the Hungarians had elevated this goal to a national ideal, a further characterization of the nationalities situation under the Magyars becomes superfluous. In order to destroy the national spirit of the subject nationalities, it was first necessary to violate their conscience. Next, it was necessary to bend their will; and, finally, it was necessary to employ force, terror, intolerance, and oppression. The violence and intolerance which are characteristic of Magyar policy vis-à-vis the subject nationalities are a natural corollary of the principles which have guided this policy.

"Unity" cannot be achieved without the sacrifice of national idiosyncrasies. When the "idiosyncrasies" fight for their lives, unity can be achieved only by force.

In a Hungary committed to unity at any price, it was inevitable that the situation of the non-Magyar nationalities should be characterized by intolerance. On the eve of World War I, Hungary had become a veritable prison for the subject nationalities.

In other parts of Transylvania, as was the case in the region inhabited by the Szecklers, the Hungarians wanted to Magyarize everything, both the land and the people. If their efforts directed against material objectives were fruitful, this cannot be said of their efforts to subdue by force the souls of the Romanian people in Transylvania. The Romanian Transylvanians were able to avoid the dangerous trap of denationalization, perpetuating, within a hostile world, the hope of a better future.

In his propagandistic work *Justice for Hungary*, which was published in London in 1928, Count Apponyi sought to present the Hungarian people to the Anglo Saxon reader as one of the best, if not the best people, living in central and southeastern Europe.

In the pages that follow, we shall deal with different aspects of Magyar propaganda directed against the Romanian nationality in Transylvania, in the hope that the myths of Hungarian "liberalism" and "cultural superiority" will forever disappear.

The Magyarization of Toponymic Names

The land of Transylvania, with its hills and valleys, rivers and woods and villages, presented much too vivid an image of its age-old Romanian spirit. One can, therefore, understand the Hungarian desire to wipe out, once and for all, those elements which spoke about a purely Romanian past and which had been handed down from father to son, from one generation to another, from one century to another.

Count Desider Banffy, the most important representative of the school of denationalization, decided to deal with this situation by replacing the old non-Magyar place names with new names, invented on the spot and bearing the characteristic stamp of Magyarism. With this end in view, he drew up "the law" dealing with names of communes and other places, which was promulgated on February 17, 1898.

According to this law, the Hungarian ministry of internal affairs was given the right to Magyarize old Romanian place names and geographic names in Transylvania, and to require the Romanian natives to use these new names officially.

This was an inequity which naturally resulted in strong protests. In their manifesto of September 14, 1897, when the law was still only a draft bill being considered by Parliament, the Romanians denounced the proposal as "an evident prejudice to their innermost feelings" and as "an inhuman attempt to destroy all the historical traces which the Romanians have left in this land, which they have defended with their blood and fertilized with the sweat of their brows."

The protests of the Romanians, as well as those of the German minority, had no effect on the policy of Magyarizing the old non-Magyar toponymic names, since this was considered an important step toward the goal of complete Magyarization to which all Hungarian governments, after the year 1867, had been committed.

Because they were unable to change the soul of the Romanian province of Transylvania, the Hungarians had to content themselves with changing certain of the external aspects. Instead of the warm Romanian names, which were of Latin or Slavo-Latin origin, the native population was obliged to use the harsh Finno-Ugrian alternatives whenever they addressed government officials. However, to the non-Magyar elements in the population, these new names were as alien as those who sought to impose them.

By imposing this kind of denationalization on the more tractable elements in the situation, the Budapest government sought to influence the inner beings of those non-Magyar citizens who persisted in calling themselves Romanian.

The Magyarization of Family Names

After the Magyarization of toponymic names, came the turn of family names. By trying to make the non-Magyars forget the original names of their native areas, and afterwards by seeking to cause them to forget the non-Magyar names under which their ancestors had lived for centuries, the Magyar leaders obviously hoped to cause the non-Magyars to forget that they belonged to another nationality.

Alexandru Celkes, the president of the Society for the Magyarization of Names, which had been set up in the Hungarian capital in 1881, produced a study confirming this viewpoint in 1898. "The Magyarization of names," he said, "is an inner effort which will one day bring about a united Magyar society instead of the mixed society which exists at present."

In the year 1896, the Hungarians celebrated the millenial

anniversary of the establishment of the Hungarian state. It was a time when the Hungarians wanted to impress western Europe with the achievements of their national genius. During this period, the movement for the Magyarization of names had achieved such proportions that it had become a source of danger for the future of the non-Magyar peoples. Thus, in 1896, the government put a lot of pressure on all the non-Magyar clerks working in the various ministries and the state administration, for the railroads, and for other enterprises, in an effort to persuade them to change their family name. Many of them were blackmailed by being told that they could lose their jobs if they did not give up their non-Magyar names, as confirmed by the Transylvanian Saxon religious leader, Bishop Teutsch.

It is easy to understand that, by making the very existence of non-Magyars depend on the Magyarization of their names, the Hungarians were able to open gaps in the ranks of the non-Magyar nationalities.

"The people," said Zenovie Paclisanu in *L'art de la manière de faire des Hongrois* ("The Art of Doing Things in the Hungarian Manner"), "succumbed under pressure and the specter of losing their jobs, which was equivalent to leaving their children without bread, firewood, and light."

As compared with other nationalities, a smaller percentage of Romanians succumbed to the pressure to Magyarize their names. This can be accounted for by the vigorous state of Romanian national consciousness and by the fact that the majority of the Romanians were plowmen and shepherds, while only a few were government clerks. Nevertheless, thanks to the monstrous system which deprived people of their own names, many people were alienated from the great family of Transylvanian Romanians. How could anyone recognize as Romanians people who had once been Albu, Chiorean, Lupu, or Budu, and who had become Zagoni, Szabo, Farkas, and Budth?

The Superiority of Magyar Culture

In *Justice for Hungary*, Count Apponyi admitted that the Hungarian people were the product of a mixture of nations (he spoke about Hungary's "mixed national composition"). This represented remarkable progress, compared with the performance of some of Count Apponyi's famous fellow countrymen, who denied this self-evident truth. But what was less praiseworthy was the manner in which Count Apponyi explained the fusion of the subject nationalities into the Magyar masses. For Count Apponyi the assimilation of these various national groupings could only be due to the superior culture of the Magyars, which had always irresistibly drawn the "inferior" Romanian, Croat, Slovak, and Serbian peoples.

For the Magyar statesman, even the spiritual leaders of the Transylvanian Romanians were viewed as bearing the mark of this superior Magyar culture, which radiated all the good things proper to a western-type culture and western civilization. Count Apponyi was not the only one who possessed such a vivid imagination. Even today, Magyar propaganda is still making efforts—which are worthy of a better cause—to spread the view that the Transylvanian Romanians owe their spiritual structure to the unrivaled Hungarian culture.

We think it is high time that the question of the so-called Magyar "superiority" is answered in a fitting manner. The time has finally come when Hungarian hypocrisy must be unmasked. At stake are not only the local Romanian-Hungarian interests, but also the security of peace in the Danubian area in the years to come.

For decades the peoples in the West have been lobbied by representatives of what passes as Hungarian liberalism. These representatives surpassed one another in praising the chivalrous quality of spirit of Arpad's descendants.

What were the "generous ideas" which inspired the Magyars when they had supremacy over the Romanian people in Transylvania, as well as over a large number of Croats, Czechs, Slovaks, and Serbs?

The answer can be simply given. The Hungarian regime was characterized by intolerance, inhumanity, oppression, and terror. Of what did the "cultural superiority" and the "civilizing mission" of the Hungarian leaders consist? Of course, they could not consist of the ruthless, inhuman, totalitarian action of denationalization, which had always been characteristic of Magyar rule. Even if the Hungarians had given the world a Beethoven, a Rembrandt, a Pasteur, or a Dante, they would have had no right to speak of the superiority of the Magyar culture because of the inhumanity which has characterized the behavior of this nation toward their neighbors of different nationality.

What cynical impudence leads them to speak of a "civilizing mission," when behind these empty words are concealed the most cruel methods of oppression in contemporary history—until the appearance of fascism in Europe? What today appears to be the unity of the Magyar nation is the product of countless intrusions carried out by the Magyars on the populations which constitute the Hungarian conglomerate, and not of the magnetic attraction exercised by the "superior culture" of the Magyars. As a matter of fact, is it a culture which bears the distinctive mark of Magyar genius? To put it differently, is it a Magyar culture, as there is a French, German, or English culture?

The German writer Otto Hauser categorically denied the existence of such a culture. Moreover, in his *Weltgeschichte der Literatur* ("History of World Literature"), he went so far as to deny that the Hungarians had made any original contribution to what might be called the cultural life of Hungary. "In the cultural life of Hungary," he said, "the Magyars have absolutely no merit."

Another German writer Franz von Loher who, in 1874, published a book entitled *Die Magyaren und andere Ungarn* ("The Magyars and Other Hungarians"), also rejected the notion that Magyar culture had participated in the civilization of Europe. Loher wrote: "We shall look in vain for the few stones which the Magyars are supposed to have contributed to the great edifice of world culture. There is not a single idea which has reached the civilized world in the fields of justice, religion, ethics, art and science, or in any other area of human endeavor that had its origin with the Magyars . . . What a terrible emptiness covers the thousand years of Magyar history! The more impetuous, the stronger, and the more vigorous their spirit appears, the more fruitless it is. Their character is and remains refractory to the concept of creation."

The most effective answer that can be given to the tendentious assertions of Magyar propaganda in other countries over the two decades following the Trianon treaty is implicit in a comparison between the treatment which Hungarians accorded their subject nationalities and the manner in which the Romanians dealt with their own national minorities after Transylvania had been reunited with the motherland in 1918.

In order to come by the truth, we shall use only statistical data and official documents.

In the countries belonging to the Hungarian crown, the rights of other nationalities who resided in the territory were established by the famous law on the "equal rights of the nationalities," which was promulgated in 1868. The title sounded promising—"equal rights of the nationalities." But that is as far as the matter went. Indeed, the text of the law began with a preamble which wiped out all the hopes aroused by the generous title of the law. As Paclisanu put it, the law in fact provided for "equal injustice" and "equal suppression" of the nationalities rather than for their "equal rights."

The preamble of this law says the following: "In Hungary there is but one nation—an indivisible one—the Magyar nation. All citizens, irrespective of their origin, are members of this Magyar nation."

We think it important to point out that this law did not speak of citizens of the Hungarian state, but of members of the Magyar nation. In other words, the Hungarian state acknowledged as beneficiaries of the law—irrespective of their nationality—only those citizens who could be counted as Magyars.

The "equal rights" to which the law referred in fact represented an onerous barter operation. The non-Magyars were granted "equal rights," but in exchange they were asked to abandon their nationality.

If, for example, the Transylvanian Romanians had asked for legal approval to convene a meeting for the purpose of changing Romanian names into Magyar ones, this approval would have been granted immediately, since such Romanians would have represented sound elements within the Magyar nation. But when the Romanian lawyer Ion Nichita, from Zalau, convened a meeting of Romanian electors on March 24, 1893, to discuss the "government's attitude toward the church" (religious freedom had been one of the rights guaranteed by the law), the sub-prefect in Salaj cancelled the meeting. He justified his action in these words:

> I shall not permit this meeting as it has been organized by the Romanian electors of the Zalau district. Hungarian law does not acknowledge the existence of electors of a different nation, such as Romanians, Serbs, Slovaks, and so forth. According to Law no. 44 of 1868 [the law which referred to "equal rights"], all Hungarian citizens, no matter what their nationality, represent, from a political

standpoint, one single nation—the unique and indivisible Magyar nation. A distinction between our citizens is possible only on the basis of the different languages they speak.

The expression of this point of view did not represent a mere abuse of authority on the part of a sub-prefect who arbitrarily forbade a meeting of Magyar citizens of Romanian nationality—and this in a land like Transylvania, which had always been Romanian. It, in fact, represented the point of view of the entire Hungarian government on the interpretation of the law dealing with "equal rights" for Hungary's various nationalities.

Since the installation of the dual monarchy, the political life of Hungary's nationalities had been carried on under the aegis of this law and in this political climate.

When one is aware of the fact that the Hungarians have always been relentless in their denationalization activities, it should not be difficult to guess the spirit in which the law dealing with Magyarization was enforced.

Let us now analyze the fundamental laws dealing with the relations between the dominant Romanian nation and the various national minorities in Transylvania after its union with Romania.

Immediately after the National Assembly convened in Alba-Julia (December 1, 1918), the government of Transylvania was taken over by the Directory Council, whose president was Iuliu Maniu, a staunch supporter of the ideals of liberty and justice and the future prime minister of greater Romania.

The fundamental ideals of the constitutional declaration of rights which was promulgated on the day the assembly convened have been mentioned in the second part of this book. The rights of the national minorities in Transylvania were stipulated in the following paragraph—implicit in which are the humanitarian and democratic motivations characteristic of all the decisions taken by the leaders of the Transylvanian national revolution:

Complete National Liberty for All the Nationalities Inhabiting the Territory. Members of each nationality are to be educated, governed, and judged in their own language, by their own representatives to the legislative

bodies and the government of the country, in proportion
to its percentage of the total population. There shall be
equal rights and complete religious autonomy for all the
official religions.

The difference between these two consecutive political conceptions of minorities' policy in Transylvania is fundamental.
The Hungarians granted individual rights, but subordinated
them to the condition of Hungarian nationality—while the
Romanians granted the Magyars their national liberty. This
radical difference was fraught with incalculable consequences
in the entire sphere of national minority rights.

The law of 1868, dealing with the rights of the subject
nationalities, in effect wiped them out. On the other hand, the
proclamation of Alba-Julia created the essential conditions for
the free development of those nationalities.

On December 9, 1919, by an addendum to the Paris peace
treaty, Romania committed itself to a formula which, on the
surface, appeared to bind it to obligations in the sphere of
minorities' policy which were not as sweeping as those which
the Romanians had spontaneously and voluntarily assumed at
the national assembly at Alba-Julia. But it must be pointed
out that the obligations assumed in Paris, in the light of their
practical consequences, today appear to be less generous than
those which the Romanian nation had assumed for
itself—because it was understood that a humane and understanding attitude toward minorities was an essential require-
ment if the various nationalities were ever to live together
harmoniously.

In the constitution of March 29, 1923, which can be considered the organic law of the Romanian kingdom, there are
to be found all the generous ideals to which the Alba-Julia
proclamation gave expression. This constitution can be likened
to a charter of liberties, which operated with the power of fundamental law, as is the case in any civilized country.

"The Romanians, irrespective of their ethnic origin, language, or religion," says Article 5 of the Romanian constitution,
"are entitled to liberty of conscience, the right to an education,
freedom of the press, freedom of association, and all the other
rights stipulated by law."

The explanatory note appended to this article stipulated
that: "By the word 'Romanian,' the constitution means any

Romanian citizen." The Magyar inhabitants of Transylvania were, therefore, included from the beginning, since they were now Romanian subjects, according to Romanian law.

Articles 7 and 8 of the constitution were animated by similar humanitarian and democratic ideals.

Article 7 said: "Differences of religious beliefs, ethnic origin and language do not constitute an obstacle to securing or exercising civil and political rights in Romania."

Article 8 said: "Within the state, no differentiation will be permitted on the basis of a person's origin or class. All Romanians, irrespective of their ethnic origin, language, or religion, are equal according to the law."

Article 22 proclaimed liberty of conscience in categorical terms. "Liberty of conscience is absolute," said the article . . . "the state guarantees liberty and protection to all religions, since their practice does not hinder the public order, ethnic harmony, and the laws of the state."

Article 23 stipulated that there shall be "freedom of speech and publication . . . there will be no need for any previous permission from any authority in order to publish anything, and no security is to be paid by newspapermen, writers, editors, typographers, and lithographers."

Finally, Article 28 proclaimed "freedom of assembly," Article 29 "freedom of association," and Article 30 "freedom to petition the government for all Romanian citizens, without exception."

The minorities enjoyed the complete freedom promised by these constitutional articles for some two decades. Among other reasons, this was so because the effects of the fundamental law were precise, devoid of any ambiguity, and categorical.

The minorities were so well organized and their interests so firmly protected by the leaders of the respective national groupings, that even the most unimportant cases of abuse—which under Hungarian rule simply would have been overlooked—were amplified, exaggerated, and brought before the eyes of the world. The English writer Carlile A. McCartney has characterized Hungarian charges with the statement that the "Hungarians were inclined to exaggeration."

It goes without saying that, under these circumstances, violating the constitution at the expense of the minority Hungarians would have constituted a crime which could not have been compensated for by all the gold in the world. Conversely, in Hungary the ostensibly favorable stipulations in their law dealing with minorities—that is, those stipulations which still remained on the books after eliminating the ones that were intended to help in setting up a unitary Magyar state—were rendered void by special decrees which departed from the general provisions of the law.

Thus, the liberties granted to the other nationalities by the law passed in 1863, with regard to the schools founded and run by them, were incrementally repealed by Law no. 18 of 1879, Law no. 33 of 1833, Law no. 15 of 1891, Law no. 26 of 1893, and especially by the famous Apponyi law (Law no. 27 of 1907), which has already been discussed in this book.

If the Hungarians had scruples about repealing the provisions of the basic law setting forth minority school policy, they were less scrupulous in their handling of the law dealing with association. By an ordinance issued by the ministry of internal affairs (no. 1508 of May 22, 1875), they rendered null and void most of the rights which had been granted to the other nationalities in 1868. This, therefore, is how their own laws were respected by the Hungarians.

Characteristic of the hypocritical methods employed by the Magyars in their propaganda abroad was that, when the initial rights ostensibly guaranteed by the law of 1868 had lost all validity as a result of special laws and many ministerial ordinances, the Hungarians went on speaking about these rights as though they continued in force.

Today it is virtually unanimously acknowledged that the Hungarian law was never put into practice because the ultra-chauvinist wing of public opinion was against it.

On this point, we possess the special evidence made public by two former Hungarian prime ministers. The first of these is Baron Desider Banffy, prime minister of Hungary from 1895 to 1899.

In his book *Hungarian Minority Policy,* which was published in 1903, Banffy showed that, thanks to considerations imposed by life itself, a large part of the law dealing with other nationalities had been rendered void because "the impossible and the absurd cannot be carried out, even when they are stipulated by law."

What emerges from this is that the men who led Hungary in 1868—according to the opinion expressed by the man who was himself prime minister in the year 1895—had behaved as irresponsibly as the members of parliament who had passed the law. In short, the outstanding personalities of that period of time had all acted irresponsibly, for only an irresponsible man would attempt to legislate the absurd and the impossible. As the French saying goes, *on n'est jamais si bien servi que par soi même* ("One is never so well served as by oneself").

Stephen Tisza, prime minister of Hungary at the beginning of World War I in 1914, surpassed his predecessor of the late 19th century by declaring in front of the Magyar House that sanctioning some of the provisions of the law of 1869 would be tantamount to madness and suicide for the Magyar state. [Session of February 20, 1914.]

The written statement presented by the Hungarians at the peace conference in Paris also represents important evidence. In this statement, one reads that "the Magyar government itself had to refuse to enforce the law," which in fact "had been rendered void by other laws."

In 1919, the Hungarians, when confronted with the overwhelming evidence against them, had to acknowledge the feebleness of the laws which governed relations between the Magyars and the non-Magyars. Later on, however, the Hungarians were able to avert this truth by charging imperialistic tendencies, irredentism, pan-Slavism, or Dacianism to those nationalities which had dared to reveal to the civilized world developments within the area governed by St. Stephen's Crown that the Magyars regarded as secret. But it was a secret that was known by everybody.

What was even more revolting was the hypocrisy displayed by the government in its campaign to undercut the very few rights which the subject nationalities could have invoked on the basis of the famous law of 1868.

The much-touted chivalrous spirit to which the Hungarians laid claim found expression in the policy of blatant duplicity. The case cited below is one of many bearing on this point.

In a town which had belonged to Hungary, the census of 1900 had reported a population of 28,764 inhabitants; 10,321 were listed at the time as Magyars, 10,451 as Serbs and Croats, and 6,483 as Germans. In accordance with the provisions of the law conferring equal rights on all nationalities, the mayor of the town decided in 1885 that the official report of the population bureau be printed in the Hungarian, Serbian, and Ger-

man languages, because of the significant proportion of the
population represented by the non-Magyar nationalities in that
town. On learning about the mayor's decision—which was perfectly legal and equitable—the minister for internal affairs
immediately instructed the local prefect that, "taking into consideration the provisions of the law dealing with the equal
rights of nationalities, I will not resort to official measures."
But he told the prefect that "in the future the official report
should be printed only in Hungarian."

This was how the basic law dealing with the minorities in
pre-Trianon Hungary was interpreted. This was the political
atmosphere in which they were put into effect.

In Romania, the constitution, which represented the basic
law of the state guaranteeing the rights of national minorities,
had a much more positive fate than the old Hungarian law
which ostensibly guaranteed "equal rights" to the non-Magyar
minorities. These were only paper rights. In Romania, on the
other hand, the law was put into effect.

All of the Romanian political leaders considered it their
duty to strictly enforce the constitutional provision governing
the minorities living in Transylvania. There were even attacks
by the ultranationalistic press directed against successive governments in the post-World War I period, charging an "excessive tolerance" toward the Transylvanian minorities. This
excess, they said, had somehow put the Transylvanian Romanians in an inferior state, especially economically, compared
to the Hungarians and the Transylvanian Saxons.

The Romanian politician who understood most clearly the
duty of the Romanians to the various minorities who lived in
Transylvania with them, was Iuliu Maniu.

In 1928, when his party was asked to form the government,
Maniu declared: "According to the spirit of justice characteristic of the Romanian people, all national and religious minorities will be treated with solicitude in the constitutional
institutions, in the spirit of our times."

In making this declaration of policy, Maniu was acting in
accordance with the traditional principles of Romania on minority matters. These were principles which he himself had
expounded on different occasions—on the first occasion, as president of the Directory Council of Transylvania, and on the next
occasion, as the leader of one of the most powerful political
parties in Romania.

"The Romanian people," said Maniu in 1918, "is too noble and too democratic not to take into consideration the wise proverb which says 'Do unto others as you would have them do unto you.' Our experience has taught us what it means to bear the yoke of oppression, and we do not want to make ourselves guilty of the same injustice from which we have suffered for centuries."

At a lecture at the Social Institute in Bucharest in 1924, Maniu set forth in the following words his party's minority program—a program he did not hesitate to put into practice when it became his duty to do so:

Among the most primitive people who are a little better than savages, the strongest always has the upper hand. Human civilization has produced laws which serve as a shield to protect the weak. A similar thing happened in the relations between states and nations that enjoyed a more highly developed civilization. Each state, and within the state its minorities, is protected by the law. The problem of the minorities, far from being determined exclusively by political relations within the state, is basically a question that has to do with human rights—rights which have been won by large sacrifices on the part of all mankind. It is a question of humanity, a question whose legitimacy is underscored by the martyrdom of many important men. It is an essential question, a question of state policy, that impinges on the harmonious development of the state.

Maniu continued:

We cannot accept in our country the abnormal situation that existed before the war in Hungary, where it was a common thing for Romanians to be unable to buy train tickets or stamps in their native town . . . because they could not ask for them in Hungarian. Enforced use of the Romanian language would change it, from the pleasant language it is to the ears of many foreigners, into a hated and harsh-sounding one.
If the Romanian national state wants to go on existing, it would also be a state with a law and a culture which protect in the same way the property of the individual and the cultural achievements of society. We must learn

from the experience of our past, and we must never commit the same mistakes which turned so angrily against those who committed them. Only by becoming the defender of all liberties and noble ideals and of all endeavors in the fields of culture and human welfare, will our country win the respect of the world.

When have similar words ever been pronounced in Hungary—words animated by the purest sentiments of brotherhood and by a profound understanding for peoples of different nationality? When had the Magyar politicians, who for centuries held the destiny of the Transylvanian Romanians in their hands, given voice to ideas as advanced as those of Maniu?

Nevertheless, these ideas were subjected to gross distortion by Magyar propaganda in those countries where it was seeking sympathizers by the simple means of denigrating Romanian nationalities policy. In his major study *Hungary and Its Successors*, C. McCartney said about Maniu, "In a speech delivered a short while after the Armistice, Maniu asked for the Romanianization of Transylvania, which was equivalent to asking for an obvious position of superiority for the Romanian element."

The purpose of this misinterpretation was to give currency to the idea that, after their experience with "Magyarization," the Romanians had embarked on a converse policy of "Romanianization." Nothing could be more inexact, more absurd, or more false.

Indeed, McCartney admits in the same book that the Hungarians had pursued a violent policy of compulsory Magyarization in Romanian Transylvania. Implicitly, therefore, McCartney admits that Transylvania was not Magyar but Romanian—otherwise, what was the point of compulsory Magyarization? If Transylvania was Romanian, then what was the point of Romanianizing it? If the Romanians had made any such effort, it would have been tantamount to knocking at an open door.

This is a question of elementary logic which has been forgotten by those who have permitted themselves to become overexcited by political passion, but it is a matter which is fully understood by all those who are not biased.

The denationalization practiced by the Hungarians before World War I was unfortunately resumed on an even larger scale after northern Transylvania was forcibly annexed by Hungary during World War II. Denationalization as a policy was inspired by the fact that the Hungarians had found it impossible, because of their relatively small numbers, to imprint a specifically Hungarian character on the large masses of Romanians, who for more than a thousand years had maintained an indestructible national unity.

The Hungarian ultranationalist Antal Kalmar, characterized Hungarian-Romanian relations in these words: "The Romanian problem is a problem of race. The hatred existing between the Hungarians and the Romanians [Kalmar called them, pejoratively, 'Wallachians'] is a racial hatred which cannot be wiped out either by good administration, or by culture, or by social and economic institutions."

What Kalmar omitted to say was that the Hungarian leaders had embarked on a war of extermination against the Romanians in Transylvania because on this Romanian land the Hungarians constituted a minority in comparison with the Romanians.

In 1913, the former Hungarian prime minister, Coloman Szell, had declared: "Transylvania is lost for the Hungarians" (*Meggoyozedesem szetrint elvesztettuk Erdelyt*).

If, under these circumstances, anyone could still talk about the Romanianization of a province where the Romanians still represented the overwhelming majority—despite the massive colonization of their territory with Szecklers and Saxons and the never-ending Magyar infiltration into the Transylvanian towns—this would have been tantamount to talking about the anglicization of England.

McCartney, himself, after studying the Transylvanian question, was obliged to admit, when confronted with overwhelming evidence, that the policy of denationalization through the forced assimilation of minorities of all nationalities was completely unknown to the Romanians. We quote again from his chapter on Transylvania:

> Even the idea of the possibility or necessity of such forced assimilation is completely alien to the Romanian mind, especially in the kingdom of Romania. This idea is preeminently a European one, which had its origin in Germany and was developed to the highest degree in Hungary.

The contradiction between these two assertions by Mc-

Cartney is obvious. On the one hand, he spoke about a program of Romanianization in Romania, carried out by the Romanians in imitation of the Magyarization actions of old, in an attempt to bring about the forced assimilation of the national minorities. On the other hand, the same author admits that the principle of assimilation was repugnant to the Romanian spirit.

But this was not everything. From the premises formulated by this English writer, there emerges a clearcut distinction between the principles that guided Hungarian minorities policy and those that guided Romanian policy. Hungary, with its mixed and polyglot population, was under pressure to pursue a policy of forced assimilation. (According to McCartney, the Hungarians pursued this policy "in the highest degree.") In contrast, Romania was in a privileged situation because of the predominantly Romanian population which existed harmoniously over the whole of Transylvania. The Romanians refused to adopt the policy of forced assimilation, of which the Hungarians had been so fond, and, conversely, put into practice the concept of complete national liberty for minorities of different ethnic origin.

The Romanians understood from the first moment that their state was reestablished within its natural boundaries, that the only way to secure the development of this state was by peaceful coexistence with the minority nationalities who shared the territory with them. This implied a policy based on a broad understanding of the vital cultural and economic needs of the minorities. One is obliged to state that Romania sincerely followed a policy of "peaceful cohabitation"—that it sought to make friends of the Magyars and other minorities in Transylvania instead of assimilating them.

The National Peasant party was not the only party to support such a conciliatory policy toward the national minorities, nor was Iuliu Maniu the only Romanian politician who demonstrated sympathy and understanding toward the former oppressors of the Romanian spirit.

The great Transylvanian poet Octavian Goga, leader of the Romanian Agrarian party, may have been the Romanian most entitled to nurture vindictive sentiments toward the Hungarian nobility, who had caused him to comprehend the tragedy of being reduced to a Romanian protestor on the Romanian soil of Transylvania. But far from nurturing hard feelings, Goga adopted an attitude of Christian forgiveness for the intolerance previously displayed by the Hungarians, and he held out to them the olive branch of conciliation, using these words:

Contrary to Hungary's traditional doctrine, which denied the right of existence to the non-Magyar nationalities, our people manifested good will toward our non-Romanian citizens. Our fundamental spirit does not accept exaggeration, and xenophobia has never been characteristic of the Romanian people. After centuries of hatred, we have held out an olive branch to our oppressors of yesterday.

The Peoples party under the leadership of Marshal Averescu, who had been one of the most important Romanian military commanders in World War I, included in its program the following statement of principle on minorities policy:

"The Peoples party does not recognize any difference between the citizens of our country, no matter what their language or religion may be."

No matter what their language or religion may be! How far we had come from the morally backward times when Arpad's most generous and liberal descendants issued ordinances stating that certain rights depended on the use of a certain language.

Similar generous principles, giving evidence of a sincere desire to cooperate with all nationalities, can be found in the program adopted by the National Liberal party under the leadership of Ion I. C. Bratianu. This great Romanian politician summarized his party's minorities policy in these words:

For us, the problem of minority rights is settled. It was settled at the point where we became aware of the need to find a complete solution to it—in the interests of justice, in the interests of internal harmony of contemporary Romanian society, which had always been attracted to sentiments of religious tolerance. . . . Our brothers and we, ourselves, were convinced from the beginning that a tranquil and enduring state life was not possible without a principled position on equal rights for minorities.

These sentiments for over twenty years inspired Romanian laws dealing with the rights of minority nationalities. Instead of hatred directed against everything Magyar, instead of intolerance, oppression and multiple contradictions, the Romanian regime adopted a policy toward the various ethnic minorities living in Romania which guaranteed to them complete equality—and what is even more important—a policy which showed profound understanding of their national aspirations within the Romanian state.

The Minorities' Press Under the Hungarians and Under the Romanians: A Comparison

In the Hungarian "paradise for nationalities" of before World War I, Romanian editors of various Transylvanian newspapers were sentenced to a total of almost 100 years in prison (they served almost their full time) for "press offenses"—that is, for the fact that they had attempted to protest against the injustices and abuses which both the government in Budapest and its Transylvanian executive bodies were committing against their Romanian subjects. This was especially true when the power of the Magyars was consolidated within the framework of the dual monarchy.

In only ten years—between 1893 and 1902—the editors of the prominent Transylvanian Romanian newspaper, *The Tribune*, were sentenced to a total of seventeen years and three months in prison and fined the enormous sum—for those days—of 56,981 gold francs.

Such were the results, before 1914, of the regulations governing minority publications in the "happy" Hungarian province of Transylvania, as the Hungarians were wont to describe it. The data given above can readily be checked, since the various court archives, and especially those of the Assize Court in Cluj, constitute dramatic evidence of the oppression and tyranny which governed Transylvania in the past.

It would be an error to believe the Romanian editors had been guilty of an excess of resistance. The reasons given for the penal actions directed against Transylvanian newspapermen will help us to understand the insignificance of their offenses. But before we come to this, let us examine the basic principles of the laws governing the operation of the press which existed at that time in Transylvania.

In contrast with the rest of Hungarian territory where the liberal press law of 1848 (Law no. XVIII) was operational, the press in Transylvania was governed by the Imperial decree of May 27, 1852, which was issued during the period of the most drastic Hapsburg absolutism.

It would have been logical, after the establishment of the dual monarchy in 1867, if the same laws had been in effect in all of the provinces ruled over by the Hungarian crown. But in Transylvania the Hungarians preferred to maintain in force the much harsher press laws decreed by the Hapsburgs—laws which originally had been used against the Hungarians in the period immediately after Kossuth's revolution. The important difference was that now the Hungarians were using this same decree against the Romanians and the other non-Magyar nationalities.

Between the two laws—the one which governed the press in Hungary proper and the Imperial decree which was enforced in Transylvania—there were important differences of detail and fundamental differences in principle.

In the first place, the Imperial decree which was operative in Transylvania did not make any basic stipulation of freedom of speech—a stipulation which can be found in the law governing the press in Hungary proper, and which said: "All people are allowed to express their ideas freely in the press."

This omission served to restrict to a very high degree freedom of the press for the Romanians in Transylvania. On the other hand, in Hungary proper the press was required to post guarantees only if the publication had a political character and if it came out at least twice a month. In Transylvania the posting of guarantees was mandatory for all publications, no matter whether they were political, religious, social, or economic in character, and no matter how often or how infrequently they were printed.

In Hungary proper, the author was held exclusively responsible for "press offenses." In Transylvania, the punishment was applied both to the author of the article and to the editor of the publication.

Nevertheless, as Paclisanu correctly points out, the most important and revolting difference was not between the text of the law and that of the Imperial decree but in the contrasting manner in which the laws were enforced in the case of the Magyar press and the press of the national minorities. Paclisanu wrote: "The Magyar governments and the entire Hungarian people looked upon this press [the minorities press] as the greatest obstacle to thwart the achievement of their ideal: the setting up of a Magyar national state."

This, therefore, accounts for the distemper which the Hungarians displayed toward the authors of articles which protested against the methods employed by the Magyar leaders in pursuit of utopian goals, and also protested against the severity of the verdicts handed down against writers for the minorities press. In these trials—or perhaps we should say sham trials—which took place in an atmosphere charged with ultrachauvinism, the Hungarian jurors were at the same time prosecutors and judges. That is why the decisions taken by the judges, *sui generis*, were regarded as so odious when directed against "offenses" of the press.

We shall deal with only three examples culled from the long history of injustice perpetrated against the Romanian press in Transylvania.

In the autumn of 1885, the official Magyar newspaper in Cluj, *Kolozsvari Kozlony*, published an article in which the principle of a unitary Magyar nation was once again featured. The article solemnly declared that the structure of the Hungary of the future should be exclusively Magyar, and that it would be a humiliation for the noble Magyar nation to take into account the other nationalities which shared the territory with them.

In its issue of November 28, 1885, the Romanian newspaper *The Tribune*, which was published in Sibiu, criticized the article in the Cluj newspaper and said that the espousal of such ideas could lead to "trouble" and civil war. The author of this article, however, made important concessions to the Magyar viewpoint in the interests of fostering better understanding between the nationalities.

"The Magyars," wrote Cornel Pop Pacurar, the author of the article in question, "should take modern circumstances into consideration and should again ponder the question of whether it is possible for them to achieve their ideal of turning polyglot Hungary into a Magyar national state. If they proceed to examine this problem thoroughly, we shall understand why they avoid discussing the national character of the land and of the state, which the peoples of all nationalities represent and which they can only defend together. They would have good reasons for not discussing it."

These were wise words, inspired by the noble concept of

living in harmony with the invaders of their land, in order to maintain peace inside the country and safeguard the peace of Europe.

The Assizes Court in Cluj did not agree with this viewpoint, and sentenced the author of the lines quoted above to one year of imprisonment, and it imposed a fine of 200 gold francs on the chief editor of the newspaper, the Romanian writer Ion Slavici.

Two years later, there was another legal action against a Romanian newspaper in Transylvania, *The Transylvanian Gazette*.

The author had written: "The Magyars wish to exterminate the Romanians, Serbs, and Slovaks if they do not agree to be assimilated into the great Magyar nation and to worship Magyar culture." This was a theme which the leaders of Magyar chauvinism had themselves repeated many times. But for his courage in putting into words what everybody already knew, the author of this article was sentenced by the same Assizes Court in Cluj to four years in prison and the customary heavy fine.

On August 14, 1890, Traian Horia Pop, the editor of *The Transylvanian Gazette*, was sentenced to one year in prison for including in an article the sentence: "Hungary is not Magyar, and this state is not Magyar—it belongs to all the nationalities." Also at issue was another sentence which pointed to the fact—as true as the previous one—that the nations of Hungary were of two kinds: the privileged Magyar minority and the non-Magyars who constituted an oppressed majority. The chief editor of the same newspaper was imprisoned for six weeks.

In writing about this trial, the newspaper, *Kronstadter Zeitung*, wrote in issue no. 191 of 1890:

> In this trial one should take into consideration another anomaly. The jurors were judging their own case. They belonged to the group who had been criticized in the incriminatory articles, and they were now called upon to hand down the verdict against their political national enemies. Moreover, the prosecutor urged the jurors to take revenge for this offense against Magyarism—that is, against the jurors.

Such was the jurors' frame of mind when they were asked

to arrive at verdicts on the various actions initiated against Romanian newspapermen. As representatives of Magyar chauvinism, the Hungarian jurors had been asked to do justice in cases which involved their innermost thinking on national matters.

Meanwhile, for their guilt in protesting against the Magyar methods of denationalization and in raising their voices against the intolerant and oppressive policy of the Magyar leaders, Romanian newspapermen in Transylvania were jailed for years, as though they were common thieves.

The severity of such verdicts did not discourage the Transylvanian journalists. They continued to do their important work in spite of the Assizes Court, which they looked upon as a blind instrument of the policy of Magyarization—until the day at last when their audacious articles brought about the liberty they had been seeking.

In order to better understand the press regime in pre-World War I Hungary, it is first of all noteworthy that newspapers and magazines printed in the Romanian kingdom were banned from circulation in Transylvania between 1879 and 1910. But Romanian newspapers were not the only publications forbidden. Many foreign newspapers and magazines—German, French, Italian, Belgian, and American (in the German language)—were subjected to similar restrictions and prohibitions, either temporarily or permanently.

Whenever a foreign journalist wrote an article dealing with the iniquity of Hungary's treatment of its minorities, his newspaper immediately came under prohibition in Hungary.

Correspondents were allowed to write only good things about Hungary, no matter how bitter or miserable the plight of the minorities. For the Romanians, the punishment was frequently years of imprisonment. For foreign newspapermen, the punishment was a ban on the circulation of their newspapers within the territory of "the noble Magyar nation."

The press regime introduced by the Imperial decree of 1853 (with small changes resulting from the ordinances of 1867, 1871, and 1872) continued in force until 1914, when the Hungarians issued a new law governing the press in Transylvania. This law maintained most of the restrictions which already existed. In any event, the law was not enforced because war broke out and it was replaced by exceptional measures. But the hour of liberty had come for the peoples whose voices had for centuries been stifled.

Because they had nothing to hide, the Romanian government granted absolute freedom to the press. But as was to be expected, the Hungarians tried to take advantage of this situation by bringing up imaginary charges or enlarging insignificant things to apocalyptical proportions.

If the Romanian press in Transylvania before World War I had written one-tenth of the articles critical of the government that the Hungarian press in Transylvania published after Trianon, all the Transylvanian Romanian newspapermen would have been in prison for life.

Let us have a look at some figures.

Under the Hungarians before Trianon, there were 15 Hungarian daily newspapers in Transylvania. In 1928 the number had increased to 28, and by 1936 to 53.

Before Transylvania was annexed to Romania, the Hungarians in Transylvania had 154 daily and periodical publications. By 1935 the number had grown to 312. Three hundred and twelve publications for a population of 1,300,000 inhabitants—while 3,000,000 Romanians living in Transylvania in 1914 had only 44 publications, only 2 of which were daily newspapers!

Professor Silviu Dragomir wrote before the Vienna *Diktat*: "Today there is at least one Hungarian newspaper, if not more, in every important town."

In Cluj, 7 of the 25 Hungarian newspapers that were published had, in 1935, a circulation ranging from 100,000 to 120,000 copies.

The Hungarian writer George Lukacs, in attempting to win English sympathizers for the cause of Magyar revisionism, wrote an essay entitled *The Injustices of the Treaty of Trianon*. (Lukacs described the treaty as an *ukase*). In it he was audacious enough to make the following statement concerning the contrast between the treatment of minorities in prewar Hungary and postwar Romania:

> If the treatment of the nationalities had been ten times harsher than our enemies say it was, it would have been a thousand times less irksome than the intolerance which today exists in the successor states [*sic!*].

Lukacs was playing with figures. He was, of course, concealing statistical data which throw light on what the real treatment of the Romanians had been under Hungarian rule and, conversely, on the treatment of Hungarians under Romanian rule. Let us fill in the blanks left by Magyar propaganda by listing the missing statistical data—and let the reader draw his own conclusion.

Between 1919 and 1933, 5,000 Magyar literary and scientific works were published in the territory of Romanian Transylvania. This is more than had been published in the preceding 50 years (1867 to 1918) of Hungarian domination. This is mentioned by the Magyar writer Iancso Elemer, in his book *The Hungarian Book in Transylvania During the Past Fifteen Years*.

Under the liberal rule of the Magyars, the Hungarians of Transylvania had no publishing house. Under the "shameful domination of the Romanians," the Hungarians were able to start a publishing house at Cluj in 1920 (Minerva), which over a period of 10 years sold over 1,600,000 Hungarian books.

Also under the "intolerant" rule of the Romanians, the Transylvanian Hungarians were able to found nine lay cultural societies, apart from others of a religious character. These societies were: the Transylvanian Literary Society in Cluj; the Sigismond Komeny Society in Tg. Mures; the E. Szigligeti Society in Oradea Mare; the I. Arany Society in Timisoara; the Fr. Kocsey Society in Arad, with branches in Careii-Mari and Baia Mare; the Teleky Society in Baia Mare; the Transylvanian Helikon of the "Transylvanian Museum"; and, finally, the Magyar Cultural Society in Transylvania (E.M.K.E.).

In addition to these important societies which provided a background against which Magyar cultural life in Transylvania was carried on, almost every Transylvanian town where a Hungarian community existed, no matter how small, had local cultural associations and literary clubs. Hungarian choral societies in Transylvania, for example, had reached the impressive figure of 162 by 1935.

Over the last decade of Magyar rule in Transylvania, there was only one Magyar magazine which could be classified as a literary review. Under "Romanian intolerance," a number of Hungarian magazines were published. Examples of these were *Pazstor Tuz, Vapkelet, Orient*, and *Erderyi Helikon*.

To the above-mentioned publications, to round out the picture, we must add the daily newspapers, the economic and religious publications, the children's magazines, the specialized publications—even the association of Magyar choral societies had its own monthly publication, *Magyar dal* ("The Magyar Song").

When all these things are put together, we shall have a complete image of what Magyar cultural life was like under Romanian rule, which came in for so much abuse.

The atmosphere of cultural freedom under Romanian rule was so auspicious from the standpoint of development of Magyar culture that the Hungarian writer Lajos Gyorgy exclaimed in 1927: "It is certain that the Hungarians in Transylvania have as active and intense a cultural life today as they did in the 16th and 17th centuries, when the center of Magyar culture was represented exclusively by Transylvania, the rest of Hungary being under the Turks."

In sum, the Hungarians under Romanian rule in Transylvania continued to enjoy a robust cultural life. Indeed, if anything, they made amazing progress in this area of activity.

So impressive were the liberties granted to the minorities by the Romanian government that the German writer Rudinger exclaimed after visiting Romania: "Romania is the most liberal of countries when it comes to the treatment of minorities (*Romanian ist das freiste Land der Behandlung der Minderheiten*)."

The author of this book, having been sent to Romania as a correspondent by the Parisian weekly, *La Tribune des Nations*, to report on the situation of the ethnic minorities in Transylvania, finished one of his feature reports with these words: "The Romanians have revived all the latent energies of this province, energies which had been idle for centuries. They brought about radical changes in the economic situation of the province, in this way contributing to its general progress. All social strata, as well as all nationalities in Transylvania, profited from this policy. I am able to declare with all objectivity that Transylvania is a real Eden for its minorities." [*La Tribune des Nations*, no. 287, May 1940.]

Despite these evident realities, Magyar propaganda continued to bang the big drum, charging that the Magyar minority in Transylvania was persecuted by an inferior people, the Romanians, who were, figuratively, breaking the wings of creative élan of the Magyar culture.

This was in the traditional Magyar pattern, no matter how liberal the Magyars, of denying the existence of any Romanian accomplishments, relying on the good will of the western reader who, for his part, found it difficult to believe that such distortion of reality was possible.

15. AGRARIAN REFORM AND THE HUNGARIAN SYMPATHIZERS

As a preeminently agrarian country, Romania, beginning with the last century, was concerned with the problem of land reform.

The first land expropriation in favor of the peasants of the Old Kingdom took place in 1866, after the union of the two principalities. This was followed by a new reform in the year 1889, after the war of independence. Both reforms, due to their limited character, were unable to settle the serious social problem inherent in the antagonism between the large landowner and the individual peasant, the fruits of whose hard labor were appropriated in the first place by the landowner.

The Romanian peasant uprising of 1907 called the attention of the government to the ever greater danger inherent in this antagonism. Land reform was imminent. But a just solution had to be found, a solution that would satisfy the millions of peasants who had no land of their own, at the same time as it avoided the complete expropriation of the landowners.

In 1915, the Parliament in Bucharest embarked on a debate on the problem of land reform. In 1917, the Parliament —which had taken refuge at Jassy, together with the royal family—put the question of land reform on its agenda. On March 22, 1917, King Ferdinand made the following declaration to the Romanian soldiers: "I, your King, declare to you that the peasants who have defended with their arms the territory of the country where they were born, will each be given land. I shall be the first to set a good example."

The first decree of the land reform program was published in the official *Gazette* of December 16, 1918, when the first 2,000,000 hectares were expropriated in the peasants' favor. Among the expropriated lands were various estates of the crown. The king had kept his word to be among "the first to set a good example."

In 1921, the scope of the land reform was enlarged by a new law, which also stipulated how land reform was to be put into practice.

We have thus far surveyed the principal stages of land reform in Romania in order to dispel one of the major mystifications the Magyars attempted to perpetrate, by seeking to persuade Western opinion that the agrarian reform had been especially designed to hurt the Magyar landowners, who owned enormous tracts of land and various properties in Romanian Transylvania.

The most important social reforms in Romania were carried out before Transylvania was united with the motherland. They represented an act of justice so compelling that it was only natural for the Transylvanian peasantry, both Hungarian and Romanian, to take full advantage of it. Land reform hurt both the Hungarian and Romanian landowners—and both Hungarian and Romanian peasants, irrespective of origin, benefited from it. The broad nature of this reform constituted the principal feature of what was a genuine social revolution—a social revolution which placed Romania in the very first ranks among the countries of the Carpathian-Danubian area.

In Hungary, in contradistinction, all the agrarian laws which had been promulgated at the end of the 19th century and the beginning of the 20th, bore the stamp of the most authentic chauvinism.

Starting from the premise that he who is the master of the land is also master of the country, the Hungarians sought by various means to Magyarize the land of Transylvania. In their colonizing activities, they colonized the land exclusively with Hungarians—even that land which had been purely Romanian and where there were enough Romanians to take the place of the Magyar counts, whose landed properties, because of their immensity, were at the best under partial cultivation. When the Magyar clique who governed Transylvania could not find enough Hungarians for their Transylvanian colonizing activities, they went so far as to bring in Hungarians from Bukovina.

Baron Banffy, the leader of the Magyar landowners, spelled out the Magyar program plainly in the newspaper *Pesti Hirlap*, of September 9, 1913: "We do not wish to consider our fellow countrymen who speak a different language our enemies, but when it comes to the problem of land ownership, we have to do so, and we have to organize ourselves accordingly."

In 1919, Transylvania had a total of 14,933,841 recorded *jugars* (one jugar equals 5,775 square meters), of which 7,613,555 were arable land; of the total arable land, 35.95 percent belonged to the state, the communes, the churches or different religions, various societies, and other groups and entities, and the balance, 60.05 percent, belonged to private citizens.

Tracts of land in excess of 100 *jugars* were owned by 8,435 landowners, only 209 of whom were Romanians. Of the total number of 8,435 large landowners, 1,190 possessed tracts of 1,000 *jugars* or more. Only 17 of these were Romanian, while 1,172 were Hungarian.

The 3,316,345 Romanians living in Transylvania at the time possessed among them 3,348,602 *jugars*, which works out to just over one *jugar* per capita. On the other side, the Transylvanian minorities of whom the Hungarians were the most numerous group, numbered 1,891,933, and between them possessed 11,233,819 *jugars*, which works out to approximately 5½ *jugars* per capita.

Statistics of the large landed estates in Hungarian Transylvania revealed the names of a few dozen families of Hungarian magnates, who governed the lives of the Transylvanian peasants from the remote heights of their fantastic rural estates in the manner of virtual despots. The counts and princes of the Eszterhazy family owned the enormous area of 314,065 *jugars*, while the various nobles of the Pesterich family lorded it over the many thousands of Romanian and Hungarian peasants living on their 117,300 *jugars*. The counts of the Szechenyi family came next with 117,257 *jugars*, and the counts of the Karolyi family came next with 111,586 *jugars*. This left at a distance other less important counts, princes, barons, and palatines of the Zichy, Pallavichini, Betthany, Philip de Coburg, Majlath, and Nadozny families.

These noblemen, who could fill a whole Gotha almanac with their names and a small kingdom with their properties, turned Hungary into a country whose character was preeminently reactionary and backward. The Hungarian peasants who lived on the estates of these princes, counts, barons, and palatines, were not men, but, as Juliu Jelyes put it in his book *The People of the Hungarian Steppe*, were "supplements of the oligarchical property."

After studying the miserable situation of the Hungarian peasants, the writer Garbay exclaimed: "Hungary is a country of famine and misery." Istvan Turi wrote on the same matter in the Magyar newspaper *Nepszaba*: "On the one side—castles and historical monuments; on the other side—Asiatic hamlets. The Hungarian villages have been the same for a thousand years, gasping for air in a countryside where large properties were predominant."

And there is the statement of Doveny Nagy Lajos in the newspaper *Uj Magyarsag*, describing what he, himself, had seen in the commune of Szeghalom—peasants eating the corn-husks out of their mattresses and pillows.

If this was the situation of the Hungarian peasants, it is not difficult to imagine the plight of the Romanian peasants who lived on landed estates belonging to the Magyar barons, who had always harbored a deep hatred for everything Romanian. When the Bucharest government put into effect in Romanian Transylvania the same agrarian measures that were already in force in the Old Kingdom, the Hungarian nobility, who were seeking to maintain their obsolete institutions in central Europe, organized a coalition against Romania in which they were joined by the less-important landowners. The agrarian reform had a well-defined goal. It sought to take part of the land that was owned—but not worked—by the oppressive Hungarian nobles and magnates and give it to the hundreds of thousands of Hungarian and Romanian peasants who had been working the land for centuries, but who did not own it.

It is worth mentioning that Hungary, which all the contemporary Hungarian writers—great and small—presented as a country of ancient liberal traditions, had known serfdom until the middle of the 19th century. Almost all of the land of the country belonged to the nobility, while the serfs had only its limited usufruct.

In 1916, the Hungarian Bishop Prohaszka came up with the idea of giving tracts of land to soldiers who returned from the front, but nothing was done about this proposal until the collapse of the monarchy in the autumn of 1918.

The agrarian law introduced by the Romanian government expropriated land totalling 1,663,809 hectares in Transylvania, as compared with the 2,776,501 hectares expropriated in the Old Kingdom.

The total number of Hungarian and Romanian peasants

who received land in Transylvania under the Agrarian Reform Law was 310,583. Of this number, 227,953 were Romanian, which represented 67 percent of the total number of Romanian peasants who were eligible to receive land. In comparison, 82,630 of those who received land were Hungarian, which represented 70 percent of the total number of Hungarian peasants who were eligible to receive grants of land under the law.

The coalition of Hungarians who were interested in perpetuating the quasi-feudal laws which protected their estates launched a furious campaign against the Romanian state when the law was put into operation.

This did not prevent the Magyar government from accusing Romania in international forums and before western public opinion of being a country that did not observe the peace treaty. The goal of the Hungarians was a twofold one.

First, they sought to maintain the same private privileges, ignoring the legitimate rights of hundreds of thousands of peasants.

Second, they sought to weaken Romania's position in terms of its standing among the peoples of western Europe.

All the competent—and incompetent—media and individuals were put on call. This gave birth to the question of the so-called "Hungarian sympathizers," who for more than a decade caused rivers of ink to flow in the international press.

First, the Hungarians brought their case before the conference of Allied ambassadors in 1923. There were two subsequent attempts to win the support of the conference. Then the Hungarians took the case to the League of Nations and to the Romanian-Magyar joint arbitration tribunal in Paris. Finally, they took their case to the International Court of Justice in the Hague. To complain against the Romanian Agrarian Reform Law, they took their case to every avenue that was open to them.

Faithful to their customary method of creating diversions from any matter which inconvenienced them, the Hungarians kept the attention of world public opinion focused on a question, which, according to international law, was exclusively a Romanian responsibility.

The litigation was reduced to the question of determining whether the Romanian state had the right to expropriate estates in Transylvania belonging to proprietors who had opted for Hungarian citizenship (and were called "Hungarian sympathizers") or who did not live in Transylvania (these were referred to as "absentees"). In other words, the various forums to which the Hungarians took their case were asked to determine whether foreigners could possess greater rights than Romanians on Romanian territory.

If this was indeed the intention of the contracting parties at Trianon, said the great statesman Nicolae Titulescu at the League of Nations, "let me tell you that no matter how long we shall turn over the pages of the Treaty signed after 1919, we shall not find anything as fascinating as the phenomenon of . . . the 'Hungarian sympathizer.' " By the skill he displayed in the course of the litigation, Titulescu brought the matter down to earth. After more than eight years of endless arguments and passionate disputes, the Romanian Hungarian conflict was settled in the Hague by a direct agreement concluded between Hungary and Romania. The agreement decided the principle of the right of expropriation in favor of the Romanian state. But, above all, the use of the phenomenon of the "Hungarian sympathizers" again underscored the unsurpassed talent of the Hungarians for jeopardizing the peace of Europe by perpetually creating conflicts, and resurrecting problems which for all practical purposes were already settled.

Part of the case had to do with claimed material damages. A limited number—167 to be exact—of "Hungarian sympathizers" claimed compensation of 45 billion lei from the Romanian state, which was twice the budget of the Romanian kingdom at that time. However, the litigation also had a purely political and propaganda aspect, in keeping with the fact that the Hungarians never missed an opportunity to point to Romania as a country where the minorities were persecuted and where the sacred and untouchable rights of the proprietor were ignored.

The real heart of the question had to do with a more equitable redistribution of the vast tracts of land which had belonged until that time to a medieval caste that had nothing in common with the aspirations of the native population. But this fact could hardly be recognized amid the torrents of sophistries employed by the Hungarians in defending their case.

As a matter of fact, the Romanians had given to the Hungarian peasants in Transylvania that minimum of social justice which the magnates of latter-day feudalism had categorically refused to grant in their own country.

Professor Ionescu-Sisesti wrote about the reform: "Never have the peasants cultivated the land with as much eagerness as they did after the reform."

For all the princes, counts, barons, palatines, and sundry other Magyar nobles who had previously governed their estates in the manner of small dictators, the Romanian expropriation represented a heavy blow. But for the Transylvanian peasantry, as for the social peace of Europe, it was a real godsend.

Always faithful to their traditional behavior, the Hungarian nobles had once more sought to block the road to social progress.

16. THE SCHOOLS: UNDER THE HUNGARIANS AND THE ROMANIANS

In 1930, in Transylvania, there were 3,207,880 Romanians and only 1,353,276 Hungarians. The ratio between the Romanians and the Hungarians was almost exactly the same when Transylvania was joined to the motherland in 1918. Looking backwards, according to the Romanian scholar, Simion Dascalul, "in the 17th century there were not only Hungarians and Saxons, but also Romanians everywhere—more than Hungarians, in any case."

It would only have been natural if the number of Romanian schools—elementary schools, at least—had been two and a half times more numerous than the Magyar schools, so that Romanian children would enjoy the possibility of learning to read and write in their native tongue.

Before 1918, however, the Hungarians had 2,588 elementary schools, 1,497 state schools, 305 communal schools, and 786 religious schools.

The Romanians, in contrast, had only 2,302 elementary schools, no state schools, 96 communal schools, and 2,206 religious schools.

The fact must be underscored that state schools for students of the Romanian language were completely nonexistent. This, despite the fact that Article 17 of the 1868 law guaranteeing equal rights for the various ethnic groups, specifically stipulated that the state had an obligation to establish, in the regions populated by ethnic minorities, schools in which the language of the respective minorities were taught.

Zenovie Paclisanu wrote that in Hungary there was no state school, primary or secondary, in any of the languages spoken by the minorities.

George Lukacs knew perfectly well how meaningless the law of 1868 was when he wrote the following words for the purpose of misleading British public opinion:

Our law of 1868, which proclaimed the equality of the various national groups, is an example of our liberal attitude toward people of differing nationalities, and it defended the elementary rights of the non-Magyars much more effectively than the so-called treaties for the protection of the minorities in the successor states." *(The Injustices of the Treaty of Trianon).*

But this tactic of bringing into the discussion inoperative stipulations of the law as though they were really operative, will already be well known to the reader, and there is no point to pursuing the matter further.

The mother tongue of the minorities, also, was not allowed in the kindergartens, where the children's age was between three and six.

The lack of state schools where the peasant children could learn to read and write in the language they spoke at home, and which they heard—exclusively—in the villages where they lived, was the principal reason for the high proportion of illiterates among the Romanians of Transylvania. With its traditional cynicism, Hungarian propaganda presented this illiteracy as a product of the Romanian intellectual inferiority. The Hungarian historian Acsady, wrote accurately: "The Transylvanian nobility was afraid that if the Romanians began to get an education, and if they had more learned heads among them, they would no longer be willing to bear their yoke."

In short, the purely Romanian villages and hamlets were completely without state schools in which the Romanian language was taught. In order to carry out their Magyarization, the Hungarians opened Magyar state and religious schools in these regions. If a child wanted to learn, he had to do so in a foreign language characterized by Finno-Ugrian harshness, which was very difficult to master for children who thought and spoke in the soft sounding neo-Latin Romanian language.

Of the total of 3,835 state primary schools which existed in Hungary before World War I, 2,839 were in regions which possessed substantial Romanian and other minorities. During the same period, Hungary possessed a total of 1,149 kindergartens, of which only 347 were situated in decisively Magyar regions, and 802 were situated in non-Magyar regions for non-Magyar children. The precise goal of this emphasis was, of course, to Magyarize the children as early as possible.

All things considered, therefore, Lukacs could go on remonstrating that the great concern which the Hungarians had for the non-Magyars was like the mutual concern existing between brothers. The only difficulty is that he forgot to name the brothers in question. The brotherly love of the Hungarians for the Romanians was like the brotherly love of Cain for Abel. Indeed, there were many schools that existed for the purpose of destroying the national existence of the minorities.

The following table illustrates the effects of the policy of Magyarization, which sought, slowly but surely, to suppress the various non-Magyar nationalities. This data is from the *Yearbook of the Hungarian Institute of Statistics*:

	1871	1890	1900
Schools in the Magyar language	5,818	8,994	10,325
Schools in the Romanian language	2,878	2,582	2,157
Schools in the German language	1,232	674	383
Schools in the Serbian language	2,547	312	135

The table shows that the Magyar schools continued to grow in number while those of the minorities showed a continuous decline.

The situation in Transylvania represented only a single aspect of the general position of the national minorities in Hungary. In the county of Bacs-Bodrog, for instance, which, in 1910, had 176,950 Germans and 267,714 Hungarians, the Germans had 20 schools and the Hungarians 261—that is, over 10 times more. In the county of Sopron, the situation for the minorities was even worse. The Hungarians, numbering 141,004, had 271 schools, while 109,160 Germans who lived in the county had no German language school at all.

In order to prevent the children from speaking their mother tongue, one teacher in a region where they had large numbers of Slovaks went to the length of dinning into the children's minds the idea that God spoke only Hungarian, so it was useless to pray in Slovak. [*The Tribune*, November 21, 1901.]

In short, all means were good so long as they served the

purpose of Magyarization—even to the point of having the Almighty speak only Hungarian.

The results of the denationalization offensive were by no means insignificant. In the school year 1913-14, 163,721 Romanian school children in Transylvania attended classes in Romanian primary schools, while 66,597 had to go to Magyar schools, since there were no Romanian schools in their respective regions.

However, so that they would not be obliged to learn to read and write in the language of their oppressors, many Romanians preferred not to learn at all. This was a logical and natural reaction because the Transylvanian Romanians wanted their sons to read and write Romanian, like themselves and like their ancestors.

A Romanian education would serve to strengthen the connection between the individual and the nation and to emphasize to the peasant child his deeply rooted affiliation to the Romanian spirit. A Magyar education, on the other hand, was meant to estrange the Romanian child from the great Romanian family.

For this reason the Transylvanian pesant chose to have an illiterate child who could still think in Romanian over one who knew the alphabet in Hungarian but who was estranged from his nation.

As we have already seen, the Hungarians were wont to ascribe the illiteracy of the Romanian peasants in Transylvania to reasons other than their own school system, in particular to a lack of ability which, they said, was characteristic of the Romanian nation. An eloquent rebuttal of this defamatory assertion is offered by the progress achieved by the same Transylvanian Romanians after they had joined the Romanian kingdom.

The percentage of literate persons in Romanian Transylvania increased from 51.5 percent in 1910 to 67 percent in 1930—that is, an increase of 15.9 percent.

The situation of the Hungarian schools in Romania after Transylvania had been joined to Romania by the Trianon Treaty was completely different from that of the Romanian schools under Hungarian rule.

In the school year 1922-23, the Hungarian minority in Transylvania had 526 state schools in which the teaching language was Magyar. Again, we would point out to the reader that the Romanians in Transylvania had no state primary schools of their own before the union with the kingdom.

During the same school year (1922-23), the Transylvanian Romanians had 1,020 Romanian state schools, but this still did not give them the proportion to which they were entitled compared with the Hungarian language state schools. This was so, first of all, because of the numerical superiority of the Romanians, and, secondly, because of the preeminently Romanian character of the places where these schools were situated. The total number of Hungarian schools was 1,669, as compared with 3,613 Romanian schools.

On the basis of a 1924 law dealing with primary education, the Romanian state had assumed the upkeep obligations for the schools in communes where the population spoke a language other than Romanian. These were, for the most part, primary schools in which the lessons were taught in the languages of the respective minorities.

In the school year 1929-30, the Romanian state spent the sum of 103,660,282 lei on the maintenance of minority primary schools [Silviu Dragomir].

In that year the Romanian state had the responsibility for 260 primary schools and for 223 sections of primary schools where instruction was in Hungarian. Thus, there were 483 state institutions at which the Hungarian minority in Transylvania could receive their education in the Magyar language at the expense of the Romanian state.

At the institutes of higher education which existed before 1918, one finds a similar discrepancy between the number of Romanian and Hungarian schools. Before their union with the kingdom, the Romanians in Transylvania had 18 institutes of higher education, compared with 196 for the Magyars.

This lack of facilities for higher education in the Romanian language accounts for the fact that the Magyars, who in 1910 represented 54.5 percent of the total population of the Hungarian kingdom, compared with 16.1 percent for the Romanians, could in 1913-14 account for 82.6 percent of the total number of students in secondary schools, compared with 5.6 percent for the Romanians.

Count Apponyi, who was aware of the truth of the minority nationalities problem in his country—he was after all a man who had often influenced the destiny of these nationalities—had the cynicism to criticize the Romanians for their lack of higher education. Judged on the scale of what he called "the economic intelligentsia," the Romanians, he said, accounted for only 6.5 percent compared with 71.7 percent for the Hungarians. Count Apponyi openly asserted that this discrepancy existed not because of "artificial repression" on the part of the Hungarians but because of racial deficiencies. But the former satrap of the Hungarian educational system purposely forgot to tell the Anglo-Saxon reader that in Austria-Hungary there existed 105 Hungarian vocational schools contrasted with no Romanian schools of this genre, and 65 Hungarian commercial schools (17 of these were in Hungary proper) compared with only one school of this kind for three million Transylvanian Romanians.

Under the Romanians, the situation was vastly different when it came to the field of higher education. Immediately after Transylvania was brought into the Romanian kingdom, the Romanians in Transylvania had 127 secondary schools (compared with the 196 Hungarian secondary schools that existed before 1918). Before the beginning of World War I, the Hungarians had had 170 secondary schools, compared with 18 Romanian secondary schools.

Under the Hungarians, the Romanians had had only five high schools, four of which taught all the grades, while one was limited to the first four grades. The four high schools were located at Blaj, Brasov, Nasaud, and Beius. In 1889, the Magyar government apparently decided that four high schools were excessive for three million Transylvanian Romanians, and so they decided to introduce the Magyar language at Beius, which had been founded in 1868, in the hope that it would serve the cause of Romanian national culture in Transylvania.

Under the Romanians, 1,300,000 Hungarians had 52 high schools. What a picture of Romanian intolerance!

Of all the secondary schools which the Romanian state supported (in doing so it went far beyond the formal obligations assumed in the treaties dealing with minority rights), there were seven schools of higher education where instruction was in the Hungarian language and two sections in a girls' gymnasium plus another two sections in commercial high schools where instruction was also in Hungarian.

At this point we must bring in the law of December 1925, which dealt with private education and in which the Romanian state made an important concession to the principles on which the Hungarian educational system was based.

From the beginning of its existence as an independent state, Romania had adopted the principle of secular education, organized, paid for, and controlled by the state.

In Hungary, education was, in principle, concentrated in the hands of communal and religious schools. Before 1867, there was in Hungary no primary school which had been founded and supported by the state. It was only after the installation of the dual monarchy that the Hungarian state began to take an interest in the way schools were organized—but this was on such a small scale that in 1880 there were only 266 state schools, compared with 1,669 communal schools and 13,772 religious schools. In 1918, the Magyar state still adhered to this principle of organization. It supported, at that time, 3,835 communal primary schools and 12,091 religious schools.

In the field of higher education, one finds a parallel situation. At that time, out of a total number of 180 high schools, only 50 were funded and controlled by the state, all the others being church schools. Of 95 teacher training schools, 30 were state schools and 65 were religious schools.

In seeking to comply with long-established traditions of the Hungarian school system, the Romanian state departed from the guiding principles of its own policy, established by law in 1925, and permitted the minorities to open new religious schools, at the same time as it approved the continued operation of the old ones.

In order to assure that the certificates which they issued possessed equal value to those issued by the Romanian state schools, the religious schools had to comply with certain conditions having to do with the curriculum and the teaching staff. Among other conditions was the one requiring that teachers be able to speak the Romanian language. Teachers and school masters were given five years' time to achieve a capability in Romanian. Teachers over fifty-five years of age and those who had served more than thirty years were exempted. Nothing could have been more logical, since the minorities teaching staff was now part of the Romanian teaching staff. Their teacher certificates had precisely the same value as any other teacher certificate in Romania.

One should not forget that the Apponyi law not only obliged the teachers to teach the Magyar language, but even extended this obligation to include the obligatory use of Hungarian by primary school children after they had graduated from the four primary grades.

The Hungarians denounced the Romanian law as an intolerable action by the Romanian government, and they rushed off to the League of Nations, to which they used to address all of their complaints against Romania.

The complaints of the Hungarians came before the Tripartite Committee of the League of Nations. After a thorough examination of the question, the committee, by its decision of March 18, 1926, rejected the accusations brought against Romania. [The finding of the committee was published in the official *Gazette* of the League of Nations for the respective year: pp. 741-42.]

Lord Cecil, who served as chairman of the Tripartite Committee, sharply criticized the exaggerated nature of the Hungarian accusations, in the following terms: "The members of the Committee point out that complaints sent to the League of Nations should be drawn up very carefully, so the League does not have to deal with any inexact data."

Addressing the Romanian government, the Tripartite Committee "congratulated it for the truly European attitude it had adopted in the question of the Transylvanian minorities." The diplomatic note addressed to Romania said: "In this very difficult problem, the Romanian government manifested the most sincere desire, the most praiseworthy one, to satisfy justice and humanity."

But the bitter lesson that the Hungarian chauvinists were taught by the League of Nations did not prevent them, even after the Tripartite Committee had handed down its decision, from defaming Romania for its handling of the school problem in Transylvania. The principle expressed by Hitler in *Mein Kampf* dealing with the ultimate effect of a persistent propaganda in an unjust cause, had found its most fruitful domain in Hungary.

Both Hungarians and foreigners should keep this lesson in mind for the future. The Hungarians must abandon their tactic of defamation at any cost. The foreigners, who in the past have fallen so easily into the trap prepared for them by chauvinistic Magyar propagandists, should investigate the facts before they make accusations.

17. THE VIENNA DIKTAT OF AUGUST 1940

We have reached the end of our exposition. However, instead of finishing this work with a final chapter, writing finis to one of the most tragic histories the European continent has known, we are constrained to dedicate the last part of this book to the first chapter of a new era of historical, geographical, and political injustice, of tragedy and nonsense.

Injustice exists today in the Romanian province of Transylvania, after an interval of only two decades during which Transylvania had witnessed a national revival that brought new life to the land which Constantin Bratianu had, with good reason, called "the heart of the Romanian spirit." Said Bratianu: "The kingdom is the brain of the Romanian nation, and Transylvania is its heart."

The new injustice took place quite rapidly. [The reference here is to the Vienna *Diktat* of August 1940.] Transylvania's territory was cut apart. No surgeon in the world would have performed such an operation—an operation which was worthy of a butcher with brutal hands.

The northern part of Transylvania was severed from the southern part. From every standpoint—historic, geographic, economic, ethnic, and ethical—such a separation constitutes an absurdity and a danger to European peace.

The shattering of Transylvania's unity was in total disregard of the most elementary notions of common sense and equity. Transylvania's existence had always been characterized by an indissoluble unity. Its history has known vicissitudes, whose tragic nature we have dealt with in this book. Whether independent, autonomous, or oppressed, whether unwillingly integrated into the Hapsburg monarchy or violently annexed to the Hungarian crown, Transylvania has had to drink the dregs from the cup of bitterness. But until recently it has never experienced the tragic situation of being cut asunder by fictitious, arbitrary, illogical, and impossible borders.

Even venturesome revisionists like Lord Rothermere had never gone as far as suggesting the destruction of Transylvanian unity.

The Transylvanian regions whose dismemberment was demanded by Lord Rothermere's supporters did not extend beyond a zone a few kilometers wide at the western border that had been established by the Treaty of Trianon. The most ardent foreign supporters of Hungarian revisionism had said that they did not demand the union of all of Transylvania with Hungary. They had said that they only wished to give Hungary the western frontier towns which Magyar propaganda, in the face of the most compelling historical, geographic, economic, and ethnic realities, had continued to describe as "citadels of the Magyar spirit."

None of the pro-Magyar propagandists abroad or their sympathizers had dared—despite the militant revisionism that characterized the twenty-year period after World War I—to formulate claims that extended as far as the Carpathian Mountains. Indeed, the most orthodox pro-Magyars did not press claims that extended beyond the western frontier area of Transylvania.

The Hungarians, during the period immediately after World War I, had not dared to formulate openly their territorial claims in their propaganda to the western nations. The memory of the chaotic state of affairs in the former Austro-Hungarian monarchy—which was essentially the work of the Hungarian leaders in Budapest—was still so contemporaneous and so vivid that even the most chauvinistic Hungarians were not foolhardy enough to ask a return to the *status quo ante*.

The Hungarians were shrewd. At the beginning they feigned deep respect for the decisions taken at Trianon. They had to deal tactfully with the Allies who, understandably, regarded the achievements of the Versailles peace conference as accomplishments to be jealously safeguarded.

The French deputy Tisseyre, a man whose pro-Magyar sentiments have already been described in this book, put the matter this way:

The Hungarians are not asking for a revision of the

Trianon Peace Treaty. They are asking that the Treaty
be put into effect, in the broadest sense of its spirit. For
the Hungarians in Transylvania they are demanding the
freedom to speak their language, to practice their religion,
and remain Hungarian.

This was at the beginning. This was how Magyar propaganda ingratiated itself with western public opinion, in particular, with political circles and the mass media. But the
content of their propaganda was completely misleading, for on
the very day that Hungary ratified the Trianon treaty, it unmistakably manifested its real revisionist intentions. After
signing the treaty, the Hungarian delegate took a solemn oath
to work to revive "the Hungary of a thousand years"—that is,
the Hungary which had lasted just five decades, from 1867 to
1918.

"In God we trust," swore the representatives of the Magyar
people in 1920. "We believe in our motherland. We believe in
the revival of millenary Hungary." Not too much time had
elapsed before an even stronger revisionist creed could be heard
on the banks of the Danube. In 1921, there took place in down-
town Budapest the unveiling of monuments commemorating
those provinces which had been separated from the dual monarchy. On that occasion, the Catholic ecclesiastic Stefan Zad-
ravet, addressed these words to a crowd whose enthusiasm was
described as "irresistible": "These monuments represent our
hatred and our revenge, which are close at hand . . . We must
be reunited at any cost!"

This exceeded revisionism. It was tantamount to a war cry
while the peoples of the world were celebrating peace. In order
to better understand the Hungarian penchant for misleading
public opinion abroad, we should mention here a remarkably
candid statement made by Count Bethlen a few years before
World War II broke out in 1939:

Count Apponyi has never uttered the word "revisionism."
The Hungarian Revisionist League was founded only
when Lord Rothermere's newspaper articles in London
had launched the slogan, in calling for a revision of the
Trianon treaty.

Was this candor or was it cynicism? Hungarian contempt

for other European peoples must have been very great if they could believe for an instant that the representatives of the European nations would be taken in by the speeches of the old Hungarian politician, Count Apponyi. Even if he did not pronounce the word "revisionism," there was widespread understanding of the real intentions of the Hungarians vis-à-vis the territories they had lost at the end of World War I.

But if the content of Magyar revisionist propaganda appeared modest at the beginning, the Magyars gradually changed their tactics and launched direct attacks to back up their territorial claims. First, they put out feelers, asking only for small "modifications" of the frontiers established by President Millerand through the approval of the Trianon treaty. Afterwards, they laid claim to the "purely Magyar towns" in the western border area of Transylvania.

What the Hungarians gained in Vienna on August 30, 1940, not only exceeded all claims which had been made over the previous few decades, but it even exceeded the optimistic expectations of the most passionate Budapest revisionists.

The Vienna Diktat

As the result of the Vienna *Diktat* of August 30, 1940—some would have us believe that the *Diktat* was the result of "arbitration"—42,243 square kilometers with a Romanian population of 1,304,894 (that is, 50.1 percent of the entire Transylvanian Romanian population) were stolen from Transylvania's territory. The area in question had, at the time, roughly 480,000 Hungarians and an equal number of Szecklers. In all, the Hungarian and Szeckler population amounted to 968,371.

According to the Hungarian statistics of 1940, the Romanians constituted 48.7 percent of the total number of inhabitants annexed to Hungary.

Of the 23 counties that were part of Transylvania, 8 were annexed to Hungary (Ciuc, Maramures, Nasaud, Odorhei, Satu-Mare, Salaj, Somes, and Trei Scaune). Another 3 counties—Bihor, Cluj, and Mures—were dismembered to create an artificial frontier in the very heart of Romanian Transylvania.

If the Szeckler enclave is not taken into consideration, the Romanians represented up to 70 percent of the entire population of the counties of Maramures, Satu-Mare, Salaj, Cluj, Somes, and Nasaud.

The rationale behind the so-called arbitration which took place in Vienna was not publicly stated, so we can only guess at the nature of the judgment which determined the present configuration of Transylvania. The shape of the new frontier between Hungary and Romania permits us to guess at some of the reasons which motivated the arbitrators. Their basic criterion must have had to do with the incorporation of the Szeckler region into Hungary. This, of course, is nonsense. The three Szeckler counties (Ciuc, Odorhei, and Trei Scaune) are surrounded by a vast Romanian ocean, in the middle of which the Szeckler concentrations remain small islands.

The "arbitrators" wished at any price to incorporate the Szecklers into the Hungarian masses. Since the territory populated by Szecklers lies on the eastern side of the province, the two arbitrarily appointed "judges" of Romanian destinies deemed it proper to give Hungary an enormous territory—a territory where the Romanians represented the overwhelming majority—in order to connect it with the Szeckler islands.

There could have been no decision more illogical, more unnatural, or more unjust. The Szecklers had come as colonists to Transylvanian land which at that time was populated by Romanians. If the Hungarians felt that the Szecklers were absolutely indispensable to the prosperity of the Magyar nation, they should have incorporated them in Magyar national territory. But in fact many Szecklers had already left these areas because of the hard living conditions imposed on them by the Hungarian nobility.

In *Die Zukunft der Szekler* ("The Future of the Szeckler") [the reference is to *Ungarn*, a pamphlet published in May 1943], Josef Venczel shows that between 1901 and 1913 only, 13,652 Szecklers had emigrated—6,753 to the United States and—an extremely interesting fact—8,599 to Romania.

A precedent, therefore, had been created.

But the incorporation into Hungary of the Szeckler minority and the territory on which they lived was nonsensical. In eastern Transylvania, where they were only colonists, the Szecklers were not at home but were on foreign territory. Historically, the colonization of European territory has never justified future demands on this territory. What rights did the Hungarians have to claim a Szeckler territory, that is, a territory inhabited by a foreign people?

Today the Szecklers may be considered Hungarians. But

in previous chapters, we saw how basically different the Szecklers were from the Hungarians. In the beginning, the Szecklers had been fierce enemies of the Magyars. The relationship was described by A. de Bertha in his work *The Hungarians and the Romanians*, [Paris, 1889]. "The Szecklers' unremitting hostility against Bathory," said de Bertha, "led many times to bloody uprisings which were harshly suppressed." Elsewhere, de Bertha adds: "Ion Sigismund de Zapolya robbed the Szecklers of their liberties, just as Bathory deceived them with all kinds of promises."

Cserey, the 17th century Szeckler chronicler, is even more explicit than de Bertha in describing the hostility which the Szecklers had always had for the Hungarians.

"Transylvania's misfortune," he said, "has always come from Hungary and the Hungarians. Because of them, we have lost both our country and our liberty."

Ciano had mutilated Transylvania in order to achieve—what an irony!—the union of the Szecklers with the Hungarians. Addressing himself to Transylvania at an earlier date, Cserey had exclaimed: "Remember this lesson, oh Transylvania, dear motherland. Never associate with the Hungarians if you don't want to suffer as you are suffering now."

If this evidence of the hostility with which the Szecklers regarded the Hungarians should not be enough, let us reinforce the picture with one very convincing incident from the history of Transylvania. When the Romanian prince, Michael the Brave, conquered Transylvania at the beginning of the 17th century, the Szecklers openly sided with him against the Hungarians. From this it may be concluded that the Szecklers preferred Romanian rule and sovereignty to the harsh domination of the Magyars.

One cannot sacrifice a native population of 1,300,000 which had deep roots in the land taken from Romania, for the sake of establishing a bridge between Hungary and the Szeckler colonists—whose only connection with the Magyars was the fact that they spoke the same language.

The Szecklers, indeed, were true-born Romanians, not colonists who had been denationalized by a tyrannical domination. If the method applied in 1940 were generalized, then the whole map of Europe would have to be changed, thus bringing about a series of insoluble situations and widespread confusion, resulting in never-ending wars.

Magyar imperialism led inevitably to claims against territories which, after the failure of the Austro-Hungarian monarchy, had been annexed by the so-called successor states, Romania, Yugoslavia, and Czechoslovakia. These claims had attracted the sympathy of Fascist Italy and Nazi Germany, which sought to use them as a platform for their own territorial claims. For the Fascists and the Nazis, the support they offered to Magyar imperialistic aspirations had a primarily political character. But the desire to rule over as large a territory as possible had a more profound meaning for the Magyars. Because there were few true-born Hungarians, they endeavored—by Magyarizing a few million non-Magyars—to eliminate the danger they saw hanging over their nation.

Ludwig Spohr, in his book, entitled *The Spiritual Reasons for Hungarian Nationalism* [Berlin, 1936], wrote:

> The supreme reason for Hungarian nationalism and imperialism is the nightmare caused by their small numbers. The fear of losing their people—who were few and decreasing in number—has impelled them to embark upon a variety of national imperialism in the form of Magyarization.

According to a study conducted by Anton Reithinger [Anton Reithinger, *Le visage économique de l'Europe* ("The Economic Face of Europe")], Hungary's population by the year 1960 would increase by 15.7 percent over its population in 1930, and the density of population would increase from 93.4 inhabitants per square kilometer to 107.7. For the same period of time, Romania would show an increase of 32.2 percent, and the density of its population would increase from 6.12 inhabitants per square kilometer in 1930 to 80.9 in 1960.

For the Hungarian nation, the danger over the coming period does not spring from lack of territory but from the low demographic density of the Hungarian people. The eight million Hungarians are not excessively crowded in their national territory. Their birth rate, as we can see, is far from constituting an obsession, as is the case with countries with more prolific birth rates. In Hungary proper—that is, the Hungary produced by the Trianon treaty—there would be ample room to cope with the normal Hungarian birth rate. By this we mean that there would be enough land to feed the population and to

offer the possibility of prosperity and progress in the economic and cultural spheres. The solution to the problem, therefore, cannot be a territorial one but is instead primarily diplomatic. It would lend itself readily to settlement by bringing back to the fold of the Hungarian nation their blood relatives and kindred nations—the Szecklers, the Hungarians living in the Bacau region and in other central European regions, including Transylvania. This would, of course, involve a population exchange on a large scale.

This would be the ideal solution—but the Romanians are not likely to impose such a solution in the light of their traditionally tolerant policy toward minorities—a policy which we hope they will adhere to in the future as faithfully as they have in the past.

There is one more aspect to the problem. The Hungary that emerged from the Trianon treaty was very much reduced in size. The thought that it would remain thus reduced kept the postwar Hungarian leaders awake at night. In a world that was now gone forever, a handful of people, wielding a rod of iron, had been able to impose their rule on enormous masses of subject nationalities in the one-time kingdom of the Holy Crown of Hungary. For these reasons the Hungarian people have lived with a mirage of a vast territory populated by a great mass of people.

Another part of the mirage was the belief that the Hungarian people were homogeneous. This homogeneity, however, had been achieved not by union but by suppression. When the Hungarians awoke from the grandeur of this dream, it was too late. They found themselves restricted to their natural boundaries. Unhappy about this situation, they embarked on a militant revisionist campaign which kept central Europe in a state of uncertainty for some twenty years after World War I. While it may be said that this uncertainty paved the way for new and bloody conflicts during the post-Trianon period, war appeared improbable except in a climate of maximum tension and incertitude.

A small state with exaggerated ambitions is the definition which best suits postwar Hungary. If these ambitions had been manifested on the plane of European spirituality, no one could have reproached the Hungarians for the disproportion between the smallness of their country and the splendor of their dreams. The dreams of territorial greatness, however, contained the seed of never-ending conflict and bloody wars.

Belgium and Switzerland are also small countries. They have become great countries, thanks to their contributions in the realm of the spirit—contributions which place them in the front rank of the great family of European states and which have made of them harbingers of a greater future which will involve the abolition of war and the federalization of Europe.

Even Francisc Herczeg, the well-known Hungarian writer who was recognized as the leader of Magyar revisionism, sang praises to small countries, comparing the small Athenian republic and the huge Persian empire, the immense British empire and tiny Portugal, the United States of America and Holland [*Pesti Hirlap*, April 4, 1931].

"Which of them is more important in the history of man?" Herczeg asked. "The small Athenian republic or the gigantic Persian empire?" Then he added:

> The first great navigators, explorers, and discoverers were not English but Portuguese. The Dutch, not the Americans, were the first to fight for civil and religious rights. Our Saviour was born in Bethlehem and not in Canterbury.

As was to be expected, Magyar propaganda gave Herczeg's statements—which did not sit well with the British and American public—ample play. Indeed, they were featured in an Italian magazine published in Budapest. [*Rassegra Ungheria*, June 1943.]

But the reduced Hungarian state did not choose to achieve greatness in the realm of the spirit. Instead, it sought to do so by the annexation of territory. This goal was fulfilled for it by two representatives of the fascist invaders, posing as arbitrators. [Ribbentrop and Ciano.] In short, Hungary grew in stature only by dealing contemptuously with the most categorical ethical imperatives.

We shall not analyze in detail the ethnic character of each of the counties that were cut off from Romania and annexed to Horthy's Hungary. It should be sufficient to relate that the Vienna *Diktat* gave the Hungarians communes such as Panoara, in Bihor County, in which, out of a total of 1,108 inhabitants, 1,101 were Romanian and one was Magyar, or Surduc, a commune in the same county where, out of a total of 830 inhabitants, 828 were Romanian and there was not a single

Hungarian. In fact, in the territory of the county of Cluj, annexed by Hungary in 1940 pursuant to the Vienna *Diktat*, the communes in the new Romanian-Hungarian frontier area had 24,843 inhabitants, of whom 24,070 were Romanian and only 393 Hungarian.

An injustice of this magnitude could exist only on a European continent that had become subject to Adolf Hitler's "new order."

A large number of Romanians, living in concentrated masses, were sacrificed in Vienna in order to arrange for the territorial incorporation of "an island" of Szecklers (not of Hungarians!) which had been artificially created. The arbitrators decided that the Romanians were to evacuate the territory—which had become Hungarian thanks to their ruling—within the brief space of fifteen days. The Romanian delegates, who received scant attention, were given a copy of the arbitrators' decision together with a map showing the Romanian territory that had now become Hungarian.

In the entire history of mankind, one can find no example of a more arbitrary or more artificial delineation of new frontiers.

The text of this decision produced by the so-called arbitration is laconic to the point of sounding like an ultimatum—which it, in fact, was. "The borderline between Romania and Hungary," says Article 1 of the Vienna *Diktat*, "will be the one shown in the annexed geographical map. The evacuation will take place within fifteen days."

The generosity of the trio who produced the Vienna *Diktat*—Hitler, Mussolini, and Horthy—was boundless!

No matter what the point of view from which one seeks to analyze the decision in Vienna, it is legally void *ab initio*.

Indeed, legally speaking, the *Diktat* would have to be considered nonexistent because the problem of Transylvania had been settled by the Trianon treaty, which had been signed by both the Romanians and the Hungarians.

More narrowly, as to the frontier between Romania and Hungary, the treaty had not provided for the possibility of later arbitration of the borderline that had been agreed upon in 1920. Nor had there been any subsequent agreement between Romania and Hungary to entrust the settling of any differences involving the Romanian-Hungarian border areas to any "arbitrators."

An official note carried over the German press agency on August 31, 1940, informed the German public and the world that "Hungary and Romania had asked the Axis powers to settle their dispute by arbitration."

The announcement made a mockery of common sense.

Romania, which had protested for two decades against Magyar revisionist claims, was presented to the world as an "applicant" for the mutilation of its own territory. The Romanians, who had fought for centuries for liberation from the oppressive yoke of Magyarism, had suddenly decided to ask the Axis countries to deprive them of 1,300,000 of Transylvania's most valued sons.

On a European continent where the rise of Nazism and Fascism had destroyed even the most elementary notions of decency and common sense, it was possible to encourage such nonsense. As a matter of fact, Hitler was continuing to apply in Europe the tactic he had invented back in 1938, at the time of the Austrian *Anschluss*. According to Hitler, this *Anschluss* had taken place in response to Austria's burning desire. Similarly, he had intervened—at Hacha's "supplication"—to establish a "protectorate" over the Czechoslovak republic.

The Vienna "arbitration" was not demanded by Romania; it was imposed on it—a small matter, but one which completely changes the character of the decision arrived at in Vienna on August 30, 1940.

But let us assume, contrary to all reason, that such juridical technicalities cannot be permitted to encumber the international decision-making process. The decision reached in Vienna would still lack one essential element, without which no verdict can be valid. The element which is lacking is the right to defend oneself and to plead one's cause before a court. Even in the most despotic trials, in which this right had been reduced to a mockery because the voice of the defense counsel had zero effect, the involved parties still retained the possibility to speak up in their own defense. Hitler and Mussolini, however, had deprived the Romanian peoples of this elementary right.

No matter how painful this may be, we have to admit that Romania's minister for external affairs had been so blinded by his pro-Nazi sentiments that—in contrast to what the most humble lawyers would have done in a similar case—he agreed to be present at the tragi-comedy presided over by the two fascist arbitrators. He agreed further to sign the *Diktat* which dismembered Transylvania and cut off 1,300,000 Transylvanians, who were the sons and grandsons of those peasants and scholars who had struggled for centuries for the triumph of the Romanian cause.

Transylvania will never forgive the Romanian delegates to the Vienna conference for not rejecting the decision which led to the Hungarian annexation of Transylvania. Such a rejection was called for by the entire history of the Transylvanian people.

What is even more revolting is the fact that there was no time to produce any of the documents which dealt with the righteousness of the Romanian cause, because the two "judges" who were deciding Transylvania's fate ruled that all documents had to be gathered and presented in less than twenty-four hours.

Hungarian avoidance of an honest debate on the matter was justly interpreted by public opinion in the neutral countries. Edouard Rossier, a Swiss professor of world history, wrote in the *Gazette de Lausanne*: "Hungary could hardly justify its claims in the matter of Transylvania, on the grounds of ethnic and demographic arguments. The Romanian element represents the majority of the population."

In these circumstances, the Hungarians demanded and obtained an arbitration which was as superficial as it was hasty. The official commentary stressed the fact that "justice" has been rendered expeditiously, in evident contrast to the cumbersome and laggard diplomacy which had preceded important decisions in international forums after World War I.

"Years of work," wrote the diplomatic reporter of the Stefani agency on August 30, 1940, "would not have been enough for the League of Nations to achieve a result comparable to that which was achieved in Vienna in forty-eight hours."

The Stefani agency was perfectly right. So absurd an outcome could only have been the product of arbitration that lasted all of forty-eight hours. Any longer discussion of the issues would inevitably have resulted in the rejection of Magyar claims on the grounds of inconsistency.

The "arbitrated" *Diktat* which took place in Vienna bears the imprint, down to the smallest details, of the haste with which the decision was reached—a haste which could only have resulted in imperfect and temporary arrangements and not in decisions of a permanent character.

The two "judges" who had been responsible for the "arbitration" were in a hurry. Matters of overriding importance for the fate of Europe demanded their presence in Rome and Berlin. The Transylvanian question was an "insignificant" matter which had to be settled quickly, and in a manner that would give satisfaction to Horthy's Hungary—for the simple reason that he had always been a friend of Nazism and Fascism.

It was for this reason that Ciano and Ribbentrop had informed Romania that "they had only forty-eight hours at their disposal to settle the Transylvanian problem and that no delay could be tolerated for a debate of the issue."

Of what conceivable importance were the historical, political, geographic, ethnic, and economic considerations which were involved in the issue?

The "arbitration" had to be over in forty-eight hours, the finding had to be handed down, a decision had to be drafted, and the Hungarian-Romanian differences over Transylvania had to be settled forever.

The mock arbitration, which took place in the Gold Hall of Belvedere Palace in Vienna, is a dramatic illustration of how much the notion of justice had deteriorated in Hitler's Europe.

Today the official statements and commentaries, as well as the telegrams sent out by the D.N.B. and Stefani agencies on the days immediately following the Vienna *Diktat*, make strange reading. One has to ask oneself if the temporary successes of the Axis countries had so blinded the Axis leaders in Rome and Berlin that they actually believed that the parody in Vienna constituted the basis for the final settlement of central European border issues. Or were they so intoxicated by their successes that they simply ignored, or ridiculed, the nations which at the time were in no position to retaliate or resist?

"The confusion in the Danubian area has been forever overcome," said a telegram from Berlin.

"A permanent peace has been established," said an official note sent out from Vienna on August 31, 1940.

And Count Ciano made this statement after the Vienna finding had been handed down: "We have settled a very difficult problem, not only with scrupulous impartiality but with the certitude that our decision will result in complete trust for the future between the two countries which have addressed us."

Finally, a declaration sent out from Vienna on August 31,

1940, emphasized the fact that leading circles inside the German ministry of foreign affairs considered the Vienna solution final and permanent.

If the Vienna "arbitrators" had taken the trouble to read the history of Transylvania, or even fragments of this history which had to do with the centuries-old struggle of the Transylvanian Romanians for liberty, they would have contented themselves with pronouncing the verdict they had reached, without attempting to comment on it. In that case they would have covered themselves with shame—but not with shame and ridicule.

For it is indeed ridiculous to pretend that the Romanians, who had fought for centuries for their national freedom and independence, would voluntarily surrender—overnight —everything they had won at the end of a centuries-old ordeal.

But then, in a Europe belonging to Hitler and company, was there any room for objections in principle? The first priority was to appease the Hungarians, in recognition of the great services they had rendered to Fascism and Nazism, among other things through their revisionist propaganda in Europe.

The Hungarians hastened to express their gratitude for the royal present they had received from the two "arbitrators." The official statement of the Magyar government, which was issued after the Vienna *Diktat*, is worth quoting verbatim: "The whole of Hungary is grateful to Führer Hitler and to Il Duce, Mussolini, for their constructive accomplishments, which, after voiding the Versailles treaty, also voided the treaty of Trianon."

Hungarian political circles observed that the Vienna "arbitration" was bound to strengthen the bonds of friendship between Hungary and the Axis powers. The official government statement said: "Hungary is proud of its future role in a new Europe, on the side of the Axis. In the future, Hungary will demonstrate the same loyalty and friendship to the Axis, for better or for worse."

The official Hungarian news agency concluded its commentary with these words: "Now that the injustice committed at Trianon has been rectified, Hungary will do everything in its power to establish good relations between the two countries, something which so far has not been possible because of the intrigues between the Entente powers."

The recognition of the relationship existing between the repudiation of the Versailles treaty and that of the Trianon treaty is worth stressing. In effect, the Hungarians were congratulating the Germans for annexing Alsace and Lorraine, for doing away with Luxembourg, for incorporating Danzig and the southern areas into the greater German Reich, and for uniting with the new German Reich not only Bohemia and Moravia but the regions as well which came under the *Générale Gouvernement* in Poland.

The government in Budapest was convinced that Hitler was making and passing laws for eternity. This was the situation that permitted them to reveal their true sentiments vis-à-vis Nazism and Fascism.

It was only natural that, in a choice between dictatorial Germany and France, with its generous ideals, the Budapest magnates would choose the former. After all, their methods of governing were in perfect harmony with the despotic Europe where intolerance and brutality were to count as guiding principles. Knowing the past, one can readily imagine the fate that Hungary had in store for the ethnic groups which had become its subjects, in a European continent impregnated with fascist conceptions.

After "proudly assuming the role awaiting it in a new Europe on the side of the Axis powers," Hungary bowed low before the Nazi and fascist adventurers who had been allotting the land of Europe to their partisans as though the whole of Europe was their estate. And they swore an oath of continuing faith, come what might, to those who had for the moment become masters of the destinies of the continent.

I should like to offer the suggestion that when, after the war, the Hungarian propagandists, with democratic effusions, try to prove to the Allies their devotion to the cause of democracy, the statements quoted above be hung on the walls of the conference room. In this way it will be possible to compare their democratic protestations with their previous frequent declarations of love for Hitler and Mussolini and of contempt for the Entente states.

If it had not been for these intrigues, said certain important Hungarians immediately after the Vienna *Diktat* was promulgated, the Romanians and Hungarians could have followed a good neighbor policy which would have formally committed them to work for improvement of Magyar-Romanian relations in the future.

The Magyar Occupation of Northern Transylvania

Within fifteen days northern Transylvania was severed from the Romanian administration. The Magyar troops triumphantly entered the land they had had to leave in 1918.

After twenty-two years of liberty, the ordeal of the Transylvanian Romanians began all over again. The acts of barbarism committed by the Hungarians against the Romanians began on the first day they set foot in Transylvania. (The reader will see later that the word barbarism does not exaggerate the situation.)

"The Hungarian fury," which had been kept alive for two decades—with a perseverance worthy of more noble ideals—by the apostles of revanchism was unleashed against both Romanian peasants and intellectuals. Indeed, this fury against everything Romanian did not even spare the Romanian churches.

Surveying the thousands of barbarous acts committed by Horthy's troops immediately after the occupation of the annexed territory, one has the impression that these acts were part of a carefully thought-out plan. This plan involved nothing less than the radical destruction of the Romanian spirit—or, to use an expression frequently used by the Hungarians—the "extermination" of the Romanians living in Transylvania. As a matter of fact, the Hungarians made no effort to conceal their intentions.

We have already dealt with the criminal intentions expressed by Ducso Csaba's hero, the young Levent, with regard to the Romanians in Transylvania. His profession of faith, while it might be considered pathological, is to be found repeated in numerous newspaper articles and in an entire Magyar ultrachauvinistic literature which was meant to keep alive Magyar hatred for the Romanians.

"The hatred for everything Romanian," says a booklet recently published in Bucharest under the title *Les assassinats* ("The Assassinations"), "had become a profession of faith with Hungarian citizens."

The following thoughts—worthy of a Jack the Ripper—were expressed in the Budapest newspaper, *Pesti Hirlap*, for April 15, 1932:

> If we occupy our country again [Transylvania], the nationalities that live in the area with us will have to adapt—and they will have to adapt within the first 24

hours. We are not going to prove weak again. The Daco-Romanians must disappear from this territory.

[When he spoke about Hungarian "weakness" in dealing with the Romanian nationality problem, the writer of this passage must have had in mind the inconclusive massacres which occurred in 1784, in 1848, and, indeed, over the entire history of Transylvania.]

The word "disappear" should be understood to mean "exterminate."

"I shall kill any Wallachian standing in my way," said the hero of Csaba's book. "I shall kill all of them; I shall be ruthless. We shall set the Wallachian villages on fire during the night . . . We shall poison the springs. And then, there will be only one nationality left in Transylvania, the Magyar one."

Such were the words of the 20th century Hungarian publicist—a publicist belonging to a people who had been Christianized a thousand years ago and who claimed the ambition of civilizing central Europe.

This, indeed, is how thousands of Csaba's fellow countrymen behaved when, on the Romanian land of Transylvania, they discovered the Wallachian residents—to whom, on this otherwise gloomy occasion, the journalist from *Pesti Hirlap* cited above paid a final homage by acknowledging their Dacian-Roman origin!

The Turda correspondent of the newspaper, *The Universe*, describes the triumphant entry of the Magyar troops into the annexed Transylvanian territory, in these terms:

The first massacres took place in five communes in the immediate frontier area. The Romanians were butchered from the very first of the occupation. The streets and the houses were covered with blood and the scene bore a marked resemblance to a slaughterhouse—legs which had been cut off by axes, dismembered women, heads which had been turned into jelly, and bright red hands which had been cut off at the wrists. Some of the dead had been hanged from the fountains and the roofs.

Csaba had been right when he wrote in his book, *Nincs Kegyelem*, that "in our veins flows the blood of Arpad, Attila, and Genghis Khan."

From August 30, 1940, the day on which the "arbitrators" promulgated their decision, until October 30, 1940—that is, in only two months—Hungarian troops on Transylvanian territory killed a total of 919 Romanians, men, women, and children. In addition, 771 people were tortured, and another 3,373 people were maltreated or seriously injured—with a brutality worthy of "the most terrible inquisitorial and terrorist regimes." [Information from two brochures, *Les assassinats* and *Les déstructions d'églises* ("The Destruction of the Churches"), part of a series entitled, *A Year of Magyar Domination in Northern Transylvania.*]

Of all the massacres committed by the Hungarians, two stand out for sheer fiendishness, the massacres committed by the Hungarian army and people in the communes of Trasnea and Ip in the border county of Salaj.

We quote from one of these brochures:

The commune of Trasnea was occupied by Hungarian troops on September 9, 1940. Immediately after the Hungarian soldiers had occupied the village, they unleashed against it, as if on orders, a virtual torrent of fire and blood. All modern weapons were utilized in giving satisfaction to their brutal instincts—rifles, machineguns, grenades, and cannons . . . After the first volley of fire, the soldiers stepped into the houses and assassinated anyone who stood in their way. Then they set the houses on fire. The case of the Romanian priest, Traian Costea, is typical. First he was shot in the head. Then his body was thrown into the wooden balcony of the presbytery. Then the soldiers set fire to the presbytery and burned it, together with the priest's body. In the course of the massacre, approximately 100 people were killed, of whom 68 could subsequently be identified. Among the victims, to the eternal glory of the civilizing mission of the Magyars, there were the children, Aurica Brumar (five years old), Victoria Brumar (nine years old), Gherasim Barjoc (seven years old), and Ion Balajan (two years old). Among the old people killed were Maria Barjoc (81 years old), Grigore Barjoc (74 years old), and many others of similar age. [*Les assassinats*, pp. 15-16.]

As can be seen, not even the children and old people were

spared. The illustrious Csaba has already told us that "he was not going to spare anybody, not even the babies in their cradles or the mothers with children in their arms."

What will surely contribute even more to increase Magyar prestige in other countries and will strengthen the conviction of those in the West who believe that the Magyar nation played a civilizing role, is the variety of methods invented by the imagination of Arpad's descendants for the purpose of exterminating the Romanians in Romanian Transylvania.

Of the 68 identified corpses in the village of Trasnea, 57 had been shot in the head, chest, or abdomen; 3 had been burned; a 65-year-old, Ana Negreanu, had had her hands cut off; 31-year old Ana Salajan, who was pregnant, was run through with a bayonet; and Vasile Nargaras was found with his head split open.

In the commune of Ip, 155 men, women, and children were massacred by 40 terrorists and soldiers. Their houses were pillaged and burned. The victims were thrown into a common grave, without the presence of a priest. The intention of the Hungarians was not only to rid the commune of all Romanians, but also to enrich themselves in the process. Thus, some 90,000 lei belonging to the village church and much other goods belonging to those who had been massacred, disappeared during the turmoil.

One could fill entire pages with a listing of all the terrible things which took place during the first two months of the Hungarian occupation. But let us limit ourselves to a few more examples.

In Cosnicul de Sus, in Salaj, on September 18, 1940, 15 men and women were massacred and buried in a common grave. At Camar, in the same county, the Magyars on September 15, killed 4 Romanian peasants. At Simleul Silvanie, they killed 7 on September 14. And at Zalau, also during the month of September, they killed an additional 21 men and women. One of the women massacred, the wife of George Vicas, was pregnant at the time. A schoolmaster was shot down in his schoolyard by a Hungarian captain.

The town of Cluj, in Cluj County, was the scene of the most abominable atrocities during the months of September and October.

On September 23, for example, a number of people were brought to the house of the Romanian priest, Andrei Bujor, where they were massacred. The victims included the priest himself and his wife, their daughters, Lucia, who had a degree in philosophy, Marioara, a sophomore student, and, Victoria, a high school student, as well as Natalia Petrea, the wife of schoolmaster Gh. Petrea, and his mother and daughter—and, finally, the Reverend Bujor's woman servant, Juhasz.

In the commune of Hida, 11 Romanians were massacred, and 9 of the bodies were left in the field for 5 days before being buried. In the Dragan valley on September 12 and 13, 12 young Romanians who were coming home from the front were killed, and at San-Mihaiul Almas Ului another 10 young men were killed.

Just as odious were the numerous individual assassinations of which Romanians were the victims. The author of *Les assassinats* recounts that "at Cluj during the first days of the occupation, many Romanians were killed in the streets or in their homes, with the same bestiality and without any reason being given." [*Les assassinats*, p. 26.]

On the night of September 14, customs officer Ion Almasul was arrested in his home by a Hungarian soldier, killed in the street outside his home, bayoneted and then trampled. On September 13, Hungarian soldiers killed a Romanian peasant in front of the railway workshop. The Romanian soldier Alexandru Badea, who was returning home from the war, was thrown out of the train by the Hungarian passengers, and he died under its wheels. In the commune of Someseni, near Cluj, the peasant Ion Pantea was killed by Hungarian soldiers, who cut the arteries of his right arm and then plunged a bayonet into his heart. This was done under the terrified eyes of his daughters, who managed to escape. In the commune of Vadasel on November 30, 1940, a gang of Hungarians from the commune of Vistea beheaded with an axe a young Romanian named Ciovanas. At Poeni, the peasant Gheorghe Bane was terribly tortured by the Hungarian soldiers, and he died two days later in excruciating agony.

But the most horrible crime committed in the county of Cluj took place in the commune of Huedin on September 10. We quote from *Les assassinats* the following account of the tortures inflicted on Archpriest Aurel Munteanu:

A Hungarian officer arrested him on the street while he was going to a funeral. The officer was joined by a gang of young Hungarian assassins. They tortured the priest in the most bestial manner for four hours, displaying diabolical perseverance and patience. They started by hitting him with their fists. They continued with clubs until he was knocked unconscious. Then, faithful to the methods of sadism, they tore his beard out together with pieces of flesh. At the same time, they tore the hair out of his head, with pieces of skin attached to it. After doing these things, the butchers twisted his arms until they broke his bones. The most bestial of all the assassins, a young man named Janos Gyepu, pushed a stick through the priest's mouth several times with such force that it came out of the nape of the neck. When the priest died as a result of these inhuman tortures, the assassins threw his body, together with that of police constable, Gh. Nicola, whom they had previously killed, into a ditch near the estate of the Magyar nobleman, Count Banffy.

We think even Attila the Hun would have been horrified by the crimes committed in the commune of Huedin by the Magyars—who claimed direct descent from Attila, "the scourge of God." Dozens of such bestialities were committed at Salonta and Santion in the county of Bihor, at Berta, Malin, Stana, Capleni, and Halmajd in the county of Somes, at Doba and Mediasul Aurit in the county of Satu-Mare, and at Agristeu in the county of Tirnava Mica where a young man, Emanuil Cristea, had his eyes burned out and his tongue pulled out of his mouth. Other atrocities were committed at Ditrau in the county of Ciuc, and at other points.

"The massacres were committed," said the author of *Les assassinats*, "by both the Hungarian army and gangs of Magyar civilians. On occasion, the tortures, inflicted with morbid imagination and insane ferocity, were carried to the outer limits of human endurance. Some people were saved only because their berserk torturers thought their victims had already died."

The Terror

Encouraged by the attitude of the Magyar troops who, instead of keeping order, themselves pillaged the territory they occupied and committed other horrible crimes, the Hungarian population in Transylvania gave free scope to their primeval instincts and engaged in a paroxysm of the most ghoulish deeds.

At Marghita in Bihor County, 3 women, one of them only 16 years old, were summoned to the mayor's office and raped by 7 Hungarian peasants. After raping them, they cut off their victims' breasts.

Several score Romanians—some 20 from Mihai Bravu in the county of Bihor, 70 from Odorhau and 40 from Nicula in the county of Satu-Mare, and 40 from Tirimia in the county of Mures—were severely wounded. In the commune of Cuzaplac in the county of Bihor, a Hungarian junior lieutenant and the civilian Szabo Iancsi forced a peasant to swallow pieces of the Romanian flag, while beating him savagely.

We might have doubted the veracity of the facts described in this brochure because of the sheer horror of some of the crimes that are detailed—if the author had not supplied precise data about the victims' names and their places of residence. Further than this, any doubts about the facts disappear when one reads Levent Ducso Csaba's profession of faith and all the threats which had been uttered by the ultrachauvinists in Budapest against the Transylvanian Romanians.

Magyar propaganda emanating from Budapest incited to rob, murder, and plunder in thousands of pamphlets spread around Transylvanian territory. We quote from one of these Magyar pamphlets targeted against the Romanians in Transylvania: "Our duty is to exterminate the Wallachian nation, to destroy every trace of this cursed people, and even to rip open the wombs of women carrying Wallachian children."

Today, in the light of all the confirmed atrocities committed by the Germans in the countries they occupied, one may wonder who are the realists and who are the political neophytes.

The brochures mentioned above, *Les assassinats* and *Les déstructions d'églises,* brought serious accusations against Hungary to the attention of the civilized world. It did this in a language of wide circulation, and with the most ample documentation. If these accusations had been false or inexact, Hungary, in order to keep its image untainted, should have produced facts to prove them groundless.

Although we are well informed about all the foreign language publications which appeared in Budapest up until the end of 1943, we have not heard about the existence of any book or brochure which sought to refute the accusations Hungary had been charged with in connection with its occupation of

Romanian Transylvania. If we had found such a book, or at the very least a newspaper article, it would have been our duty to mention it. But until refuted or seriously challenged, all the accusations brought against Hungary will continue to stand.

It is to be noted that all of the data concerning Hungarian bestialities in occupied Romania have to do with only the time interval from August 30, 1940, to October 30, 1940.

All the statistical data available at a later period demonstrate that there was a recrudescence of the previous terror unleashed by the Magyars. Horthy's regime wanted to liquidate the problem of the minorities once and for all. It would exterminate them, and then offer a radical settlement of the problem.

Some of the Romanians were sent to prison. Others were sent to the front or to Germany to be used in forced labor battalions. And some went away never to return.

As of December 30, 1941, the total number of Romanian prisoners was 13,000. By the end of 1943, this figure had increased threefold. During World War I the Hungarian prisons had been full of Romanians. In World War II, the Hungarian detainee camps again held many thousands of Romanians—in Budapest, in Debrecen, in Pospokladany, in Bichie-Ciaba, in Kistracsa, and in other centers.

Confronted by the evident acts of barbarism and cruelty, what could the master tricksters in Budapest and their emissaries in London and the United States of America say in their defense?

"The Defenders of Christendom" in the Role of Church Destroyers

The Hungarians were not only guilty of acts of cruelty committed against the Romanian populace. They sought to destroy the Romanian nation by directing their blows against the churches as well, because these had been unconquerable citadels of the Romanian spirit in Transylvania.

In 1789, the petitions of the two Romanians, Ionache Navrodim and Ion Constantin of Cluj, for permission to build a Romanian church in that town had been rejected by the Jurors' Council.

"If we granted approval for the building of a Romanian church in Cluj," read the decision of the honorable jurors, "it would mean that we assented to the growth and affluence of the Romanian population, which is a race of thieves." This intolerant and reactionary decision, it is to be noted, dated from 1789, the year in which the banner of liberty, equality, and brotherhood had been raised in western Europe.

In the year 1940, the Hungarians carried their religious intolerance even further than had their predecessors in 1789. In occupying Transylvania, they set upon the Romanian churches, Orthodox and Greek-Catholic, with a fury that was decidedly unworthy of those who called themselves "defenders of Christendom."

In the annexed territory, there were, as of August 30, 1940, 422 Orthodox parishes with 339,448 believers and 977 Greek-Catholic parishes with 1,066,145 parishioners. Knowing from past experience that the church had always been a strong fortress behind whose walls the Romanians had been able to maintain their nationality unaltered, the Hungarians made great efforts to denationalize them forcibly, using religion as an instrument. Thousands of Romanians were compelled to give up their ancestors' faith and turn to one of the Magyar religions, thus becoming totally lost in the Hungarian mass.

But this time the Hungarians made use of a more oppressive method than their forefathers. They did not content themselves with the violation of Romanian conscience; they began to tear down the churches. We quote verbatim from *Les déstructions d'églises*:

In the eastern counties, at least 12 Romanian Orthodox and Greek-Catholic churches were destroyed. The Hungarians, armed with axes, mattocks, and hatchets, descended upon the churches and, in a few hours, razed to the ground edifices that had been erected to the "glory of God" by the Romanian faithful, with many years of labor.

The counties in which these churches were located were inhabited primarily by Szecklers. In times gone by, Szecklers had been sworn enemies of the Magyars, but by this time they were almost completely denationalized. In Odorhei County, six churches were razed to the ground, and the authorities made no effort to prevent the destruction.

The Greek-Catholic church of St. Nicolae of Racosul de Sus (Felso-Rakos) was the first in the area to be destroyed. During the month of October 1940, the Holy Trinity Church at Mereny (Homorod Almas) was also destroyed, as well as the Orthodox Church at Biborteni (Bibarczfalva). In December of 1940, the Greek-Catholic Church at Ocland (Okland) was destroyed, and after this act of vandalism, the Hungarian peasants used the debris as construction material. In January 1941, a mob also destroyed the Greek-Catholic Church in Craciuneni (Karac-sonyfalva). Finally, in February 1941, the Greek-Catholic church of St. Mihai in Varghis, after being desecrated, was also destroyed.

In the county of Trei Scaune, two Orthodox churches were completely destroyed. One of these was situated at Capeni (Kopecz). The authorities in this town notified the Romanian population that, by a fixed date, they either had to give up their old religion and become Protestants or undergo expulsion. [*Les déstructions d'églises*, p. 20.]

The second church was at Comalen (Kamalo), which was set on fire by a Szeckler mob in September 1940. Again, the Romanian population in the village was forced to affiliate with one of the several dominant Magyar religions.

Romanian churches were either destroyed or sacked in Odorhei, in Sinmartin (Homorod-Szentmartou), in Singeorgi de Padure, in Panet, in Borsec, in Batanii Mari, in Borosineul Mare (Nagyborosyno), in Aiata-Mare, in Belini, in Bicsar, in Osun, and in other places.

A chandelier belonging to the Romanian church in Sin-georgi de Padure was taken to Odorhei to be used in the local casino. In Trei Scaune, a Szeckler mob stole valuable sacred objects from the churches. During the night of September 14, Hungarians removed the cross from the top of the Romanian Orthodox church in St. Gheorghe and replaced it with a Magyar flag. In Zabala (Zabola), the roadside crucifixes, which had been put in place by the Romanians so that all Christians, Romanian or Magyar, might stop and pray, were pulled out of the ground.

"This was the answer to the regime of tolerance and civilized treatment with which the Romanian state governed and is still governing the Magyar minority," says the author of *Les déstructions d'églises* [p. 23].

Nor were the cases which have thus far been listed the only ones where the Hungarians desecrated Romanian holy places after the annexation of Transylvania.

The Orthodox churches in Praid (Odorhei County),

Gheorghieni (Cluj County), and Miercures Ciuc (the capital town of Ciud County) were turned into cereal warehouses. The same fate befell the Orthodox church in Odorhei. At Dej, the foundation of the Greek-Catholic church which was in the course of construction, was destroyed. In Bicaz-Centru (Ciuc County), the Hungarians turned the Greek-Catholic church into a billet for the motorized forces. In Zalau the Orthodox church was burned down on Easter Eve, 1942.

The fate of the Romanian priests in Transylvania was increasingly difficult. When Magyar rule was reimposed, the Romanian clergy was submitted to a trying ordeal. According to *Les déstructions d'églises* [p. 33]: "The offending measures are without end. One would have to have a body and soul made of steel to be able to endure the tortures to which the priests are subjected."

Here are a few examples:

On the night of September 8, 1940, a group of Hungarian soldiers surrounded the house of the Romanian priest in Haideu, Bihor County, and, after breaking into his house, beat him to a pulp. The reason invoked by his attackers was the victim's Romanian citizenship. "You are a Romanian," the attackers told the Romanian priest, "and you contributed to the existence of greater Romania." After giving him this reason for their unexpected visit, the blows came.

In June of 1941, the Romanian priest Juliu Ardeleanu, of Sat-Sugatag, was sentenced to compulsory residence. That is, he could go on exercising his profession, but he had to report every day to three different authorities in three separate villages. Within a twenty-four hour period, therefore, he had to appear personally at the police station at Harnicesti, at the notary's office at Giluesti, and at the mayor's office in Sat-Sugatag.

There was also the case of the priest Ion Dan, of Spurcani, Bihor County. Reverend Dan was also the village schoolmaster. On January 21, 1942, he was forbidden to exercise his profession as a priest. Three weeks later, he was sent to the commune of Tisza-Suly in Hungary proper, where there were no Romanian pupils. On March 27, 1942, the Inspectorate sent him back home, and then expelled him from the ranks of the teaching staff. Finally, on April 30 the village notary in Ciutolea, Arad County, obliged him to leave his office in the local school which belonged to the Orthodox church.

Even the Orthodox bishop of Cluj, Nicolae Colan, suffered under the arbitrary methods employed by the Hungarians in Transylvania in the field of religion.

A bishop of a church with more than 350,000 believers, he was one day summoned to appear before a recruiting commission, where he was weighed and measured like a simple recruit. Then they asked him—since he had become a Hungarian soldier!—to swear allegiance to Regent Horthy.

Many other instances of petty persecution, violation of conscience, and daily oppression are dealt with in this booklet (*Les déstructions d'églises*) which details the religious terror imposed in Transylvania by the representatives of the Hungarian state—a state whose coat of arms shows the symbol of Christendom—a cross—tilted to one side.

Without exception, all the Romanian priests in the Szeckler region were compelled to leave their home. Those who were not expelled had to seek refuge on Romanian territory.

Such were the vicissitudes of the Romanian clergy in the province of Transylvania which had been annexed by the "holy crown of Hungary" after the *Diktat.*

Under these circumstances, it becomes easy to imagine the plight of Romanian intellectuals in the annexed territory, to say nothing about that of the simple peasants.

We were able to talk to several peasants who took refuge in Romania a long time after the annexation of Transylvania by crossing the frontier illegally. These people left behind their homes, their plots of land, and virtually all of their small possessions.

Their action appeared all the braver to us because, once they had reached the other side of the Carpathians, they had to start their lives over from the beginning—a task which inevitably involved many difficulties.

A Romanian peasant can make up his mind to leave his land only when he is motivated by reasons of overwhelming importance. The reason invoked by all of the peasants who took refuge on Romanian territory was the inhuman treatment to which they had been subjected by the Hungarians from the first day of the occupation. A militant propaganda had saturated the hearts of the younger Hungarian generation with the venom of vindictiveness, so that on the day when the Magyars again became masters of dismembered Transylvania the Romanians began to be treated like the deadly enemies of the

Hungarian state. Each activity, each gesture, was suspected. The atmosphere in the annexed region became unbearable. The only consolation open to the Romanians was the enjoyment of their limited worldly goods. But this, too, was affected by the harshness of the new Magyar oppression. All their crops, which they had grown by the sweat of their brows, were confiscated, and they were left with only small quantities of food, which were not even enough to meet their daily needs.

Confronted with this situation, numerous Transylvanian Romanian peasants chose to leave their land, their homes, and their families, rather than to be turned into the vassals of foreigners. It almost appeared that the Romanian peasantry in Transylvania, despite all their past suffering, had not yet drunk to the dregs the cup of their tragic destiny.

The flight of Romanian refugees over the frontier that had been artificially established at Vienna calls to mind parallel movements of their ancestors over a frontier—also an artificially established one—which separated the Romanians in the old days.

"Every day, every hour, the population migrates toward the principalities," says Volume XXI of the *Transylvanian Diet Documents*, in the chapter dealing with the migration of the Transylvanian Romanians from Alba-Julia in 1698. [Magyar Academy, 1899.]

"One-third of the entire population in Fagaras County left their homes and migrated to neighboring Wallachia," continues the account of the Magyar Academy. Thus, almost two and one-half centuries before World War II, a large part of the Romanian population in Transylvania had fled from their own country, basically for the same reason that motivates the current influx of refugees—that is, because of Magyar intolerance.

At a certain moment in this earlier migration, the refugee influx reached such proportions that, in 1669, Emperor Leopold I demanded strong measures to prevent the population from migrating into Moldavia and Wallachia.

A report drawn up by G. Rall and G. G. Obst, dated May 20, 1777, was devoted to the illegal movement of the Transylvanians across the frontier. The report ended with these words: "Oppression has forced thousands of Romanian families in Transylvania, over a period of the past 120 years, to migrate to Moldavia or Wallachia."

Speaking about the same phenomenon, the Austrian consul Konig, in a report dated February 15, 1785, refers to "the migration of 24,000 families from the counties of Distrita and Nasaud to Moldavia."

These facts are completely ignored in a recent book published in Geneva by Herbert van Leisen. [Herbert van Leisen, *Des Siebenburgische Problem*, Kundig, Geneva, 1943 ("The Transylvanian Problem").]

Van Leisen states that the Romanians in the two principalities in question had originally come to Transylvania to colonize it beginning with the year 1700. If van Leisen had said that the Saxon peoples, who have for centuries been an integral part of the Anglo-Saxon people, first came from Britain in the 18th century, the aberration from historical fact could not have been greater.

One is constrained to ask: What about Emperor Leopold's appeal of 1699, and all the official documents of the 18th century which had to do, not with the efforts to prevent Romanian immigration to Transylvania, but precisely the opposite—migration from Transylvania?

Van Leisen does not make his only mistake in this erroneous interpretation of history. If we were to quote all the errors in his bulky bilingual work, we would have to dedicate a volume of similar magnitude to this task.

This is how history is written in Budapest. We should not be surprised, therefore, if a few decades from now, another writer—as objective and well informed as van Leisen—were to sponsor the theory that, beteween 1940 and 1942, many Romanians in Romania proper, out of eagerness to enjoy the superior civilization of men like Ducso Csaba, migrated to Transylvania.

The Culprits

It goes without saying that it is not our intention to accuse the entire Magyar nation of the excesses and atrocities committed against the Romanian people in northern Transylvania after the imposition of the Vienna *Diktat* by Galeazzo Ciano and the champagne salesman, Joachim von Ribbentrop.

In this book we have had occasion to speak about the deep abyss that existed between the Magyar nobility and the Romanian peasantry, but also between these noblemen and the Hungarian peasantry, which had to endure similar oppression on the immense estates of the land magnates.

The Hungarian magnates of the 20th century were as reactionary as their ancestors during the Middle Ages. The hatred they had instilled into the hearts of the Hungarian peasants against everything Romanian was a diversion intended to perpetuate the advantages they derived from their privileged status, without taking any measures to improve the lot of the peasantry.

According to the Magyar professor Juliu Szecfu, the Hungarian peasants in the regions of Cerepfalda, Kacs, Nosvai, and Szomolya, lived in grottos as they did in prehistoric times. Their condition was akin to that of the era of slavery.

In his study on *Public Health in the Mezokovesd District*, K. Stuman wrote that the dwellings of the Hungarian peasants in the region bore a marked resemblance to prehistoric caves.

From all this it is clear that the Hungarian peasant, because of his miserable living conditions, must have carried in his heart a seething hatred, but, with characteristic perfidy, the Magyar nobility were able to divert this hatred to the Romanian populace.

In addition to the reactionary nobility, the Magyar intellectuals were also to blame for the situation that existed because, instead of enlightening the peasantry, they led them onto the dangerous ground of anti-Romanianism.

It is not natural for peoples to hate each other as long as the upper classes do not abandon the noble mission of preaching brotherhood between the social classes and between nations of different origins.

In Hungary, unfortunately, the intellectuals sided, body and soul, with an oppressive aristocratic clique in maintaining an atmosphere of chauvinistic ultra-Magyarism. This atmosphere killed in the cradle every striving toward national emancipation by the large national groupings that lived in the area with them.

There can be no doubt that, on the day when a sincere and honest democratic regime comes to power in Budapest, the Transylvanian problem will cease to exist for the Hungarian government. It is to be recalled that Lajos Kossuth, when he had put some distance between himself and the chauvinistic hatred that was endemic in Hungary, had frankly conceded the essentially Romanian character of Transylvania.

A final solution of the Transylvanian question is available only through a reunited Transylvania, under a Romanian regime, within the limits established by the Trianon treaty.

Transylvania is a Romanian province, and it must remain Romanian, as the Trianon treaty stipulated. The British and French knew better than anyone else that the frontiers initially established by their experts at the peace conference exceeded, in favor of the Romanians, the frontiers that were finally accepted by the conference itself as the border line between Romania and Hungary.

We must never forget that agreement on the establishment of a "Romanian Transylvania" would mean the end of a thousand-year-old struggle. Conversely, the dismemberment of Transylvania is a result of the special circumstances of World War II—circumstances that bear a disturbing similarity to those that resulted in the dismemberment of other states in central Europe and the Balkan areas.

In a world that has been moved to accept the sound principle of peaceful co-existence between nations, the problem of the Szeckler minority will, by the nature of things, be settled in a simple manner. Nevertheless, in order to avoid a future situation similar to the one that led to the outbreak of the most destructive war in the history of mankind, we believe that an exchange of populations would be recommended. The Szecklers, as their own name tells us (Szek-el Szikoli), have historically been the guardians of the eastern frontier of Transylvania. Deprived of this historic function, it would be logical for the Szecklers to return to Hungary proper, whose people have always looked upon them as the most distinguished branch of the Magyar nation, and who should be happy to be reunited with them in this way.

In exchange, the Romanians who now live in Hungary should be brought back to Transylvania. In this way the problem of the low Hungarian birthrate would be solved, in addition to the problem of the age-old conflict between the Romanians and the Magyars. If the Transylvanian question is settled, there is no doubt that peaceful relations can be established between Romania and Hungary.

After the Trianon treaty, the great Romanian statesman Nicolae Titulescu suggested to Hungary on many occasions that they should forget their futile hatred of the past, in the light of the fact that, at the Alba-Julia Conference in 1918, the entire Romanian nation had expressed its will to live freely on the land of Transylvania.

Titulescu, as did his predecessor at the Romanian ministry

for external affairs, Take Ionescu, dreamed that the Little Entente, uniting the three Danubian states—Czechoslovakia, Romania, and Yugoslavia—could one day become a decisive factor in maintaining the peace of Europe by bringing Hungary into the partnership.

"The Union," said Titulescu to a Hungarian reporter from the Budapest newspaper, *Az-Est,* "will never be successful if it is set up against the will of the other parties. However, it will always be successful if it is set up for the purpose of achieving something concrete."

While Romania, through its authorized minister, suggested that Hungary and Romania commit themselves to a policy of sincere cooperation, Magyar propaganda was obstinately trying to prove to those in the west, especially in Great Britain, that the Little Entente intended to subjugate Hungary. It was the old Magyar method of distorting the truth, in the interests of propaganda and revisionism.

Refusing to be diverted by Magyar provocations, Titulescu advanced a plan for future cooperation with Hungary—a plan which, had it been put into effect, could have avoided many of the subsequent political events, perhaps even World War II, by creating an indissoluble political unity in the heart of Europe which would have been able to offer much more resistance to Hitler's pressures than the separate nations.

"Hungary and Romania," said Romania's minister for external affairs, "produce a large variety of raw materials, and it is in their common interest to sell them. . . . In order to sell its products, Hungary could make use of Romanian sea and river lines. To put such a program into effect [Titulescu had an entire program that dealt with the problems of trade and transportation], only one formula is possible. There must be an understanding between the central European countries —Hungary, Austria, Czechoslovakia, Yugoslavia, and Romania—on preferential customs tariffs and the observance of the rights of the respective nations, and which will also take into consideration the special interests of certain of the states in central Europe."

The great Romanian statesman concluded:

This is the right formula for the future. The central European states have only to choose—either to unite in order to achieve prosperity, or to remain isolated and fight each

other and live in misery. This is the only solution that
could endow our frontiers with a moral nature.

Hungary chose the road leading to isolation, rejecting the
friendship which the Romanian government had repeatedly
proposed.

Hungary obstinately turned down all proposals for cooperation with its neighboring states, because it had formal promises from Fascist Italy and the Nazi Reich that it would receive
its share of the loot when the Axis reorganized Europe for "one
thousand years."

One has to agree that the clique of Budapest nobles were
very well looked after by their fascist patrons. When the attention they received did not satisfy them, they looked after
their own interests, taking advantage of the misfortunes of
their neighbors, primarily the Romanians, the Czechs, and the
Slavs.

This policy was bluntly explained in the *Nouvelle Revue
de Hongrie* of December 1943. The revisionist countries had
refused an alliance with neighboring countries, since any alliance between them would have meant giving up revisionism—which was unacceptable.

Thus, the twenty years of revisionism were tantamount to
twenty years of propaganda against peace.

Moreover, by helping to create a more receptive atmosphere for German revisionism, Hungarian revisionism also
helped to pave the way for the most destructive war in the
history of mankind.

After World War I, various writers and newspapermen
insisted that the Hungarians had really been responsible for
the outbreak of the war.

Today, the role of the clique of Magyar magnates in paving
the way for World War II is becoming more and more evident.

Are these two circumstances the result of simple coinci-
dence—or are they the product of a systemic and more profound
cause?

It is our firm conviction that central Europe became the
hotbed of war, replacing the Balkan peninsula, and that this
was caused primarily by the reactionary mentality of the Budapest aristocracy.

Instead of offering the people conditions that would have
permitted them to prosper economically and culturally, the

clique of Magyar nobles sought to divert attention from other social problems by offering them the cheap satisfaction of a vindictive policy.

Instead of offering bread to the people, they offered incentive for noisy protest demonstrations. Instead of offering land to the people, they improved the quality of their own lands. And, finally, instead of liberty they promised their people—somebody else's liberty. Nothing could be more illustrative of the situation of the Magyar masses in Horthy's Hungary than the famous exchange in the Hungarian parliament in which the Romanian government was called the most intolerant of all governments—to which the reply was heard: "Give us the rights that the Magyars have in Romania!"

In Budapest, however, the just claims of the people were considered as in the time of Coriolanus in Rome. They were regarded as plots meant to weaken the power of the nobility, little by little.

Needless to say, they were brutally rejected. In order to maintain their centuries-old privileges, the Hungarian nobility incited the people against the Romanians—this at the time when the Transylvanian problem had for all practical purposes been settled in perpetuity at Alba-Julia on December 1, 1918.

On the day when the despotic regime in Budapest is replaced by a sincere and democratic regime, nothing will stand in the way of cooperation between the two neighboring European peoples, the Hungarians and the Romanians. But the condition sine qua non for such cooperation is the unity of Transylvania within the natural frontiers of Romanianism.

March 1944

EPILOGUE

The Vienna *Diktat* was imposed on Romania by the Nazi and fascist forces and signed by the two delegates from Romania, Mihai Manoilescu and Valer Pop, who were in reality delegates of Romanian Nazism and their participation in the conference, from a moral standpoint, was from the beginning null and void.

The *Diktat*, however, was never ratified by the Romanian people. The Romanian people almost to a man rejected the Vienna *Diktat* as an act which might be binding on its signers but not on the Romanian people. This became clear from the first day that this infamous decision was publicly known. Indeed, the entire nation protested against the mutilation of Transylvania, which the Romanians regarded as one of their most cherished provinces.

All Romanian patriots, no matter what their political affiliation, condemned the procedure employed by the two ad hoc "judges" who, from the lofty height of their boundless ignorance, chose to decide "forever" the fate of Transylvania. Needless to say, Transylvania was a land whose past meant nothing to them and whose future left them completely indifferent.

The Association of Transylvanian National Guard Veterans was the first to denounce the Vienna decision as an act that was bound to create a central Europe which was a hotbed of war. "The Vienna verdict," said the Transylvanian National Guard Veterans, "instead of promoting a climate of peace between the Hungarians and the Romanians, further aggravates the ancient feud existing between them."

In a comment a few days later, the newspaper *The Universe*, concluded in much the same terms: "A dangerous hotbed of war has appeared in Europe." [*The Universe*, Bucharest, September 5, 1940.]

At the same time, Romania's former ambassador in Rome Ion Lugosianu, wrote these inspired words in connection with the August 30 *Diktat*:

Romania loses 45,000 square kilometers and 2,500,000 people in 24 hours. Transylvania is dismembered. Hungary is now Moldavia's neighbor. The new frontier is now only 22 kilometers from Brasov. The county of Maremures, where one of the first Romanian principalities had been founded; Cluj, the birthplace of our culture; Masud, with its frontier guards; the thousands of purely Romanian villages and the much larger number of hardworking Romanian peasants—all are now behind a foreign frontier.

The Transylvanians are important to us from more than a statistical standpoint. Transylvania is the cradle of our nation. A dismembered Transylvania means not only that the land of a nation has been artificially carved up—it also means that the history of past centuries has been buried and that the very soul of a law-abiding, liberty-loving, but unlucky nation, is bleeding. This soul cannot die!

The Romanian nation submitted to the annexation because the decision came to them in the form of an ultimatum. But it never resigned itself to the annexation.

Unfortunately, the wave of initial protests was also the last to be heard. It was the will of the dictatorial regime that had come to power in Romania—a regime which was at the beck and call of the invading Nazis—to turn the Transylvanian problem into one of their taboos. Nothing was permitted to be written in Romania critical of the dismemberment of Transylvania. The odious Baron von Killinger, one of the most sinister Nazi figures, and his Gestapo brutes kept their eyes and ears open, and any protest was nipped in the bud.

When a Romanian politician or newspaperman dared to face up to the anger of the Romanian dictator and Baron von Killinger by violating the orders, he was sooner or later sent to a concentration camp or prison. Among many others there was the case of Anton Ionel Muresanu, chief editor of *Transylvania*, the newspaper of the Transylvanian refugees. After being expelled from Transylvania by the Hungarians because of his nationalistic attitude, he was sent from one concentration camp to another and from one prison to another, this time by the Romanians, that is, by the dictatorial regime of Ion Mihai Antonescu.

On August 23, 1944, as a result of the skillful and extremely courageous actions taken by four leaders of the Romanian political parties (Iuliu Maniu of the National Agrarian party, Constantin I. C. Bratianu of the National Liberal party, Constantin Titel Petrescu of the Social Democratic party, and Lucretiu Patrascanu of the Communist party)—a policy which had the full approval of King Michael I—the dictatorial regime of Ion Antonescu collapsed, bringing with it the withdrawal of the Nazi forces from Romania.

Immediately after the coup of August 23, Romania returned to its normal and traditional foreign policy—on the side of the United Nations. For their part, the great western Allies—the United States of America, the Soviet Union, and Great Britain—acknowledged the lawfulness of the Romanian claim on Transylvania and, in the Armistice agreement itself, they declared the Vienna *Diktat*, which had been imposed on Romania by force, null and void.

The attitude of the United Nations in the Transylvanian question should be emphasized because it represented one of the first occasions when the ideological principles for which millions of Romanians, Americans, and British had given their lives in the war were put into practice.

In a Europe which had been governed by the Nazi-Fascist new order, the righteous Romanian cause had been trampled underfoot by establishing an artificial frontier dividing Romanians who were citizens of the same country. But in the new world, whose principles have now sunk deep roots in Europe, the righteous Romanian cause has triumphed again. Transylvania was acknowledged as belonging to the Romanian nation, based on the sacred principle of ethnic unity.

Having been born on the territory of free America, I derive deep satisfaction and a justifiable pride from the fact that my native country warmly embraces the cause of Romanian Transylvania as part of the larger cause of liberty.

SELECTED BIBLIOGRAPHY OF WORKS CITED BY MILTON LEHRER

Apponyi, Albert, et. al., *Justice for Hungary*. London: 1928.

Bell, Mathias. *Geographical Compendium of Hungary*. 1779.

de Bertha, A. *The Hungarians and the Romanians*. Paris: 1889.

Bragan, N. *The Romanians Between the Ninth and the Fourteenth Centuries*. 1932.

Bratianu, I. *The Foreign Policy of King Carol I*.

Clark, Charles Upson. *Greater Romania*. New York: 1922.

Clopotel, I. *Revolutia din 1918 si Unirea Ardealului cu Romania*. Cluj: 1926.

Csaba, Ducso. *Nincs Kegyelem*. Budapest: 1939.

Csaplovits, J. V. *Gemälde von Ungarn*. 2 vols. Pesta: 1829.

Czornig, Karl F. Annex to *Ethnographie des Österreichischen Monarchie*. Vienna: 1857.

Donald, Robert, *The Tragedy of Trianon*. London: 1928.

Dragomir, Silviu. *Avram Iancu*. Bucharest: 1924.

Erzberger. *Souvenirs de Guerre*. Paris: 1921.

Florianus, M. *Chronicon pictum Vindobenense*. Vol. of Historiae Hungaricae Fontes Domestici. Lipsiae, Quinque Ecclessiis. 1883.

de Geza, Magistri Simonis. *De Originibus et gesta Hungarorum*. Ed. Podhradetzky. Buda: 1833.

———. *Chronicon Hungaricum*.

Gyarfas, E. *A roman grog katolikusok autonomiaja*. Budapest: 1905.

Homan, B. *Geschichte des ungarischen Mittelalters*. Berlin: 1940.

Homan, B., and Szektii, J. *Magyar történet*. Budapest: 1939.

Horvath Eugen. *So Starb der Friede*. Berlin: 1930.

Iaszi, Oscar. *Revolution and Counterrevolution in Hungary*.

Iorga, N. *Ce sint si ce vor sasii din Ardeal*. Bucharest: 1919.

———. "Les Nationalités en Transylvanie roumaine." *Revue de Gènève*. 1923, p. 229.

———. *Contra dusmaniei dintre natii: romani si unguri*. Bucharest: 1931.

———. *Réponse aux conférences données à Cambridge par le Comte Bethlen sur la révision du traité de Trianon*. Bucharest: 1933.

———. *Seconde réponse au Comte Bethlen*. Bucharest: 1933.

———. *Istoria romanilor*. Bucharest: 1936-39.

————. *Histoire des Roumains de Transylvanie et de Hongrie.* 2nd ed. Bucharest: 1940.

Juhasz & Ladislas, ed. *Gesta Hungarorum (Anonymus quondam Bela regia notarius.)* Anonymi Bela Regis Notarii. Budapest: 1933.

Kazsonyi. *La Parenté des peuples danubiennes.* Vienna.

Kiepert, H. *Volker und Sprächenkarte von Österreich und Unterdonauländer.* Ethnographic map based on 1869 census in Austria. Berlin: 1869.

Kiritescu, C. *The History of the War for the Realization of Romania.*

Korabinszky, I. M. Geographical Lexicon of Hungary. Presburg: 1786.

Loucarevici. *Jugoslawiens Enstahung.* Vienna: 1938.

Lukacs, George. *"The Injustices of the Treaty of Trianon."*

Lupas, I. "Individualitatea istorica a Transilvaniei." *Studii, conferinte si communicari istorica.* Bucharest: 1928.

————. *Istoria unirii romanilor.* Bucharest: 1937.

Moga, I. "I Romani di Transilvania nel Media Evo." Vol XIX *Revue historique du sud-est européen.* 1942, p. 183.

Moroianu, G. *Les Luttes des Roumains Transylvains pour la liberté et l'opinion européene.* Paris: 1933.

Nistor, I. "Rumanische Wanderungen aus Siebenburgen." Vol. XVIII of *Revue historique du sud-est européen.* 1941, p. 140.

Pacatian, T. V. *Cartea de aur sau luptele nationale ale romanilor de sub coroana ungara.* Sibiu: 1904-1915.

Paclisanu, Zenovie. *L'art de la maniere de faire des Hongrois.*

————. "Statistique des Roumains de Transylvanie au XVIIIᵉ siècle." Vol. I *Revue de Transylvanie,* 1934, p. 203.

————. *Luptele politice ale romanilor ardeleni din 1790-1792.* Analele Academiei Romane. Bucharest: 1923.

Popa-Liseanu, G. *Sicules et roumains: Un procès de dénationalisation.* Bucharest: 1932.

————. *Isvoarele istoriei romanilor.* 1934.

Pauler, Gyula. *The History of the Magyar Nation under the Arpad Kings.*

Rogerius. *Miserabile Carmen.* Monumenta Germaniae Historica. Hanover: 1892.

Rössler, Robert. *Rumänische Studien.* Vienna: 1871.

Seton-Watson, R. W. *A History of the Romanians: From Roman Times to the Completion of Unity.* Cambridge, England: 1934.

————. *Treaty Revision and the Hungarian Frontiers.* London: 1934.

Spohr, Ludwig. *The Spiritual Reasons for Hungarian Nationalism.* Berlin: 1936.

Steed, Wickham. Preface to *Les Luttes des Roumains Transylvains pour la liberté et l'opinion européene,* by George Moroianu. Paris: 1933.

Török, Pál. *Der Vergangenheit des Ungarischen Staatslebens.*

Valyi, A. *Magyarorszagnak Leirasa.* Buda: 1796.

BIOGRAPHICAL NOTE

Milton G. Lehrer was born in Brooklyn, N.Y., in May 1906, of Romanian-Jewish immigrant parents. He received most of his education in Romania and Paris. In Paris, he took a degree in international law, and in the 1930s, he began writing. He soon became a correspondent for the well known Paris news weekly *La Tribune des Nations*. He returned to his career as a journalist after World War II, writing again for *La Tribune des Nations* and for the Israeli newspaper *Al-Hamismar*. He wrote articles as well for many other European publications.

For a period of years after the war, Lehrer was vice-president of the foreign correspondents' association in Bucharest. However, when the Communists came to power, following the forced abdication of King Michael in December 1947, life became increasingly difficult for foreign correspondents in Romania. Lehrer found himself writing things which would not affront the Communists. Among other things, he translated writings of Victor Hugo and Alexander Dumas, and the wartime speeches of Franklin D. Roosevelt.

Although Lehrer was an American citizen by birth, the Communist regime treated him as a Romanian citizen, which meant that he had to have an exit permit before he could leave the country. The American embassy could do nothing to help him at the time because of the strained condition of Romanian Communist relations with the USA. He and his wife repeatedly applied for exit permits, naming Israel as the country of their intended destination, because this appeared safer than naming the USA. Finally, after countless requests had been turned down by the Romanian government, Lehrer died in Bucharest in November 1969.

Lehrer is survived by a widow who was given permission to leave Romania two and a half years after her husband died, and who now lives in Tel Aviv.